Problems of International Administrative Law

Problems of International Administrative Law

On the Occasion of the Twentieth Anniversary of the World Bank Administrative Tribunal

Edited by

Nassib G. Ziadé

MARTINUS
NIJHOFF
PUBLISHERS

LEIDEN • BOSTON
2008

This book is printed on acid-free paper.

Library of Congress Cataloging-in-Publication Data

Problems of international administrative law : on the occasion of the twentieth anniversary of the world bank administrative tribunal / edited by Nassib G. Ziade.
p. cm.
Includes index.
ISBN 978-90-04-15712-5 (hardback : alk. paper)
1. International administrative courts. 2. International officials and employees. 3. World Bank. Administrative Tribunal. 4. Judicial review of administrative acts. I. Ziade, Nassib G.
KZ5274.P76 2008
342'.0664—dc22

2008017249

ISBN 978-90-04-15712-5

Koninklijke Brill NV incorporates the imprints Brill, Hotei Publishing, IDC Publishers, Martinus Nijhoff Publishers and VSP.

PRINTED IN THE NETHERLANDS

TABLE OF CONTENTS/TABLE DES MATIÈRES

OPENING SESSION

REVIEW OF MANAGERIAL DISCRETION BY INTERNATIONAL ADMINISTRATIVE TRIBUNALS

Chair: *A. Kamal Abul-Magd*

ANNEXES

INTRODUCTION

Nassib G. Ziadé*

The present book seeks to open to a larger audience the proceedings of a Conference on international administrative law ("Conference") held in Paris on May 16, 2000. The occasion of the Conference was the celebration of the twentieth anniversary of the World Bank Administrative Tribunal. The Conference was attended by two former Presidents of the International Court of Justice, judges of international administrative tribunals, high-ranking officials of international organizations, scholars and international law specialists. The presentations and debates have not lost any of their impact or relevance since the event. To the contrary, they provide a useful framework for understanding issues that remain salient and still debated today.

In addition to the proceedings of the Conference, two additional documents have been included in this book as annexes. The first is a reprint of an article by Judge Robert A. Gorman discussing his experiences while judge and later president of both the World Bank Administrative Tribunal (WBAT) and the Asian Development Bank Administrative Tribunal (AsDBAT). The second is an article by Ms. Celia Goldman, Registrar of the International Monetary Fund Administrative Tribunal (IMFAT), on selected issues addressed by that Tribunal.

At the Conference, the participants discussed in great depth the topic of judicial review of managerial discretion, as well as procedural and practical issues relating to the work of international administrative tribunals. There was a general convergence of views by various contributors to this book with respect to questions of judicial review powers, while views diverged with respect to procedural and practical issues.

As concerns the judicial review of managerial discretion, we were reminded throughout the various interventions that all international administrative tribunals have asserted jurisdiction to conduct limited reviews of cases involving the exercise of discretionary power by an administration (p. 28), and that the general standard of review with respect to individual administrative decisions is that a tribunal will not interfere with an organization's

* Deputy Secretary-General, International Centre for Settlement of Investment Disputes (ICSID); former Executive Secretary, World Bank Administrative Tribunal.

exercise of discretion, absent abuse of discretion or improper motive (p. 195). Judge Prosper Weil reminded us that this standard is similar to the one used in French administrative law, according to which a judge reviews merely the legality (*légalité*) of an administrative decision and not its wisdom (*opportunité*) (*id.*). A source of complication resides in the fact, noted by Judge Gorman, that it is often "a matter of fine judgment and delicate line-drawing to differentiate an arbitrary management decision from one that is merely unsound or unwise" (p. 218).

We were also reminded throughout the Conference that international administrative tribunals have consistently invoked the idea that discretionary power is not synonymous with "arbitrariness" (pp. 25–26). Judge Francisco Orrego Vicuña cited the example of the WBAT, which requires that discretionary decisions be taken by the World Bank in the Bank's genuine interests (p. 45). According to Judge Orrego Vicuña, discretionary powers must always be exercised in observance of the rules, general principles of law and the applicant's employment contract; hence, the power of the administration is limited (*id.*). This conclusion was shared by Judge Nicolas Valticos, who observed that international administrative tribunals have balanced the freedom of decision with which an administration needs to act against the tribunal's obligation to ensure that international civil servants are protected by a legal framework (p. 36).

Having recalled that discretionary power must be subject to review, and that judges should not substitute their own assessments for that of the organization, Judge Michel Gentot introduced two caveats. He first noted that the scope of a judge's review of the administration's exercise of its discretion depends on how much discretion the judge decides to allow the administration (p. 27). He then observed that as such a review can be properly undertaken only when the judge perceives the real, as opposed to the claimed, motivations of the administration, a trend has emerged favoring a deeper level of scrutiny of the decisions of international organizations (pp. 28, 30).

It is in this context of judicial review of managerial discretion that several speakers discussed the issue of the imposition of disciplinary measures by different organizations. Judges C.F. Amerasinghe (p. 38) and Orrego Vicuña (p. 46) pointed out that in so doing, administrations exercise a quasi-judicial function which is different from their other discretionary powers. Reflecting on the experiences of the United Nations Administrative Tribunal (UNAT), WBAT and International Labour Organization Administrative Tribunal (ILOAT) (pp. 38–39), Judge Amerasinghe opined that in disciplinary cases, the control of an administration's exercise of its discretion by international administrative tribunals is stricter than that applied to the exercise of other discretionary powers, "though it may fall short of a substitution of judgment" (p. 39). In a similar vein, Judge Valticos, in pointing to the practice of the Council of Europe Administrative Tribunal (CEAT), indicated that in reviewing whether a sanction imposed by the Council of Europe's Administration is adequate, the Tribunal cannot judge the wisdom of the sanction or substitute its assessment for that of the Administration (p. 35).

In exercising their control over the imposition of disciplinary measures upon staff members for engaging in misconduct, the WBAT and the AsDBAT have, according to Judge Gorman, added to the detailed staff rules adopted by the respective institutions "various due-process requirements, and have also made clear the importance of 'proportionality' in the imposition of discipline [i.e.,] that there be some reasonable 'fit' between the wrongdoing and the severity of the punishment" (p. 221). A similar requirement of proportionality has been imposed by many other international administrative tribunals, including the CEAT which, according to Judge Valticos, can censure those sanctions which are disproportionate to the objective and subjective circumstances in which the misdeeds were committed (p. 35).

Although judges of international administrative tribunals agree on the importance of the principle of proportional discipline, the application of this principle in certain instances may result in what Judge Gorman aptly described as "a significant disparity of attitudes based upon [the judges'] differing cultural and societal backgrounds" (p. 221). Indeed, in the *Carew* and *Planthara* judgments decided by the WBAT in 1995, the Tribunal found on the basis of the principle of proportionality that the discharge by the World Bank of two staff members who had falsified their records for overtime work was an excessive sanction. Commenting on these two judgments, Judge Gorman acknowledged candidly: "If I were deciding the cases myself . . . I almost certainly would . . . have sustained the discharges" (p. 222). He added: "Yet my colleagues were inclined to find that the wrongdoing – about which we had no doubt – was not so grave as to warrant termination. . . . I deferred to my colleagues' assessment, based on their own cultural norms, on the issue of 'proportionality,' because I thought it inappropriate to push for the application of stricter sanctions that I believe squared more with U.S. values" (*id.*).

The former General Counsel of the World Bank, Dr. Ibrahim F.I. Shihata, criticized the WBAT's handling of the *Carew* and *Planthara* cases. Referring to the special values and goals of the World Bank with respect to the fighting of corruption, Dr. Shihata cautioned international administrative tribunals, when evaluating the proportionality of discretionary measures imposed in disciplinary matters, against rendering judgments "by isolating the cases from the underlying policies and values of each institution"

(p. 63). Thereafter, Judge A. Kamal Abul-Magd, who had presided over the WBAT at the time of the *Carew* and *Planthara* judgments, reassured the Conference's participants that "[n]o administrative tribunal wants to make decisions in isolation from the real needs of both the staff and the institution" (p. 65).

Several participants discussed the controversial issue of whether, in Judge Abul-Magd's words, "the reviewing power of [an international] administrative tribunal is limited to individual administrative acts, or can be expanded to policy-making or quasi-legislative powers of the administration" (p. 20). Two approaches are conceivable in this regard. The first one, which has been adopted by the WBAT and a number of other international administrative tribunals (pp. 48, 194), allows the review of the validity of a general policy decision only when the tribunal reviews an individual application of that policy by the organization. In this respect, the WBAT has emphasized that it is not empowered to provide advisory opinions concerning the validity of general rules. The second approach, which was adopted in the IMFAT's Statute (pp. 111, 153, 230–31), gives the IMFAT jurisdiction to review a regulation, not only in the context of its review of its individualized application, but also directly. While IMF Executive Board decisions are included among those which the IMFAT can review, the IMFAT's Statute explicitly excludes from the Tribunal's jurisdiction resolutions taken by the Board of Governors.

Opinions differed at the Conference with respect to the propriety of each approach. According to Judge Orrego Vicuña (pp. 48, 64), it would be inappropriate for the WBAT, or any other international administrative tribunal, to assume the role of a policy-reviewing body. Such a role, which could lead to the nullification of rules enacted by the governing bodies and could result ultimately in the supremacy of one organ over another, pertains more to a constitutional tribunal than to an administrative one. In a similar vein, Judge Weil (pp. 194–95), pointing to the experience of the French Conseil d'Etat, questioned the right as well as the positive provisions pursuant to which international administrative tribunals may review the validity of an institution's policy decisions. Echoing the same concerns as Judge Orrego Vicuña, Judge Weil observed that an international administrative tribunal cannot be a super-General Assembly or a super-board of directors, and must know how far it may go. For his part, Judge Bola A. Ajibola (p. 182) cautioned tribunal members against "making [themselves] the policy-makers" and "putting [themselves] in the position of management."

Other speakers took a different approach. Judge Spyridon Flogaitis (p. 131) invited the WBAT to accept some of the principles introduced by the statutes of other international administrative tribunals, "particularly with respect to applications brought against administrative acts of a general character." Mr. Dominick Devlin (pp. 165–66), then Legal Adviser of the International Labour Office, expressed concern over the position taken by the ILOAT, according to which a measure of a general nature which could lead to individual decisions could be challenged only to the extent that it served as the basis of an individual decision. Mr. Devlin observed that under this system, a staff rule could be found to be invalid twenty years after its enactment even though the organization had been acting upon it consistently for that entire period of time.

The phenomenon of the proliferation of international administrative tribunals was examined carefully by several contributors. Judge Stephen M. Schwebel remarked that "it was the World Bank itself that launched the course of proliferation, a phenomenon that has both advantages and disadvantages" (p. 152). Judge Valticos recalled that the idea of an international administrative tribunal was first introduced in 1927 at the initiative of the first Director of the International Labour Office (p. 32). Judge Gorman elaborated on the topic, noting that "[t]he League of Nations in 1927 established *its* tribunal, whose structure was taken over by the International Labour Organization in 1946; the United Nations Administrative Tribunal was created in 1949; the World Bank Administrative Tribunal was founded in 1980; and its related institution, the International Monetary Fund (a much smaller employer) created a separate tribunal in 1994" (p. 209). Judge Gorman added that "[t]here are a myriad of other international organizations which have their own separate administrative tribunals; and some 50 organizations subscribe to the ILO Tribunal, which disposes of dozens of cases each year concerning the rights of staff members of those many organizations" (*id.*).

Judge Gilbert Guillaume observed at the outset of the Conference that the proliferation of international administrative tribunals has not posed a serious risk of divergence in international administrative law. He attributed this situation to the following factors: (i) the permanence and wisdom of the judges, who sometimes sit on different tribunals at the same time; (ii) the case law created at the inception of the tribunals is closely followed through the years by successive judges, with only necessary adjustments being made; (iii) the judgments are rarely undermined by dissenting opinions; and (iv) the judges never hesitate to refer in their judgments to the judgments of other international administrative tribunals (pp. 10–11). With respect to the latter point, Professor Raul C. Pangalangan asserted that "[e]ach international administrative tribunal . . . must draw wisdom from the case-law of other tribunals" (p. 50). As to the idea mentioned by Judge Guillaume of judges serving simultaneously on different tribunals, Mr. Giovanni Palmieri stated that it was favored by staff representatives (p. 173). Mr. Palmieri considered that such experience would help tribunal judges to become specialists in international administrative law and would promote further consistency in the law (*id.*).

Judge Valticos expressed a concern that the number of international administrative tribunals had become excessive (p. 182). He asked whether the stage had been reached when administrations and staff associations should review whether it was desirable for the sake of jurisprudential uniformity to recombine jurisdictions which have common sources of law and similar functions (p. 183).

By contrast, several speakers viewed the proliferation of international administrative tribunals as a rather positive phenomenon. Judge Ajibola noted that "[i]f all the activities of these tribunals were handled by a single institution, the caseload would be daunting or overwhelming" (p. 182). Mr. Chris de Cooker stated that as the European Space Agency "is different from other institutions," it needs its own Appeals Board, which "understands [the Agency's] culture, . . . and is able to explain the judgments in clear and concise terms" (p. 161). Judge Jean Massot similarly pointed out that it is preferable that the rules of procedure of each tribunal take into account the specific characteristics of the organization within which the tribunal must function (p. 147). Judge Massot further downplayed the risks associated with proliferation by noting that it is in any event always possible to allow judges to sit on different tribunals (*id.*).

With respect to the composition of international administrative tribunals, the Conference participants discussed the qualifications required of tribunal members and the possibility of renewing their appointments. Judge Massot (p. 148) and Mr. de Cooker (p. 160) assessed positively the practice of the European Space Agency Appeals Board (ESAAB) with respect to the appointment of non-lawyers as well as lawyers to that tribunal. The two speakers found the appointment of persons with practical experience in the highly technical work of the organization, and having an informed insight into the functioning of the organization, to be very useful. This view was supported by Judge Hubert Thierry (p. 155), who argued that the criteria for the selection of tribunal members should not be so restrictive as to exclude the participation of qualified persons who do not have standard legal qualifications. Taking a different view, Judge Amerasinghe (pp. 183–84) expressed the opinion that as tribunal judges are neither conciliators nor mediators and must reach decisions according to law, lawyers are required for the task and cannot be replaced with administrators or diplomats.

With respect to the renewal of tribunal members' appointments, three views were advanced during the Conference. According to Judge Thierry (p. 156), a once-renewable four-year term would be the most practical solution with respect to the length of members' terms. Judge Amerasinghe (p. 183), on the other hand, opposed any renewal of appointments and favored a longer term (e.g., a seven-year term) with no renewals. Dr. Shihata, recalling his experience as the World Bank's General Counsel, mentioned that, given the complexities of the World Bank, he had taken the position that the WBAT would be weakened if its members were changed every three years (p. 192). According to Dr. Shihata, the renewal of the Tribunal's members "enabled the Tribunal to establish a doctrine on many issues and to take strong stands in spite of the complexities of the situations that it has had to address" (*id.*). It may be noted in this respect that the Bank's approach toward renewal was altered in 2001, following Dr. Shihata's departure, with the WBAT's Statute's being modified to provide, *inter alia*, that Tribunal members were in the future to be appointed for five-year terms which could be renewed only once.

With respect to the more specific issue of uniformity of opinion within tribunals, the present author notes that tribunals (or panels constituted within tribunals) will always strive in their judgments to draft language which reflects a consensus that is acceptable to all members. In cases where tribunal members are unable to agree on the draft of a judgment, the question arises as to whether a tribunal member can file a dissenting opinion. The statutes and rules of procedure of some tribunals expressly allow for the filing of dissenting opinions. The majority of such texts are, however, silent on the question of whether dissenting opinions are permissible. They merely state that a tribunal may reach its decision by a majority of the members present at a session. In the absence of a provision expressly allowing for the filing of dissenting opinions, members of the UNAT and the ILOAT have availed themselves, albeit exceptionally, of their judicial right to file dissenting opinions, while no such opinions have ever been filed in the African Development Bank Administrative Tribunal (AfDBAT), the OECD Administrative Tribunal (OECDAT), the NATO Appeals Board (NATOAB) or the ESAAB.

Several judges at the Conference spoke in favor of international administrative tribunals rendering consensus judgments. According to Judge Thierry, the practice of issuing separate and dissenting opinions is inadvisable in international administrative tribunals, and particularly regrettable when important cases are decided by panels, since this may lead to a judgment being adopted by two judges out of three constituting a panel in a tribunal composed of seven judges (p. 156). Dissenting opinions, in the words of Judge Ajibola, "could become an expensive exercise, a kind of undesirable luxury that many of [the] administrative tribunals could ill afford" (p. 181). By contrast, the fact that each judgment of the IMFAT has been rendered unanimously has contributed, according to Ms. Goldman, to the "articulation of a measured and carefully reasoned jurisprudence" (p. 230). In explaining how the WBAT has managed to render all of its judgments unanimously without any separate opinion or dissent, Judge Gorman recalled that since the early days of that Tribunal, all the judges "have given great weight to the belief that [the] judgments have greater force and clarity, and that the Tribunal will have greater credibility, if [they] speak with one voice rather than several" (p. 224). To reach such a goal, Judge Gorman acknowledged that "differences of view . . . are accommodated in the course of preparing and issuing judgments" (p. 4), and that "deeply rooted cultural differences . . . must be submerged in an effort to identify an international standard" (p. 5). Taking a more permissive approach, Judge Amerasinghe stated that "the authority of the operative decision is [not] affected by separate or dissenting opinions, although unanimity in every respect could be useful" (p. 184).

In regard to procedural matters, and more specifically the issue of oral hearings, it is well known that several international administrative tribunals, such as the AsDBAT, the IMFAT, the ILOAT, the UNAT and the WBAT, either decide their cases on the basis of the written pleadings alone, or hold oral hearings very rarely. Other tribunals, such as the Inter-American Development Bank Administrative Tribunal (IDBAT), the CEAT, the NATOAB and the OASAT, hold oral hearings systematically in every case.

Mr. Devlin saw as a goal having an efficient tribunal which works as quickly as possible, and expressed a preference for dispensing with oral proceedings altogether (p. 164). The majority of the participants, however, favored the holding of evidentiary hearings on the grounds that these are "important to claimants even if they lose their cases" (de Cooker, p. 161), are generally favored by individual applicants and staff associations (Sicault, p. 176), and promote the staff's perception of enjoying full due process (Rivero, p. 168). Taking a middle approach, Judge Gorman expressed his readiness to defend the general practice of the AsDBAT and the WBAT to decide cases on the pleadings alone, while conceding that there may be cases in which it would be useful for a tribunal to question witnesses (pp. 225–26). He added that in the handful of cases where the WBAT had held oral hearings, these had proved to be helpful in addressing very significant issues (p. 226). Similarly, Mr. Ko-Yung Tung acknowledged that while evidentiary hearings may not be necessary in every case, the WBAT's willingness to schedule them serves to "underscore the Tribunal's commitment to a fair and complete review of every case that comes before it" (p. 15). For his part, Judge Weil stressed that the uncertainties presented by highly fact-intensive cases could perhaps be relieved by evidentiary hearings or more extensive written proceedings (p. 197).

If a Tribunal were to dispense with oral hearings, great reliance could instead be placed, in the words of Mr. Devlin, on "a high-quality internal Appeals Committee" which "could sift the facts and give the Tribunal a taste of how 'normal' officials in the organization think" (p. 164). Mr. David Rivero, however, expressed reservations to this idea since "[t]he World Bank has not yet developed rules of evidence at the level below the Administrative Tribunal and the fact-finding [at that lower level] is not very reliable" (p. 169). Professor David Ruzié pointed out that it is obvious from the jurisprudence of the ILOAT and the UNAT that in many organizations the internal grievance committees perform a rather poor job (p. 185). He nevertheless stated that efficient internal mechanisms would greatly facilitate the work of tribunals (*id.*).

At the Conference, several speakers discussed the topic of abusive or frivolous applications, with which many international administrative tribunals had been confronted. Mr. de Cooker stressed that the "existence of one such [vexatious and frivolous] case every few years is the price to pay to have an open system" (p. 161). Other speakers, however, viewed the problem differently. As the present author emphasized, such applications add to the workload of a tribunal and impede its ability to deal expeditiously with the meritorious cases which come before it (p. 93). They are furthermore costly to the respondent institution that has to defend the cases in addition to bearing the expenses of the tribunal (*id.*).

One option available to a tribunal to deal with this situation is to award compensation to the respondent institution. The Statutes of the IMFAT, the AfDBAT, the CEAT, the OASAT and the NATOAB in fact allow for the imposition of a penalty on an applicant who brings a "clearly frivolous claim" (OASAT), or one which constitutes an "abuse of process" (NATOAB). In support of this approach, Mr. Rivero observed that it would be "a matter of simple justice, to the organization in some cases, to have [costs] awarded" (p. 168). Taking a different view, Mr. Palmieri criticized the tendency of certain organizations unjustifiably to accuse applicants of submitting abusive claims (p. 174). Judge Flogaitis for his part warned against the imposition of severe penalties, as this would create the impression that the right of access to justice is constrained (p. 187). Judge Flogaitis added that even when a tribunal's statute foresees punitive cost awards against applicants, these will be very difficult to impose as it must be established before the tribunal that the case is frivolous or brought merely to harass the institution (pp. 187–88).

Judge Flogaitis' observation is confirmed by the fact that among those tribunals referred to above whose statutes allow for the imposition of penalties, only the OASAT has ordered applicants in some instances to reimburse the organization for its expenses and attorneys' fees, and the organization did not then seek such reimbursement. It may be noted, however, that the ILOAT, the Statute of which is silent on the issue, asserted in the *Vollering (No. 15)* judgment rendered in 1999 that "it possesses the inherent power" to impose such a penalty. The UNAT stated six years later in the *Fayache* judgment that the ILOAT's wisdom in the *Vollering (No. 15)* judgment was fully recognized by the UNAT, and that the UNAT "will have no hesitation in acting accordingly, should the occasion arise." In the meantime, the ILOAT had imposed cost penalties in the *Müller-Engelmann (Nos. 14 & 15)* judgment rendered in 2003, in which the Applicant, who had prevailed in a previous judgment, introduced thirteen further complaints before the Tribunal. The ILOAT emphasized that it would not impose such penalties "in every case in which a persistent litigant such as the complainant loses," but that a complainant may expect to suffer cost consequences where he or she has actually had success before the Tribunal and "nonetheless refuses to accept the limitations which such success imposes."

As this author submitted in his Conference paper (pp. 95–97), the option of imposing a penalty on an applicant who has brought a frivolous claim may lead to unexpected consequences. The threat of a penalty may discourage applicants who have meritorious cases from submitting them to the tribunal. Paradoxically, the threat may not necessarily have a deterrent effect on those who would submit frivolous claims. Fortunately, the texts governing a number of tribunals provide a safer and more efficient device to deal with frivolous claims. These tribunals may summarily dismiss a case on the basis of the application alone if it is clearly or manifestly irreceivable or inadmissible, or if it is devoid of all merit. A skillful use of the summary dismissal mechanism by a tribunal may prove to be beneficial to all those involved in the process, including the applicant who is made aware at an early stage that he or she has no case. It may also diminish the perceived need to impose penalties on an applicant for what may be considered a frivolous case.

The issue of frivolous applications before international administrative tribunals is comparable to that of a dissatisfied party who attempts to use, as a cover to appeal a judgment, the limited exceptions to the principle of the finality of judgments provided for in the statute or rules of a tribunal, such as allowances for requests for revision, interpretation or rectification. It is here submitted that a tribunal faced with such abusive requests should deal with them firmly from the outset. In this respect, Judge Massot made it clear that at the OECDAT and at the ESAAB, a request for revision, rectification or interpretation of a judgment, which is in reality an appeal of an unfavorable judgment, is addressed according to a streamlined procedure by the president after consultation with the two other members of the panel (p. 149).

The related question of whether there should be a specific right of appeal against judgments of international administrative tribunals was raised by

Judge Ajibola (p. 61) and discussed by various speakers during the Conference. Some speakers dismissed the idea of creating an appellate body, stressing that "[t]he finality of [judgments] is a very legitimate consideration" (Abul-Magd, p. 66), and that the granting of "a right of appeal will entail further delay and expense" (Fernando, p. 138). In the words of Mr. Devlin, "[w]e are prepared to put up with wrong decisions from time to time in order to ensure greater speed" (p. 165). By contrast, other speakers were in favor of creating a procedure that would allow applicants to appeal international administrative tribunal judgments. Mr. Palmieri likened such a procedure to the situation prevailing in domestic administrative law (p. 174). Judge Ruzié for his part proposed an appellate system which would concern itself solely with issues of law, with a view to tackling jurisprudential divergences (p. 186). In his concluding remarks, Dr. Shihata took a clear position in favor of the former approach, as he warned against the "continuing proliferation of grievance mechanisms within each institution" (p. 192). He then advocated the adoption of "limited [means] that are fair and efficient in addressing the complaints" (*id.*).

Several speakers at the Conference proposed that as long as there exists no right of appeal of international administrative tribunal judgments, the admissibility of requests for revision should be broadened. In this respect, Judge Ruzié recommended that the requirement of discovery of new facts be reconsidered (p. 186). Judge Mark Fernando suggested in relation to the ILOAT that other grounds beside the discovery of new facts be allowed, "includ[ing] a breach of natural justice, a serious violation of the rules, or even an inconsistency between two judgments of the same Tribunal which involve the same issue" (p. 141). Professor Jean-Didier Sicault recalled approvingly the case law of the ILOAT, starting with the *de Villegas (No. 4)* judgment of 1981, which has allowed for the revision of judgments on grounds other than the discovery of new facts, such as an omission by the Tribunal to pass judgment on a claim or to take account of essential facts, or a "material error, i.e., a mistaken finding of fact which, unlike a mistake in appraisal of the facts, involves no exercise of judgment" (p. 177). While Professor Sicault considered the grounds for revision authorized by the *de Villegas (No. 4)* judgment to represent important safety valves for losing applicants (pp. 177–78), the present author expressed his disapproval of the *de Villegas (No. 4)* jurisprudence on the basis that the grounds it allows for the revision of judgments pertain more to an appeal than to a revision (p. 187). The present author preferred the more recent *Sethi (No. 4)* judgment rendered by the ILOAT in 1999, according to which "the stability of the judicial process requires that final judgments . . . be set aside only on limited grounds and for the gravest of reasons" (*id.*).

At an early stage of the Conference, Judge Abul-Magd raised the issue of how to foster an "interaction between tribunals and institutions that does not violate the independence and integrity" of the international administrative tribunals (p. 65). The first and most direct means of achieving such communication would consist of holding a meeting between members of the tribunal and its secretariat on the one hand, and senior officials of the organization on the other, in the presence of representatives of the staff association. Such meetings have taken place in the context of the WBAT (Gorman, p. 144), the IMFAT (Schwebel, p. 153) and the ILOAT (Devlin, p. 165). The purpose of such meetings would presumably be to discuss ways of collectively improving tribunal procedures, and to allow the tribunal to draw to the attention of all parties concerned some trends encountered in the course of deciding cases.

There is a second, subtler way of communicating that involves a tribunal undertaking an educational function. According to Judge Gorman, the WBAT "serves a useful non-judicial function by seeking to communicate to the Bank, its staff members and its management guidelines for proper management practice and treatment of staff members" (p. 143). This can be done through the use of *obiter dicta* in tribunal judgments. In Judge Gorman's words, "it is often appropriate [for an international administrative tribunal], when the opportunity and context present themselves, to go beyond strictly the issue to be decided and give the institution some gentle advice as to how it might alter and improve its rules and treat staff members more fairly" (p. 144). This educational function of a tribunal, which would allow the tribunal not to limit itself to deciding specific issues brought before it, was assessed differently by Dr. Shihata. According to him, the educational role "is not advisable as a general matter," and a tribunal "would do best if it [were to] limit its role to what is stated in its [s]tatute" (p. 192).

Whether a tribunal should restrict itself to deciding the issues raised before it or should also allow itself to give guidance going beyond the scope of the case presented remains an open question. It was established, however, that the WBAT's judgments "have provided to the Bank Group invaluable guidance for future actions" (Tung, p. 14), and that "senior management [is provided] with summaries of the Tribunal's [judgments]" (Rivero, p. 169). Indeed, the mere existence of an international administrative tribunal to which an aggrieved party may have recourse has provided great support to general counsels and legal advisers within organizations, and strengthened their efforts to persuade their respective administrations not to pursue certain courses of action (Schwebel, p. 153; and Devlin, p. 164).

Prior to the closure of the Conference, several speakers suggested that the presidents and members of international administrative tribunals should meet together on a regular basis (Thierry, p. 157), and that the Conference "be viewed as the beginning of a series of continuing conversations" (Gorman, p. 198). It is worthy of note that these suggestions have since been implemented.

With respect to the present work, it may be noticed that as the Conference was bilingual (with English and French), the text of every presentation or paper is preceded by a summary in the other language. I take sole responsibility for the preparation of these summaries, as they were not reviewed by the authors.

This work would not have been possible without the support and encouragement of the judges of the WBAT, and particularly Robert A. Gorman who presided over the WBAT at the time of the Conference. I would further note that my former colleagues in the WBAT Secretariat assisted me greatly in organizing the Conference. I would like particularly to acknowledge the exceptional efforts of Howard Dean in this respect. I would also like to thank Marie Bonhomme for her valuable administrative assistance. With respect to preparing this book for publication, I would like to thank my colleagues Peter C. Hansen, Adjunct Professor of International Law at the American University in Washington and a former WBAT Counsel, and Fady E. Béchara, Associate Professor of Civil Law and Private International Law at the Saint-Joseph University of Beirut and a member of the Beirut Bar Association, for their advice and suggestions throughout the various stages of the preparation process. Maureen MacGlashan, former British Ambassador to the Holy See, and currently editor of *The Indexer*, contributed her valuable expertise in preparing the index.

The usual disclaimer applies, and I take full responsibility for any defects in the preparation of this book.

Washington, D.C.
December 2007

OPENING SESSION

OPENING REMARKS

Robert A. Gorman*

Résumé

Au début de l'an 1980, Robert McNamara, qui assumait à l'époque la présidence de la Banque mondiale, m'a informé de la création par le Conseil des Gouverneurs de la Banque d'un Tribunal dont l'objectif était – et demeure toujours – d'assurer que les décisions des cadres de la Banque soient conformes aux règles de droit et d'améliorer, par conséquent, le moral des employés de la Banque et l'efficacité de leur service.

Dès sa constitution, le Tribunal administratif de la Banque mondiale (TABM) a développé une méthode de travail qui demeure toujours en place. Il s'agit pour sept juges venant de pays différents reflétant des traditions juridiques, des cultures et des pratiques sociales diverses de dépasser les particularismes et les différences de vues et d'aboutir à des jugements unanimes, intellectuellement rigoureux, scrupuleusement impartiaux et faciles à lire. Tous les jugements rendus à ce jour par le Tribunal sont unanimes et ne comportent ni opinions séparées ni opinions dissidentes.

Le caractère unanime des jugements rendus par le TABM est d'autant plus remarquable en matière de harcèlement sexuel ou encore en matière disciplinaire, deux domaines qui reflètent des différences culturelles profondes. De telles différences doivent pourtant être dépassées afin d'identifier des critères internationaux applicables aux agents internationaux. Tel a été le plus grand défi pour moi durant mes années passées aussi bien au TABM qu'au Tribunal administratif de la Banque asiatique pour le développement.

L'objectif de la conférence d'aujourd'hui est multiple: d'abord, partager nos expériences et nos interrogations dans un cadre relativement informel; ensuite, publier les présentations et les interventions d'aujourd'hui dans un livre qui puisse servir de référence à l'avenir aux chercheurs, juristes et praticiens; enfin, nous permettre de mieux faire connaissance afin de faciliter des échanges futurs qui conduiraient à des conférences et réunions régulières.

* * *

As President of the World Bank Administrative Tribunal, it is my great pleasure to call to order this conference that marks the 20th anniversary of the creation of the Tribunal. I recall being invited to meet, in early 1980, with then President of the World Bank, Robert McNamara. He

* President, World Bank Administrative Tribunal; Professor of Law, University of Pennsylvania.

informed me of the approval by the Bank's governing board of the creation of a Tribunal, to be modeled along the lines of the Tribunals at the International Labour Organization and the United Nations. He firmly stated that the time had come to provide a court-like agency to hear and decide cases brought by any staff member of the Bank. President McNamara mentioned two important purposes, which still motivate the work of the Administrative Tribunal today, and of other administrative tribunals: to assure through an impartial agency that the decisions of Bank management conform to the rule of law, and as a consequence to achieve an improved level in the morale of staff members and in the efficacy of their service.

The Tribunal's first major action in 1980 was to adopt our rules of operation, and we then decided our first case, which presented questions of importance, difficulty and nuance. We also very quickly developed our style of work, which remains to this day – thoroughly collaborative, a submergence of individual personalities to the common end of reaching judgments that are intellectually rigorous, scrupulously impartial, intelligible and readable. The Tribunal has issued 225 judgments over the course of 20 years. The overwhelming number have been decided by all seven judges sitting as a plenary panel; it was only after some 17 years had transpired that the exigencies of handling a mounting docket induced the Tribunal to divide into panels of three and four judges. Every one of these 225 judgments has been unanimous, without any separate opinion and without any dissent. There are differences of view; but they are accommodated in the course of preparing and issuing judgments that have greater force and clarity by virtue of the single voice with which the Tribunal speaks.

These very positive elements in the work of the Tribunal – particularly rigor and collegiality – are in the greatest measure attributable to the remarkable individual who served as President of the Tribunal for some ten years, Eduardo Jiménez de Aréchaga, who at the time was a former President of the International Court of Justice. It was a great privilege for me, particularly as one whose special competence was in labor and employment law and not in international administrative law, to have served with Judge Aréchaga. I would ask you to take a moment, by your silence, to pay tribute to his memory – and to the memory of the three other judges who have served on the Tribunal and who have passed away: Taslim Olawale Elias, Charles Onyeama, and Fred Apaloo. I also hope you will reflect upon the very recent passing of Heribert Golsong, who was the Vice President and General Counsel of the World Bank at the time the Administrative Tribunal was created and who played a major role in its establishment.

When I speak of my work on the Administrative Tribunal to my lawyer colleagues in the United States, the aspect that we all find most intriguing is the common core of values – both substantive and procedural – that all seven judges from around the world bring to bear upon our judgments. At present, the Tribunal judges come from France, Chile, Australia, Egypt, Nigeria, Singapore and the United States – obviously different legal systems, reflecting different histories, cultures and social practices. And yet, even though the terminology and the language used to express it may be different, there is an overwhelming congruence of views about the interpretation of the documents that govern the rights of staff members, about the elements of due process and fair procedure that must shape the Bank's decisions, about the nuanced criteria that divide a reasonable exercise of managerial power from an abuse of discretion, and about the proper remedies to be awarded.

Surely one could expect, for example, that notions of sexual harassment, an increasing concern in workplaces throughout the world, would reflect deeply rooted cultural differences. The same might also be expected in cases of discipline for improper conduct, in which a central issue in the jurisprudence of tribunals is whether there is "proportionality" between the seriousness of the staff member's offense and the severity of the punishment imposed by the institution. Nonetheless, these differences must be submerged in an effort to identify an international standard that is appropriately applied in the context of international agencies. That has been a most challenging and instructive exercise for me during my years on the World Bank Administrative Tribunal, as well as my fewer years on the Asian Development Bank Administrative Tribunal.

My colleagues and I on the World Bank Administrative Tribunal decided that the convergence of our 20th anniversary and the year 2000 warranted more systematic reflection upon our jurisprudence and our operations. We also thought it would be greatly instructive to have a conversation with, and among, our colleagues in many other international juristic bodies – colleagues not in the sense that we work side by side, but rather in our common efforts to shape a system of just rules for the governance of an international civil service.

Our purpose today is therefore several: first, to share experiences, concerns and questions in a relatively informal and conversational setting, so that we may possibly enhance our jurisprudence and our internal operations; second, to produce a printed volume that will preserve the papers and the comments of our many distinguished participants today, to be available in the future for scholars, jurists and practitioners; and third, to enable us to become better acquainted, thus facilitating future conversations among our tribunal judges and secretariats and, I very much hope, leading to future regular conferences and other forms of meetings on these and other subjects of common interest.

I am pleased that a major role will be played today by three of my most cherished colleagues on the World Bank Administrative Tribunal, who were appointed along with me when the Tribunal was established in 1980, who have served for all or nearly all of the intervening years, and who preceded me as President of the Tribunal: Kamal Abul-Magd will preside at this morning's discussion; Eli Lauterpacht at this afternoon's; and concluding remarks will be delivered by Prosper Weil (as well as by Ibrahim Shihata, whose term as Vice President and General Counsel coincided with almost all of the Tribunal's existence, and who has been strongly supportive of the role and work of the Tribunal). A major role in planning and organizing this conference has been played by Nassib Ziadé, the Executive Secretary of the Tribunal. He has been of incalculable assistance to the Tribunal in gathering information about the work of other administrative tribunals, in identifying issues that can usefully be discussed today, in identifying and contacting speakers, and in overseeing the conference arrangements.

I would now like to introduce my colleagues for this morning's opening remarks. I am so pleased to introduce Gilbert Guillaume, who is presently the President of the International Court of Justice. I would also parenthetically like to welcome Stephen Schwebel, who will participate in this afternoon's discussion and who is the former President of the International Court of Justice. And also delivering opening remarks is Ko-Yung Tung, who is now the Vice President and General Counsel of the World Bank.

Again, I welcome you all, with the hope that this conference will be both a pleasant celebration of the Tribunal's birthday and a stimulating forum for the many of you who have traveled to Paris for this unique event.

DÉCLARATION D'OUVERTURE

Gilbert Guillaume*

Summary

The International Court of Justice (ICJ) has ruled on several occasions on questions involving international civil servants. Two important advisory opinions were delivered in 1949 and 1954. In the first opinion, the Court noted that the United Nations (UN) might find it necessary to entrust its agents with important missions to be performed in disturbed parts of the world. The Court stated that these agents must be assured effective protection, and concluded that the UN had the capacity to seek adequate reparation for damages suffered by it as well as by the agent and those holding rights under the agent. In the second opinion, which like the first had been requested by the UN General Assembly, the Court found that judgments of the United Nations Administrative Tribunal (UNAT) were binding on the UN. It concluded that the General Assembly had no right on any ground to refuse to give effect to an award of compensation made by the UNAT in favor of a UN staff member. In the same opinion, the Court recognized that international administrative tribunals have the power to examine requests for interpretation of their judgments, even when their statutes are silent on this point.

There followed a series of more technical judgments that were heard by the ICJ pursuant to a then-existing procedure that allowed the ICJ to entertain requests for review of UNAT and International Labour Organization Administrative Tribunal (ILOAT) judgments. With respect to the judgments of the UNAT, this procedure was strongly criticized as being unfair, and it was therefore ultimately eliminated by the UN General Assembly. At present, only judgments of the ILOAT can be contested before the ICJ on the basis of either a lack of jurisdiction on the Tribunal's part or a fundamental procedural irregularity by the Tribunal. Such a procedure has not been used since 1956.

In such conditions, the future contribution of the ICJ to the field of international civil service law will likely be through advisory opinions rather than through direct intervention in specific cases brought originally before international administrative tribunals.

The proliferation of international administrative tribunals has not posed a serious risk of divergence in international administrative law, as is the situation with respect to general international law given the many criminal and other specialized and regional international tribunals now operating. International administrative case law on the whole remains extremely consistent. This situation results from the following factors: (i) the permanence and wisdom of the judges, who sometimes sit on different tribunals at the same time; (ii) the case law created at

* Président de la Cour internationale de Justice.

the inception of the tribunals is closely followed through the years by successive judges, with only necessary adjustments being made; (iii) the judges never hesitate to refer in their judgments to the judgments of other international administrative tribunals; and (iv) the judgments are rarely undermined by dissenting opinions. These factors have unfortunately not been applied in the area of general international law. In this respect, the ICJ may need to institute procedural mechanisms that will expand its role and thereby ensure consistency in international law.

* * *

Monsieur le Président, Mesdames, Messieurs,

Je voudrais tout d'abord remercier les organisateurs de cette conférence et tout particulièrement vous-même, Monsieur le Président, ainsi que Monsieur Nassib Ziadé, Secrétaire exécutif du Tribunal administratif de la Banque mondiale, pour leur aimable invitation à participer aux travaux d'aujourd'hui.

Ayant à multiples reprises et en des qualités diverses été amené à m'intéresser au contentieux administratif international, j'ai avec grand plaisir accepté cette invitation.

Puis je me suis demandé quelle contribution je pourrais apporter à cette conférence en tant que président de la Cour internationale de Justice.

Encore que brève, cette contribution m'a paru devoir être double. Elle concerne d'une part le passé et d'autre part l'avenir.

*

Dans le passé, la Cour a en premier lieu été amenée à plusieurs reprises à se prononcer sur des questions d'importance concernant les fonctionnaires internationaux.

Elle l'a fait pour la première fois à la suite de l'assassinat du Comte Bernadotte en 1948 à Jérusalem. Saisie alors d'une demande d'avis de l'Assemblée générale des Nations Unies, la Cour a, le 11 avril 1949, rappelé que l'ONU peut avoir à confier à ses agents des missions importantes dans des régions troublées du monde. Elle a estimé que, dans ces cas, ces agents doivent disposer d'un appui et d'une protection appropriés. Elle en a déduit que l'Organisation a capacité pour demander une réparation adéquate des dommages subis tant par elle que par la victime et ses ayants droit.

Puis, dans un deuxième avis du 13 juillet 1954, la Cour a estimé, là encore sur une demande de l'Assemblée générale, que les jugements du Tribunal administratif des Nations Unies (TANU) avaient force obligatoire à l'égard de l'ONU. Elle en a déduit que l'Assemblée générale n'avait pas le droit, pour quelque raison que ce soit, de refuser d'exécuter un jugement accordant une indemnité à un agent. Dans ce même avis, elle a reconnu aux juridictions administratives internationales compétence pour connaître des recours en interprétation dans le silence même des statuts.

Ces deux avis fondamentaux ont été suivis d'une série d'autres, plus techniques. Ceux-ci ont été rendus selon les procédures de réformation des jugements du TANU et du Tribunal administratif de l'Organisation internationale du Travail (TAOIT), alors en vigueur. Le 23 octobre 1956, la Cour a reconnu au Tribunal administratif de l'OIT une compétence plus large que ne le souhaitait en l'espèce l'UNESCO, en précisant que les requérants avaient pu se prévaloir devant ce tribunal non seulement de leurs contrats et du statut applicable, mais encore d'une simple note de l'administration "annonçant que tous les titulaires de contrats de durée définie se verraient en principe offrir le renouvellement de leurs contrats".

Puis, le 12 juillet 1973, la Cour a été amenée à se pencher sur une plainte d'un agent des Nations Unies endossée par le comité des demandes de réformation. L'intéressé soutenait que le TANU avait omis d'exercer sa juridiction et avait commis dans la procédure une erreur essentielle ayant provoqué un mal jugé. La Cour a écarté ces griefs.

Elle a, de même, le 20 juillet 1982, écarté une demande de réformation d'une décision du TANU présentée en 1981 par le Gouvernement des Etats-Unis. A cette occasion, elle a estimé en effet que le TANU n'avait pas en l'espèce outrepassé sa compétence et n'avait méconnu aucune disposition de la Charte.

Enfin, le 27 mai 1987, la Cour a reconnu la validité d'un jugement du TANU reconnaissant la licéité du non-renouvellement par le Secrétaire général d'un contrat à durée déterminée, le détachement de l'intéressé auprès des Nations Unies par son administration nationale ayant pris fin.

Les deux premiers avis ainsi donnés par la Cour ont été d'une importance évidente. Ceux qui ont suivi ont eu une portée plus limitée. Par ailleurs, la procédure selon laquelle la Cour pouvait être saisie des demandes de réformation des jugements du TANU a été vivement critiquée par une partie de la doctrine comme inégalitaire. Aussi l'Assemblée générale a-t-elle finalement décidé de la supprimer et, à l'heure actuelle, seuls les jugements du TAOIT demeurent susceptibles d'être déférés à la Cour. Ils peuvent être contestés pour incompétence ou faute essentielle dans la procédure suivie. La Cour peut être saisie par le Conseil d'administration du Bureau international du Travail (BIT) ou le Conseil exécutif de l'organisation internationale ayant accepté la compétence de la Cour. Cette procédure n'a pas été utilisée depuis 1956.

Dans ces conditions, la contribution future de la Cour internationale de Justice au contentieux de la fonction publique internationale semble devoir être avant tout le résultat de demandes d'avis consultatifs. Ainsi la Cour a-t-elle récemment dû préciser à deux reprises l'étendue des immunités et privilèges des experts de la Commission des droits de l'homme des Nations Unies sur demande du Conseil économique et social par deux avis du 15 décembre 1989 (affaire *Mazilu*) et du 29 avril 1999 (affaire *Cumaraswamy*). Une telle contribution est loin d'être négligeable, mais elle n'implique pas une intervention directe dans les contentieux portés devant les tribunaux administratifs internationaux.

*

Cette situation ne va cependant pas sans poser un problème qui n'est d'ailleurs pas propre aux juridictions administratives: celui de la cohésion future du droit international.

Ce problème est particulièrement aigu en droit international général. Il est né de la création des juridictions criminelles internationales, de la mise sur pied du mécanisme de règlement des différends de l'Organisation mondiale du Commerce, de l'institution du Tribunal international du droit de la mer et de la multiplication des juridictions régionales. Cette prolifération des juridictions a en effet créé des risques sérieux de divergences de jurisprudence qui se sont concrétisées récemment quand, dans l'affaire *Tadič*, le Tribunal pénal international pour l'ex-Yougoslavie a pris volontairement et explicitement des positions de principe différentes de celles de la Cour internationale de Justice.

En ce qui concerne les juridictions administratives internationales, la situation à cet égard me paraît cependant comporter moins de risques. Certes, comme l'a noté Monsieur Ziadé dans son rapport soumis à la séance de cet après-midi, ces juridictions se sont, elles aussi, multipliées, tout particulièrement en ce qui concerne les institutions financières internationales. Mais en même temps, elles ont développé une jurisprudence conservant dans l'ensemble une certaine cohérence.

On peut s'interroger sur les raisons de cette cohérence et sur les leçons à en tirer. Mon impression personnelle est que cette situation résulte pour l'essentiel de la permanence et de la sagesse des juges. La jurisprudence du TANU et celle du TAOIT ont été fixées assez rapidement, sous l'influence de deux grands juristes français, Mme Suzanne Bastid et M. Maxime Letourneur. Leurs successeurs sont restés fidèles à cette jurisprudence en lui apportant bien entendu les retouches nécessaires. Le même phénomène peut être noté dans d'autres juridictions administratives internationales.

En outre, on ne saurait oublier que les mêmes personnes siègent parfois dans divers tribunaux et surtout que ceux-ci n'hésitent pas à se référer aux jugements rendus par les uns ou les autres. C'est ainsi que, récemment encore, en tant que président de la Commission de recours d'Eutelsat, j'ai été amené dans un jugement rendu par cette commission à m'appuyer sur la jurisprudence du TANU ou celle du TAOIT et sur le premier jugement rendu par le Tribunal administratif de la Banque mondiale dans l'affaire *de Merode*.

Dans le même sens, on doit noter que les jugements des tribunaux administratifs internationaux ont rarement été affaiblis par des opinions individuelles ou dissidentes, celles-ci étant le plus souvent exclues et de toute manière utilisées avec mesure.

Ces leçons ne sont malheureusement pas complètement transposables en droit international général, à tout le moins au niveau mondial. Elles pourraient toutefois être méditées avec fruit par les juges qui ne sauraient, sans danger grave, entrer en compétition sauvage les uns avec les autres au risque d'accroître l'insécurité juridique et d'affaiblir la confiance des Etats dans le droit international.

La Cour internationale de Justice a, dans cette perspective, un rôle important à jouer et si la sagesse des juges ne suffisait pas, peut-être faudrait-il envisager d'instituer des mécanismes procéduraux permettant dans l'avenir d'assurer la cohérence du droit en étendant le rôle de la Cour.

Mais tel n'est pas le propos de notre conférence d'aujourd'hui qui se place bien au contraire dans une perspective de meilleure compréhension entre des juges appartenant à des juridictions distinctes, mais au service d'un même droit. A cet égard, elle constitue sans aucun doute un exemple que je tiens à saluer et un événement auquel je suis heureux de participer.

OPENING REMARKS

Ko-Yung Tung*

Résumé

Depuis vingt ans, date de sa création, le Tribunal administratif de la Banque mondiale est aux prises avec les problèmes les plus ardus qu'ait connus la Banque. On se souvient du premier jugement rendu par le Tribunal dans l'affaire *de Merode et al. c. Banque mondiale* où le Tribunal avait posé les fondements de sa jurisprudence ultérieure. Au fil des ans et de 225 jugements rendus, le Tribunal a défini, pour le personnel et la direction de la Banque, la bonne pratique du pouvoir discrétionnaire ainsi que la notion du traitement équitable du personnel.

Les buts assignés au Tribunal par le Président de la Banque de l'époque, Robert McNamara, ont ainsi été réalisés: remédier, à l'instar d'autres organisations spécialisées des Nations Unies, à l'absence de tribunal administratif au sein de la Banque mondiale, et assurer, en cas de litige, le déroulement d'un procès juste et équitable. En effet, les membres du personnel ont toute opportunité aujourd'hui de présenter leurs cas au Tribunal administratif par écrit et de l'accompagner d'une documentation parfois volumineuse.

Je suis heureux d'apprendre qu'en plus des plaidoiries orales ayant eu lieu dans deux cas durant les premières années de son existence, le Tribunal administratif a organisé au mois de janvier dernier sa première séance d'audition de témoins, ce qui renforce la confiance des membres du personnel quant à l'opportunité qui leur est donnée de faire valoir leurs droits.

La Banque mondiale a récemment opéré une refonte complète de la procédure des recours. Un nouveau système est né, appelé le Système de résolution des conflits, qui favorise une solution rapide et amiable des conflits entre la direction et le personnel. La médiation volontaire y remplace l'ancienne revue administrative obligatoire. Elle constitue la première étape du Système de résolution des conflits.

Toutefois, il appartiendra toujours au Tribunal de trancher les cas difficiles et complexes qui ne se résoudront ni par la médiation ni par les autres moyens mis à la disposition des parties. Les jugements du Tribunal seront finaux et obligatoires à l'égard des plaideurs.

* * *

Good morning Mr. President, Judges of the Administrative Tribunal, and distinguished guests. I would first of all like to thank you for the opportunity

* Vice President and General Counsel, World Bank; former Partner, O'Melveny and Myers, New York.

to attend this important conference. I am also grateful for the invitation to speak to this gathering on this noteworthy occasion.

We observe today the twentieth anniversary of the establishment of the World Bank Administrative Tribunal. In the twenty years since the decision to establish an Administrative Tribunal for the World Bank Group, this Tribunal has wrestled with some of the most complex, and often intractable, issues that have arisen within the Bank Group. In its first decision, *de Merode et al. v. The World Bank*, the Administrative Tribunal articulated the principles that would serve as the cornerstone for the jurisprudence that would follow in later years. Those principles have found application in a host of different situations arising over the past twenty years.

Those attending today's conference will well appreciate the difficult cases presented to the Tribunal for resolution. Whether the cases involved termination of employment, disputed performance evaluations, promotions that were denied or benefits that were disputed, the issues coming to the Tribunal have always been complex, the facts in dispute, and the answers never straightforward. Nonetheless, the Tribunal has judiciously managed to find the right outcome. Its decisions are always lucid and its reasoning cogent. Most significantly, its decisions have provided to the Bank Group invaluable guidance for future actions.

Staff and management have learned from the Tribunal's decisions. They have learned about the legitimate exercise of management discretion, and about abuse of managerial discretion. They have learned about essential elements of employment. These important principles and others, articulated first in June 1981 and elaborated upon in some 224 subsequent decisions, have provided everyone in the World Bank Group with a better understanding of good management practice and just treatment of staff.

Twenty years ago, in recommending to the Executive Directors the establishment of an Administrative Tribunal for the Bank Group, then President Robert McNamara noted several reasons for the establishment of a Tribunal. These included the need to deal with the desire to remedy an unequal position of the Bank staff in relation to other specialized agencies of the United Nations that already had an administrative tribunal.

Twenty years ago, the Bank held 5,000 employees; today there are more than twice that number. With more diversity of staff, the issues will no doubt become more complex.

Circumstances have changed, but one additional reason given by Mr. McNamara remains equally if not more essential. He observed that wherever administrative power is exercised, there should be the possibility, in cases of disputes, of a "fair hearing and due process." Mr. McNamara called attention to the fact that this principle is enshrined not only in numerous national constitutions but is also reaffirmed in the Universal

Declaration of Human Rights. As General Counsel, I have personally promoted the rule of law, not only for our borrowing members, but also within the Bank itself.

I believe that the most important contribution made by the Administrative Tribunal over the past twenty years has been to provide staff with the assurance of an impartial, fair and thorough review of their grievances. While some staff may go away from the Tribunal disappointed that the decision did not go their way, all staff go away knowing that they have had their day in court. They are accorded ample opportunity to make their case to the Administrative Tribunal, through written argumentation and through the submission of documents, sometimes volumes of documents! There can be no doubt that all staff who have wanted to exercise it have enjoyed the right to the "fair hearing and due process" that Mr. McNamara envisaged.

In its early years, the Administrative Tribunal scheduled oral arguments in two cases where it concluded that such argumentation would further illuminate the issues before it. I was very encouraged to learn that in January of this year, the Administrative Tribunal held its first evidentiary hearing, where witnesses were called and subject to direct and cross-examination by lawyers for both parties. This is an important development in the practice of the Tribunal, and serves to further meet the expectations of staff that they will be afforded every opportunity to make their case. Evidentiary hearings of this sort may not be necessary in every case. However, the Tribunal's willingness to schedule such a hearing and to devote the time necessarily associated with such a proceeding, serves to underscore the Tribunal's commitment to a fair and complete review of every case that comes before it.

Many of you may have already heard that the World Bank Group has recently completed a comprehensive review of its grievance processes. The result is a new system called the Conflict Resolution System. Various authorities from around the world have reviewed the new system and have described it as state of the art. This system emphasizes the early and hopefully amicable resolution of conflicts between staff and management. It provides staff with multiple channels of help at various times in the course of a dispute.

Voluntary mediation replaces mandatory administrative review as one of the first entry points into the conflict resolution system. It is our hope that mediation will result in satisfactory outcomes to all sides in many cases. Early indications are that this objective may well be achieved.

Mediation, however, will not succeed in all cases. And there will always be some instances where, regardless of the number of avenues open to staff, disputes will remain. It is these, the hardest and most complex cases, that the Administrative Tribunal will be called upon to adjudicate in the years to come. It will have to provide staff with full opportunity to make their case. Most importantly, its decisions will necessarily be the final, and binding, decision on both staff and Bank management that brings these disputes to an end. I remain confident that, as it has in the past twenty years, the World Bank Administrative Tribunal will, in the years to come, continue to work hard and well to find the just outcome.

Today, the World Bank and other international organizations are under attack from many fronts. Our immunity is challenged in many jurisdictions. Our best defense will be the unassailable integrity of the rule of law as established by the Administrative Tribunal. I would like to conclude by thanking the Judges of the Administrative Tribunal, both past and present, for the hard work, long hours, and wise judgment they have each brought to the cases coming before them. I would also like to recognize the contributions of the Administrative Tribunal's Executive Secretaries and staff, past and present, to the functioning of the Tribunal. I wish also to pay tribute to my predecessor, Ibrahim Shihata, who has left behind a rich legacy for me.

I look to the coming years with confidence that the Tribunal will succeed in meeting the challenges that surely await it.

Thanks to all of you for making time to attend this conference. I look forward to an interesting and robust exchange of views concerning the topics on today's agenda.

REVIEW OF MANAGERIAL DISCRETION BY INTERNATIONAL ADMINISTRATIVE TRIBUNALS

INTRODUCTORY REMARKS

A. Kamal Abul-Magd*
Session Chair

Résumé

L'avis rendu en 1925 par le comité de juristes nommé par la Société des Nations dans l'affaire *Monod* déclarait déjà que l'administration publique se devait, dans chacun de ses actes, de toujours s'inspirer de l'intérêt public et de respecter les principes de la justice. L'avis ajoutait que si l'administration excédait ses pouvoirs pour des fins privées on non autorisées par la loi, elle commettrait des actes illégitimes.

Il importe de noter que cet avis confirmait le principe selon lequel, dans une organisation internationale, l'administration demeure soumise à la règle de droit et au contrôle judiciaire. En outre, l'avis introduisait déjà le concept subtil et moderne de détournement de pouvoir.

Il reste que l'étendue du contrôle judiciaire variera suivant l'étendue des pouvoirs accordés à l'administration: il ne sera pas le même en cas de compétence liée ou de pouvoir discrétionnaire.

Deux questions surgissent dans le cadre du contrôle judiciaire exercé par les tribunaux administratifs: d'abord, celle relative au principe suivant lequel, en matière de pouvoir discrétionnaire, les tribunaux ne font que contrôler les actes de l'administration sans leur substituer leurs propres jugements; ensuite, celle de savoir si le contrôle judiciaire se limite aux actes administratifs individuels ou s'il s'étend aux actes réglementaires de l'administration.

En cette ère de globalisation, il est sain d'échanger nos idées et de découvrir les points communs entre nos différentes cultures sur la question.

* * *

Distinguished Judges of the Administrative Tribunals, dear guests, ladies and gentlemen. After an opening session where three eminent international lawyers have made their valuable contributions to the work of this conference, there may be no need for further introductory notes. I wish, however, to make a very brief introduction to the topic to be addressed during this first working session. I have no intention whatsoever to abuse the minimum discretion usually allocated to the Chair in order to make a separate presentation. After having read most of the papers, I simply felt that a very brief comment on the topic would not be out of order.

* Judge and former President, World Bank Administrative Tribunal; Professor of Law, Cairo University.

Perhaps the best way to introduce this morning's topic is to quote a few lines from the opinion of the committee of jurists nominated by the League of Nations in 1925 in the *Monod* case: "This does not mean that a public administration can exercise its powers in an arbitrary manner. The public administration must always, in all its acts, have regard to the public interest and respect the principles of justice. If it exceeds its power for private ends or ends not authorised by law, or if it commits an injustice, it is guilty of unlawful acts."

The importance and relevance of this particular statement is not limited to the fact that it confirms that public administration in international organizations remains subject to the rule of law and, hence, to judicial review. It also introduced the very advanced and sophisticated concept of *détournement de pouvoir.* When this statement refers to following illegal ends or ends not envisioned by the legislator, it in fact refers directly to abuse of discretion in the technical sense of *détournement de pouvoir.* One does not have to adopt the classical French distinction between *compétence liée* and *pouvoir discrétionnaire* to recognize that the scope of review in any international tribunal does indeed vary according to the amount of discretion allocated or given to the administration itself.

Having said so, I need not dwell on the fact that almost all international administrative tribunals have operated on the basis of such a distinction, no matter what form or what technique they have opted to follow, or in what manner they have expressed their acceptance and adherence to this distinction.

It remains, however, to examine issues relating to the exact scope of the power of judicial review in administrative tribunals. More specifically, when it comes to discretionary power, one must determine whether the principle referred to in all decisions of administrative tribunals – namely that they review but do not substitute their own judgment for that of management – is in fact respected. What counts in the last analysis is not what the tribunal says it is doing, but what the tribunal is actually doing. Another difficult issue is whether the reviewing power of the administrative tribunal is limited to individual administrative acts, or can be expanded to policy-making or quasi-legislative powers of the administration.

Here, I must refer with all modesty to one of the very first decisions made by the World Bank Administrative Tribunal. In the *de Merode* case, very subtle distinctions were made, paving the way for subsequent decisions and hopefully for other administrative tribunals as well.

As the President of our Tribunal, Robert A. Gorman, has said, we need to exchange ideas. I might add that we also need to discover common points as we head into this period of globalization, during which different cultures will meet. Whether they relate to law, politics or other areas, we need to identify commonalities and to cooperate in implementing and strengthening them. In summary, we have come here to learn, knowing that while not every concern is usually expressed in decisions, many concerns remain inside of us.

I am privileged to welcome the main speakers in this session: Mr. Michel Gentot, President of the International Labour Organization Administrative Tribunal and a Judge on the International Monetary Fund Administrative Tribunal; and Mr. Nicolas Valticos, former Deputy President of the Council of Europe Administrative Tribunal and President of the Curatorium of the Hague Academy of International Law.

LE CONTRÔLE DU POUVOIR DISCRÉTIONNAIRE PAR LES TRIBUNAUX ADMINISTRATIFS INTERNATIONAUX

Michel Gentot*

Summary

In the World Bank Administrative Tribunal's (WBAT) first judgment, *de Merode*, the Tribunal made a distinction between those essential conditions of an employment contract which cannot be amended without the consent of the affected staff member, and those less fundamental and essential conditions which the Bank has the discretionary power to amend so long as such power is not used in an arbitrary manner for reasons alien to the proper functioning of the organization. One can find in *de Merode* an echo of the opinion of the committee of jurists appointed by the League of Nations in the *Monod* case: "The public administration must always, in all its acts, have regard to the public interest and respect the principles of justice. If it exceeds its power for private ends or ends not authorized by law, or if it commits an injustice, it is guilty of unlawful acts." The same idea, i.e. that "discretionary" is not synonymous with "arbitrary," has consistently been restated by other international administrative tribunals. It can be found, for example, in the *Ballo v. UNESCO* judgment of the International Labour Organization Administrative Tribunal (ILOAT): "Discretionary authority must not . . . be confused with arbitrary power." Similarly, the WBAT held in *McNeill* that while the Administration had a widely discretionary power to determine during or at the end of a probationary period whether the probationer should or should not be confirmed, such power is balanced by the Administration's duty to meet "the appropriate standards of justice." The WBAT also determined in *Barnes* that "[a]lthough the Applicant did not have a right to either conversion or extension of her fixed-term contract, the decision not to convert or extend her contract was nonetheless a decision which, like any other exercise of discretion by the Respondent, must be reached fairly and not in an arbitrary manner."

Organizations need not be paralyzed by the fear that their administrative decisions and policies will be systematically challenged before a judge. Nor should they be able, on the other hand, to evade the application of the rule of law to them by invoking the needs of the organization.

It is difficult to provide a clear and precise definition of "discretionary power." In English, the concept of "discretion" or "discretionary power" is commonplace. In French, however, the term most often used – and with great caution – is simply "*pouvoir d'appréciation.*" The scope of a judge's review of the administration's exercise of its discretion depends on how much discretionary power the judge decides to allow the administration to exercise.

* Président du Tribunal administratif de l'Organisation internationale du Travail; Juge au Tribunal administratif du Fonds monétaire international.

The question is often raised at the outset whether a case is one of an organization's discretionary power or, alternatively, of its *compétence liée* (a concept of French administrative law which refers to an administrative body having jurisdiction over a matter but being bound by law or otherwise to decide the matter in a specific manner). Sometimes, it is a combination of both. Organizations are bound by the provisions of their statutes, by those general principles recognized by tribunals, and by the employment contracts concluded with their staff. In many cases in which *compétence liée* is at issue, a tribunal must simply compare a particular decision referred to it with the rules under which the employee claims his or her rights. For example, an employee is clearly entitled to the salary and allowances established for his or her category of employment, and the administration has no discretionary power over such an entitlement. However, if the rules provide for the awarding of an allowance based on the staff member's performance, the administration's determination is discretionary in this respect. Such discretion will be subject only to a minimum or a limited review.

All tribunals have asserted jurisdiction to conduct limited reviews of cases involving the exercise of discretionary power, although the language used to describe such reviews is not always identical, even within the same tribunal. It is a widely held belief that while discretionary power is not synonymous with arbitrariness and must therefore be subject to review, judges should not substitute their own assessments for those of the organizations. Their scope of review is thus limited.

Judges have the right – and the duty – to censure decisions, even those resulting from the exercise of discretionary power, which: (i) were issued by an authority that was not competent to act in the situation; (ii) were taken in violation of procedural rules; (iii) were based on errors of fact or law; or (iv) indicate the existence of a *détournement de pouvoir* (abuse of power) or misuse of authority. Oft-cited examples of such decisions include those in which there have been obvious errors occurring during an evaluation of the facts, disregard of the rules of proportionality in the case of disciplinary measures, and, more generally, unreasonableness or abuse of discretion. This scope of review may appear limited, but it is actually quite broad. Indeed, such review can be properly exercised only when the judge perceives the real, as opposed to the claimed, motivations of the administration through the exchanges between the parties before the tribunal.

The trend has been toward the convergence of "normal" and "limited" reviews of the decisions of international organizations. In all cases, the principles of due process and proportionality must be respected. Similarly, the real motives behind an administrative action need to be scrutinized by the judges.

Are there still any acts of international organizations which are completely immune from review? Probably not. All decisions of international organizations regarding employment matters must be founded on legal and reasonable grounds. The question arises, however, whether general policies issued by an organization's governing body are immune from review. In this respect, the ILOAT held in *Niesing (No. 2)* that "the political and administrative bodies that frame personnel policy have a duty as employer at all times and more particularly when amending conditions of service to abide by [the] general principles [of law]."

* * *

Après vous avoir entendu, Président Kamal Abul-Magd, je serais tenté de renoncer au temps de parole que vous m'avez si généreusement alloué car vous avez dit l'essentiel de ce que je m'apprêtai à dire. Je ne ferai donc que prolonger les pensées que vous venez de développer en des termes très précis.

1. *Les sources du contrôle du pouvoir discrétionnaire*

Ce n'est pas un hasard si les organisateurs de cette belle conférence ont choisi comme premier thème de discussion le contrôle du pouvoir discrétionnaire par les tribunaux administratifs internationaux. Comment ne pas rappeler – et vous l'avez fait Monsieur le Président comme d'autres avant vous – que le premier jugement rendu par le Tribunal administratif de la Banque mondiale, juridiction créée en 1980, a été rendu sur le recours de Monsieur de Merode?

Dès cette première affaire, le Tribunal administratif de la Banque mondiale doit trancher la question relative à la manière de concilier le pouvoir dont dispose tout employeur d'organiser le service et de fixer les conditions d'emploi, d'une part, et les droits des fonctionnaires internationaux d'autre part. Le Tribunal souligne avec force qu'il faut distinguer entre les conditions essentielles du contrat d'emploi, qui ne peuvent être modifiées sans l'accord de l'agent, et les règles qui sont moins fondamentales et moins essentielles et que la Banque a le pouvoir discrétionnaire de modifier par voie d'amendements aux statuts. Dans ce dernier cas, le Tribunal ajoute que ce serait un abus du pouvoir discrétionnaire que d'exercer ce pouvoir de manière arbitraire pour des raisons ou des finalités étrangères au fonctionnement convenable de l'organisation. Il rappelle que la Banque a le devoir de s'assurer qu'elle a un personnel possédant les standards les plus élevés d'efficacité et de compétence technique.

On trouve bien dans ce premier jugement l'écho des conclusions de ce collège, auquel vous faisiez allusion Monsieur le Président, créé il y a soixante-quinze ans par la jeune Société des Nations (SDN) et chargé de se prononcer sur une réclamation présentée par Monsieur Monod, placé en disponibilité *sine die* et, en fait, licencié. Ce collège de juristes préfigurait ce qui allait devenir le Tribunal administratif de la SDN, lui-même à l'origine de tous les tribunaux administratifs internationaux. Ce comité de juristes a donné un avis dont je rappellerai la conclusion: "l'administration doit toujours, dans chacun de ses actes, s'inspirer de l'intérêt public et respecter les principes de la justice. Si elle excède ses pouvoirs pour des fins privées ou non autorisées par la loi, elle commet des actes illégitimes".

On retrouve cette idée dans un grand nombre de jugements. Je me bornerai à citer le jugement *Ballo c. UNESCO* du Tribunal administratif de l'Organisation internationale du Travail (OIT) (Jugement No. 191 du

15 mai 1972) qui, en termes plus laconiques, développe une idée forte qui nous inspire tous: "le pouvoir de libre appréciation ne doit pas être confondu avec le pouvoir arbitraire". Discrétionnaire n'est donc pas synonyme d'arbitraire – comme le reconnaissent tous les tribunaux.

Ces citations montrent l'ancienneté et la permanence des problèmes posés par le contrôle juridictionnel des appréciations dites discrétionnaires. Les organisations ne doivent pas être paralysées dans l'exercice quotidien de leurs responsabilités par la crainte de voir leur politique et leur gestion mises en cause systématiquement devant un juge qui peut être tenté de corriger toutes les déviations et tous les excès. Mais les organisations internationales ne doivent pas non plus échapper à l'application de la règle de droit en tentant de légitimer leurs actes, comme elles le font souvent, par la recherche de l'intérêt du service. Même si leurs pouvoirs ne sont pas encadrés par des règles statutaires strictes, comme lorsqu'il s'agit par exemple de mesurer la valeur d'un agent, de l'opportunité de l'affecter à tel ou tel emploi, de renouveler son contrat ou de l'intérêt qu'il y aurait à modifier la réglementation en vigueur, les appréciations discrétionnaires auxquelles se livrent les organisations internationales pour prendre leurs décisions doivent pouvoir être censurées par un tribunal si elles sont arbitraires.

Je voudrais aussi brièvement que possible examiner l'étendue de ce que l'on appelle le pouvoir discrétionnaire des organisations internationales tel qu'il est défini par la jurisprudence avant d'en venir à l'analyse de la nature, de l'intensité et de l'adaptabilité du contrôle exercé par les tribunaux sur les appréciations discrétionnaires.

2. *L'étendue du pouvoir discrétionnaire*

A. Difficultés d'une définition: Le pouvoir discrétionnaire est difficile à définir. On s'en rend d'ailleurs particulièrement compte lorsque l'on procède à des exercices de traduction. Sur la base de données Triblex du Tribunal administratif de l'OIT, j'ai relevé 463 utilisations des mots *discretion* ou *discretionary power* dans la partie anglaise et n'ai pu relever aucune utilisation dans la partie française. En langue française, on parle le plus souvent, avec plus de circonspection, d'un simple pouvoir d'appréciation. Il semble donc que l'on répugne un peu en France à utiliser le terme de "discrétionnaire" sans doute parce que l'on associe à ce mot une connotation d'arbitraire. En anglais, en revanche, le mot *discretion* correspond davantage à l'exercice de la liberté de faire ou de ne pas faire, d'organiser son service avec la plus grande efficacité et, éventuellement, d'apprécier les agents en fonction de leur efficacité. Cet exemple montre en tout cas qu'il est difficile de donner une définition claire et précise du pouvoir discrétionnaire. On serait donc tenté de dire qu'est discrétionnaire le pouvoir d'appréciation que le juge ne contrôle qu'avec le souci de ne pas se substituer à l'autorité administrative compétente.

B. C'est donc plutôt par une analyse des cas dans lesquels les tribunaux reconnaissent l'existence d'un tel pouvoir qu'il conviendrait de délimiter le champ du pouvoir discrétionnaire. Plusieurs exemples peuvent être donnés. Je pense tout d'abord à l'opportunité de modifier une réglementation. C'est un cas d'exercice du pouvoir discrétionnaire et c'est d'ailleurs ce que rappelle le jugement *de Merode*. Mais les tribunaux administratifs internationaux, dont le Tribunal administratif de l'OIT, sont souvent confrontés à une question difficile: dans quelle mesure les organisations peuvent-elles modifier les conditions et la méthodologie de l'ajustement des rémunérations des fonctionnaires placés sous leur autorité? Je pense également à l'organisation des services. Dans quelles conditions peut-on modifier un organigramme ou répartir les agents dans les départements et bureaux? C'est là aussi une activité de gestion qui relève des appréciations discrétionnaires. Mais cela ne veut pas dire, pour autant, que les administrations peuvent agir dans l'arbitraire. Il en va de même des affectations et des mutations dites dans l'intérêt du service et qui, quelquefois, recouvrent des mutations à caractère disciplinaire, de l'appréciation des mérites des agents au moment des évaluations et des refus de promotion et du maintien en fonction des stagiaires. Il s'agit également des appréciations portées sur la manière de servir qui vont justifier un refus de renouvellement de contrats à durée déterminée. Dans tous ces cas, l'Administration peut très légitimement se prévaloir d'un pouvoir de libre appréciation, d'un pouvoir discrétionnaire.

3. *L'intensité du contrôle du juge*

Lorsque l'on se trouve dans le cadre des appréciations discrétionnaires, quelles sont la nature et l'intensité du pouvoir du juge? Il semble que ce contrôle est en fait modulé en fonction du caractère plus ou moins étendu du pouvoir d'appréciation que le juge, de manière souveraine et sous réserve du contrôle de la Cour internationale de Justice, va pouvoir laisser au gestionnaire.

1. A. Pouvoir discrétionnaire ou compétence liée?: On se demande toujours dans un premier temps si l'on se trouve dans un cas de pouvoir discrétionnaire ou de compétence liée. Les organisations sont liées par les dispositions des statuts, par les principes généraux reconnus par les tribunaux et naturellement par les stipulations des contrats passés avec les agents. Dans bien des cas, le travail du tribunal est simple. Il s'agit de confronter la décision individuelle qui lui est déférée avec la norme supérieure

dont le fonctionnaire revendique l'application. Il est clair qu'un agent a droit par exemple aux traitements et aux indemnités qui sont allouées à sa catégorie. Il peut exister un litige sur le caractère fondé du droit invoqué par l'agent. Mais il n'y a aucune marge d'appréciation par les services de l'organisation dont la compétence est liée pour donner à l'intéressé ce qui lui est dû. Pourtant, cet exemple simple montre qu'il peut exister une combinaison de compétence liée et de pouvoir discrétionnaire. L'intéressé a droit à son salaire et aux indemnités statutaires. Mais si les statuts prévoient une indemnité donnée en fonction de la manière de servir de l'intéressé, le pouvoir d'appréciation exercé par l'Administration relève alors de sa discrétion et peut être soumis uniquement à un contrôle que l'on qualifie de contrôle minimum ou de contrôle restreint.

B. Sur les appréciations discrétionnaires, tous les tribunaux reconnaissent que l'existence d'un contrôle restreint s'impose même si les formulations retenues pour caractériser ce contrôle ne sont pas toujours homogènes. Il faudrait conduire une étude pour repérer les différentes rédactions, y compris à l'intérieur d'un même tribunal, qui caractérisent ce contrôle restreint. Il me semble que l'on trouve partout l'idée que le pouvoir discrétionnaire n'est pas synonyme d'arbitraire et qu'il faut donc le contrôler mais que les juges ne doivent pas substituer leur appréciation à celle des organisations. De fait, le contrôle doit être limité.

Quelles que soient les formules utilisées, il semble que le juge ait le droit et le devoir – mon professeur Madame Bastid disait, il y a quarante ans, que la compétence était le droit et le devoir d'agir – de censurer des décisions, même fondées sur l'usage d'un pouvoir discrétionnaire, qui émanent d'une autorité incompétente, qui sont prises en violation des règles de forme ou de procédure, qui sont fondées sur des erreurs de fait ou de droit ou qui révèlent l'existence d'un détournement de pouvoir ou d'un *misuse of authority*. L'existence d'erreurs manifestes, qui ne peuvent pas échapper à un esprit moyennement éclairé, commises dans l'appréciation des faits, d'une méconnaissance des règles de proportionnalité, notamment dans le cas des sanctions disciplinaires, et, plus généralement, *d'unreasonableness* ou *d'abuse of discretion*, est souvent relevée dans les jugements en langue anglaise.

L'intensité de ce contrôle, même s'il apparaît limité, est en réalité considérable. Ce contrôle ne peut être exercé – et c'est le point le plus important – que si le juge connaît les motifs réels de l'Administration. Que le contrôle soit limité ou qu'il ne le soit pas, dans tous les cas, le juge doit être mis en mesure, par le biais des discussions entre les parties, de se forger une conviction sur les motifs réels et non les motifs affichés qui ont inspiré l'action administrative. C'est en fonction de la connaissance de ces motifs que le juge peut dire s'il y a *misuse of authority* ou non, s'il y a arbitraire.

2. Exemples de jugements: Quelques exemples récents, relevés dans la jurisprudence du Tribunal administratif de l'OIT, du Tribunal administratif de la Banque mondiale et du Tribunal administratif du Fonds monétaire international montreront la diversité des formulations, mais la convergence des solutions.

a) *Tribunal administratif de l'OIT*
8 juillet 1999 (No. 1855 – Wright c. OEB): refus d'accorder un congé spécial
8 juillet 1999 (No. 1860 – Gupta (No. 5) c. OMS): rejet d'une candidature à un emploi
3 février 2000 (No. 1907 – Reis-Ekelund c. OIE): services insatisfaisants
3 février 2000 (No. 1929 – Beaucent c. UPU): mutation prétendument dans l'intérêt du service
b) *Tribunal administratif de la Banque mondiale*
11 avril 1997 (No. 157 – McNeill): non titularisation d'un stagiaire et placement en congé administratif spécial pendant les deux derniers mois de son stage
18 novembre 1997 (No. 176 – Barnes): refus de prolonger un contrat de durée déterminée
15 mai 1998 (No. 185 – Ezatkhah): absence d'efforts pour offrir une nouvelle affectation à un agent
c) *Tribunal administratif du Fonds monétaire international*
2 avril 1996 (No. 1996-1 – Mr. M. D'Aoust): fixation du grade initial et du salaire
22 juillet 1997 (No. 1997-1 – Ms. "C"): mutation et prolongation de contrat

J'aimerais évoquer deux jugements de 1997 du Tribunal administratif de la Banque mondiale. Le jugement *McNeill* concerne un agent dont la nomination n'est pas confirmée à la fin de la période probatoire et qui est mis en congé spécial. Il allègue le détournement de pouvoir. Le Tribunal reconnaît que l'Administration a un pouvoir largement discrétionnaire pour déterminer si, à l'issue d'une période probatoire, il convient ou non de confirmer la nomination. Mais ce pouvoir doit être équilibré par le devoir de se conformer aux *appropriate standards of justice.* En l'espèce, le Tribunal considère que diverses erreurs ont été commises dans la procédure d'évaluation de l'intéressé et donc dans l'information donnée au requérant. Le Tribunal octroie à l'intéressé une indemnité de 25000 dollars.

Le jugement *Barnes* du 18 novembre 1997, sur recours de Madame Barnes, concerne un cas fréquent pour la plupart des tribunaux: le refus de renouveler un contrat à terme fixe. Le Tribunal administratif de la Banque mondiale reconnaît que l'intéressée n'a pas un droit au renouvellement mais ajoute que, comme tout exercice du pouvoir discrétionnaire par le défendeur, la décision doit être prise avec le souci de la justice et pas de manière arbitraire. Or le motif de non-renouvellement était lié à des évaluations concernant le travail fait qui semblaient un peu biaisées. Le Tribunal octroie alors une indemnité égale à un an de salaire à l'intéressée et dit que l'ensemble des erreurs reconnues par le tribunal "*amount to unreasonableness and arbitrariness.*"

Conclusion

En guise de conclusion, je poserai deux questions. D'une part, n'assistons-nous pas actuellement à un rapprochement entre le contrôle "normal" et le contrôle "restreint" exercé par les tribunaux administratifs internationaux sur les décisions des organisations internationales? Dans tous les cas, les principes du *due process of law* et de la proportionnalité doivent être respectés. De même, les motifs réels de l'action administrative, les finalités et les intentions des organisations doivent être scrutés par leurs juges. Les Administrations ne peuvent plus se réfugier dans le silence. Les organisations internationales semblent croire que les tribunaux ne comprennent pas suffisamment qu'il faut qu'elles puissent exercer un pouvoir libre d'appréciation. Les tribunaux sont naturellement conduits à faire respecter la règle de droit. Les quelques difficultés qui demeurent entre les organisations et leurs juges tiennent sans doute au fait que les tribunaux n'expliquent pas assez que la règle de droit doit dans toute hypothèse être respectée.

D'autre part, y a-t-il encore des actes des organisations internationales qui échappent à tout contrôle? Probablement non. C'est un vieux problème toujours courant dans les droits nationaux. En matière internationale, il me semble que toutes les décisions des organisations internationales concernant la gestion du personnel doivent reposer sur des motifs légaux et raisonnables. Mais la question se pose toujours pour les normes générales émanant des conseils d'administration des organisations pour lesquelles les conseils croient pouvoir invoquer le caractère souverain de leurs pouvoirs. Sur ce point, l'arrêt *Niesing (No. 2) et consorts* du Tribunal administratif de l'OIT (Jugement No. 1118 du 3 juillet 1991) soutient qu'une fois que l'Administration est constituée sur la base d'une totale autonomie, "les organes politiques et administratifs chargés, en qualité d'employeur, de la gestion du personnel, doivent respecter les principes [généraux du droit] dans toutes leurs actions, notamment lors de la modification des conditions d'emploi". Il en résulte que même la modification des règles statutaires n'échappe pas à un contrôle. On retrouve ici les principes qui fondent la solution du jugement *de Merode* du Tribunal administratif de la Banque mondiale. Cela prouve que celui-ci nous inspire toujours.

A PROPOS DU CONTRÔLE DU POUVOIR DISCRÉTIONNAIRE PAR LES TRIBUNAUX ADMINISTRATIFS DES ORGANISATIONS INTERNATIONALES

Nicolas Valticos*

Summary

The idea of an international administrative tribunal was first introduced in 1927 at the initiative of the first Director of the International Labour Office. Over the years, the existing administrative tribunals (i.e., those of the International Labour Organization (ILO) and the United Nations) saw their authority recognized by a growing number of international organizations, and other administrative tribunals were created and developed.

It was sometimes felt in the beginning that since the authority of the ILO's Administrative Tribunal (ILOAT) was a strictly defined one (i.e., a *compétence d'attribution*), the Tribunal had no right to review the discretionary power of an administration. This absolutist conception of discretionary power began to erode as early as 1953, when the ILOAT issued its judgment in *Desgranges*. Though the Tribunal's judgment did not refer explicitly to discretionary power, it dealt implicitly with the issue. The principle that an international organization's administration needs to be subject to the rule of law logically implied that there are certain limits to the notion of discretionary power.

Control by international administrative tribunals over the discretionary powers of administrations is nowadays generally accepted. The main point in this respect was stated by President Gentot when he observed that discretionary power is not synonymous with arbitrary power, but that judges should not substitute their own assessments for those of the organization.

Numerous judgments of the Council of Europe Administrative Tribunal (CEAT) have formulated the principles which it applies in reviewing the discretionary powers of the Council of Europe's Administration. The gist of these principles is that the Secretary-General has broad discretionary powers in certain areas, but that these must always be exercised within the bounds of the law, with respect for due process and for procedures set forth in the organization's rules, and without any *détournement de pouvoir* (abuse of power) undertaken to the detriment of the staff member. In the event of a dispute arising from personnel management, it is incumbent upon the CEAT to ascertain not only whether the contested decision emanated from a competent body and was taken in a regular manner, but also whether procedures were properly followed and, in terms of internal legality, whether the administrative authority took all relevant factors into account, whether erroneous

* Président du Curatorium de l'Académie de droit international de La Haye; ancien Président suppléant du Tribunal administratif du Conseil de l'Europe.

conclusions were drawn from the file or, finally, whether there had been an abuse of power.

The CEAT has emphasized that the requirement that an administrative action must be properly motivated helps to ensure the transparency necessary in personnel matters. It declared in one case that in the assessment of the subjective qualifications of civil servants, the scope of discretionary power on the part of the relevant authority is not as broad as the Administration seemed to believe.

On the subject of sanctions, the CEAT has pointed out that it is the right of the Council of Europe's Administration to determine the sanction to be imposed and that the Tribunal cannot substitute its assessment for that of the Administration. The CEAT has stated, however, that like other such administrative tribunals, it can, without judging the wisdom of a sanction, review whether the sanction is adequate, and can also censure those sanctions which are disproportionate to the objective and subjective circumstances in which the misdeeds were committed.

In conclusion, discretionary power still exists, but only to a limited extent. In their desire to avoid having the term "discretionary" interpreted as being synonymous with "arbitrary," international administrative tribunals have balanced the freedom of decision with which administrations need to act against the tribunals' obligations to prevent the administrations from succumbing to the temptations of absolute power and to ensure that international civil servants are protected by a legal framework.

* * *

Il y a trois quarts de siècle, en 1927, l'idée d'un tribunal administratif pour les organisations internationales a été lancée, peu après la création de la Société des Nations et réalisée, sur l'initiative d'Albert Thomas, le premier directeur du Bureau international du Travail. Depuis, cette institution a été consacrée, sous l'une ou l'autre forme, par la plupart des organisations. Le contrôle, par les tribunaux administratifs, du pouvoir discrétionnaire de l'Administration se situe à la limite – mais maintenant à l'intérieur de celle-ci – de la compétence des tribunaux en question, ce qui aurait paru, il y a certes déjà quelque temps, une contradiction dans les termes. Ce contrôle est maintenant généralement consacré, il est vrai, dans un certain cadre et à certaines conditions.

L'essentiel a été dit par le Président Gentot lorsqu'il a observé que le pouvoir discrétionnaire n'est pas synonyme d'arbitraire, mais que les juges ne doivent pas substituer leur appréciation à celle des organisations. Le Président Gentot a d'ailleurs également traité de la question en 1994, dans le cadre de la Société française pour le droit international[1]. Il y a cité une phrase du Professeur Prosper Weil qui a été juge et président au Tribunal

[1] M. Gentot, "Le contrôle de la légalité et les limites du pouvoir discrétionnaire", in *Le contentieux de la fonction publique internationale: Actes des journées d'études des 9–10 décembre 1994*, Société française pour le droit international, 1996, p. 243 et s.

administratif de la Banque mondiale: c'est bien "la politique suivie par le juge [administratif] qui dessine les contours du pouvoir discrétionnaire"[2]. Je ne vais pas répéter ici ce que le Président Gentot a déjà dit avec une inégalable compétence. Je me dois cependant de rappeler ce qu'il a dit en termes simples et significatifs: le juge est appelé à censurer ce qui lui paraît manifestement erroné et déraisonnable.

Mon intervention sera en partie subjective. En effet, elle sera fondée, jusqu'à un certain point, sur une expérience personnelle, d'ailleurs variée, car j'ai été associé au fonctionnement des tribunaux administratifs à divers titres au cours des ans, à celui de l'OIT, il y a très longtemps, comme plaideur, et à celui du Conseil de l'Europe, plus récemment, comme juge.

I. *Un arrêt significatif du Tribunal administratif de l'OIT en 1953*

A l'origine, on avait parfois estimé, comme un auteur qualifié[3] l'estimait en 1954, que la compétence du Tribunal administratif de l'OIT "étant strictement une compétence d'attribution, le tribunal n'a pas à contrôler le pouvoir discrétionnaire de l'administration". Cela n'était pas inexact dans une certaine mesure, mais le pouvoir discrétionnaire avait déjà commencé à devenir une sorte de peau de chagrin. En effet, l'arrêt *Desgranges* avait, dès 1953, commencé à sonner le glas d'une conception absolutiste du pouvoir discrétionnaire. En l'occurrence, il s'agissait du licenciement d'une employée du Bureau dit de correspondance du Bureau international du Travail (BIT) à Paris et, à l'époque, ce Bureau extérieur n'était couvert ni par le statut du personnel du BIT ni par la législation française. Je fus chargé de défendre l'intéressée devant le Tribunal administratif du BIT, dont le vice-président était le Professeur Georges Scelle.

La sentence ne s'est pas référée expressément au pouvoir discrétionnaire, mais, tout en ayant une portée plus générale, elle a implicitement visé la question car, si elle avait admis que certains fonctionnaires internationaux ne possèdent aucun statut, cela aurait pu signifier le pouvoir discrétionnaire de l'Administration à leur égard. On lit donc dans l'arrêt que "c'est une norme fondamentale de toute technique juridique qu'aucun tribunal ne peut s'abstenir de juger sous prétexte de silence ou d'obscurité de la loi" et que "l'absence de dispositions de droit positif en ce qui concerne les employés des bureaux de correspondance rendrait extrêmement précaire la situation de ces salariés et risquerait de les soumettre à des décisions

---

[2] *Id.*, p. 250.

[3] F. Wolf, "Le Tribunal administratif de l'OIT", *Etudes et documents du Conseil d'Etat*, Paris, fasc. No. 22, 1969, pp. 33–72.

arbitraires, sans qu'ils disposent d'aucun recours ni devant les tribunaux nationaux ni devant le Tribunal administratif". L'Administration fut condamnée et, peu après, les "Bureaux de correspondance" du BIT furent dotés d'un statut.

Le principe de la nécessité, pour les administrations internationales, d'être liées par des règles de droit entraînait logiquement une certaine limitation de cet îlot de résistance connu sous le nom de pouvoir discrétionnaire. Comme dans les ordres juridiques nationaux, et notamment en France, le contrôle du juge sur les actes dits discrétionnaires a été élargi. Il porte non seulement sur le détournement de pouvoir mais aussi sur l'erreur de droit, l'exactitude matérielle des faits et l'erreur manifeste de jugement. Parallèlement, avec les années, les tribunaux administratifs existants (ceux de l'OIT et des Nations Unies) virent leur compétence reconnue par un nombre croissant d'organisations internationales et d'autres juridictions furent créées et se développèrent. Nous célébrons ainsi, aujourd'hui, l'anniversaire – peut-on dire la majorité? – de l'un d'eux.

II. *La jurisprudence du Tribunal administratif du Conseil de l'Europe*

Je me référerai ici en particulier à la jurisprudence, en matière de pouvoir discrétionnaire, du Tribunal administratif du Conseil de l'Europe dont j'ai fait partie comme président suppléant pendant une dizaine d'années, et dont le travail du président, le Juge Carlo Russo, et celui du greffe ne sauraient être assez soulignés.

1. *L'exercice du pouvoir discrétionnaire par le secrétaire général*

Nombreux sont les arrêts qui, souvent explicitement, ont formulé les principes appliqués par ce Tribunal en matière de contrôle du pouvoir discrétionnaire de l'Administration[4]. L'essentiel de ces principes, pour citer certains des arrêts explicites, est que le secrétaire général dispose, dans certains

---

[4] On peut notamment citer, parmi les plus récentes, les sentences suivantes du Tribunal:
29 septembre 1995 (recours 187 et 193: Roose I et II): caractère adéquat des sanctions;
29 septembre 1995 (recours 189 et 195: Ernould I et II): *id.*;
29 septembre 1995 (recours 190, 196, 197 et 201: Lelegard I, II, III et IV): *id.*;
5 avril 1995 (recours 194: Fernandez-Galiano): gestion du personnel (qui cite plusieurs sentences antérieures dans le même sens);
29 mars 1996 (recours 208: Maréchal);
26 avril 1996 (recours 210: Sixto);
27 janvier 1997 (recours 216, 218 et 221: Palmieri);
20 mai 1999 (recours 245 et 249: Bouillon);
22 octobre 1999 (recours 351: Baechel).

domaines, d'un large pouvoir discrétionnaire qui doit toujours s'exercer dans la légalité et dans le respect de la procédure prévue par le statut et dans le respect des droits de la défense, et sans qu'il y ait de détournement de pouvoir au détriment du requérant.

En matière de gestion du personnel, le Tribunal a souligné que le secrétaire général, investi du pouvoir de nomination, dispose d'un pouvoir discrétionnaire, mais que celui-ci doit toujours s'exercer dans la légalité. En cas de contestation, la juridiction internationale ne peut substituer son appréciation à celle de l'Administration. Mais elle a le devoir de vérifier si la décision contestée a été prise conformément aux dispositions réglementaires de l'organisation ainsi qu'aux principes généraux du droit tels qu'ils s'imposent dans l'ordre juridique des organisations internationales.

2. *Le contrôle du Tribunal*

Il appartient au Tribunal d'examiner non seulement si cette décision émane d'un organe compétent et si elle est régulière en la forme, mais aussi si la procédure a été correctement suivie et, au regard de la légalité interne, si l'appréciation de l'autorité administrative a tenu compte de tous les éléments pertinents, si des conclusions erronées n'ont pas été tirées des pièces du dossier, ou enfin s'il n'y a pas eu détournement de pouvoir.

Le Tribunal a souligné que motiver de façon suffisante un acte administratif est une exigence dont le respect contribue à assurer, en matière de gestion du personnel, la transparence indispensable. Il a précisé, dans un cas, qu'en matière d'appréciation des qualifications subjectives des fonctionnaires, l'exercice du pouvoir discrétionnaire de l'autorité chargée de leur appréciation ne saurait être aussi étendu que semble le penser l'Administration, qui revendique une très large marge d'appréciation. Il y a donc là un équilibre à trouver.

3. *La question des sanctions*

S'agissant des sanctions, le Tribunal a souligné qu'il appartient à l'autorité administrative d'apprécier la sanction à infliger et que la juridiction internationale ne peut substituer son appréciation à celle de l'Administration, mais qu'en revanche, sans être juge de l'opportunité des sanctions disciplinaires, les tribunaux administratifs ont la possibilité de contrôler si la sanction est adéquate et de censurer les sanctions hors de proportion par rapport aux conditions objectives et subjectives dans lesquelles les faits reprochés ont été commis[5]. Il existerait alors erreur de droit. L'Administration

---

[5] A cet égard, référence a été faite au jugement No. 203 – *Ferrecchia* – du Tribunal administratif de l'OIT du 14 mai 1973.

ne doit donc pas excéder sa marge d'appréciation quant à la nature des faits reprochés et quant au comportement du requérant dans l'exercice de ses fonctions. Récemment, le Tribunal a ainsi annulé une décision disciplinaire de révocation qu'il n'a pas estimée proportionnée et qu'il a donc considérée comme entachée d'illégalité.

Je conclurai sur une question. Peut-on encore parler de pouvoir discrétionnaire? Le pouvoir discrétionnaire existe encore sans doute, mais non sans aucun doute, et dans une mesure limitée seulement. Soucieux d'éviter la synonymie de "discrétionnaire" avec "arbitraire", les tribunaux administratifs ont reconnu une marge plus ou moins grande, selon les cas, aux pouvoirs des administrations internationales, mais ont entouré ces pouvoirs de ce qu'on peut appeler sans impertinence des garde-fous, combinant ainsi la latitude nécessaire à l'action des administrations en question avec la nécessité d'éviter que celles-ci ne cèdent aux tentations du pouvoir absolu et d'assurer que les fonctionnaires internationaux soient protégés par un cadre suffisant de règles de droit.

COMMENTS

DISCRETION IN DISCIPLINARY CASES

Ranjan (C.F.) Amerasinghe*

Résumé

Même si les tribunaux ne peuvent pas substituer leur appréciation à celle de l'administration, le pouvoir discrétionnaire exercé par cette dernière n'est pas synonyme d'arbitraire.

Les pouvoirs discrétionnaires (tels le pouvoir de transférer, d'accorder une promotion, de classer, de licencier) sont nombreux. Mais le pouvoir disciplinaire en est un exemple très particulier où l'administration exerce un pouvoir "quasi-judiciaire" (pour reprendre une expression consacrée par le Tribunal administratif des Nations Unies (TANU) dans une série de cas à partir de 1998). Dans le but d'empêcher l'arbitraire en ce domaine, le TANU exerce un contrôle encore plus strict que dans les autres domaines du pouvoir discrétionnaire de l'administration. Le Tribunal administratif de la Banque mondiale (TABM) ainsi que le Tribunal administratif de l'Organisation internationale du Travail (TAOIT) ont suivi la même approche.

Concernant l'établissement des faits, les Tribunaux sont presque arrivés à substituer aux conclusions de l'administration leurs propres jugements quant à la justesse et à la nature des griefs qui sont reprochés aux membres du personnel. Les Tribunaux appliquent le critère du caractère raisonnable des griefs. Ils réexaminent les faits comme une Cour d'appel le ferait dans le cadre des juridictions nationales: ils s'assurent que les griefs contre les membres du personnel sont justifiés.

Dans le domaine de la proportionnalité des sanctions, les Tribunaux sont très stricts dans la protection des membres du personnel contre l'injustice.

Les Tribunaux sanctionnent également l'erreur de droit de l'administration quant à la qualification du manquement des membres du personnel à leurs obligations.

Le jugement *Kiwanuka* du TANU a posé les principes généraux concernant le contrôle du pouvoir disciplinaire. Il en ressort que le contrôle se focalise sur trois points principaux: l'établissement des faits, la qualification du manquement par les membres du personnel à leurs obligations et la proportionnalité des sanctions. Cette approche est similaire à celle adoptée par le TABM dans les affaires *Carew*, *Planthara* et *Mustafa*.

Tout en reconnaissant l'intérêt de l'administration à assurer des standards exigeants de conduite, les tribunaux ont à cœur, en matière disciplinaire, de protéger les membres du personnel contre toute injustice qui pourrait provoquer des dommages graves à leurs carrières.

* * *

---

* Judge, United Nations Administrative Tribunal; former Executive Secretary, World Bank Administrative Tribunal.

We have heard two experienced speakers on the subject of discretionary powers. I do not think that there can be any doubt that discretionary power exercised by administrations (indeed, it is better to refer to the exercise of administrative power rather than "managerial" power because such power may be exercised by administrators who are not "managers" in the narrow sense) is not arbitrary or absolute power.[1] This proposition is not generally questioned. On the other side of the coin, tribunals do not substitute their own judgment for that of the administration.[2] What they do is look for particular defects in the exercise of discretionary power which, broadly speaking, amount to an abuse of discretion.

My comments will be largely devoted to exploring the nature of the control exercised by tribunals in regard to disciplinary powers, because I think that this is a very important area, especially in the context of the United Nations and the World Bank, and that there have been some significant developments in this area.

Let me say, first, in general, that many of the cases that come before tribunals do not concern the exercise of discretion by the administration. They involve the application of what may be described as poorly drafted staff regulations and rules which purport to give staff members specific rights, and the question is whether those rights have been respected in the application of the instruments by the administration (e.g., the question whether a widow's entitlement may be commuted under a particular pension regulation or whether nursery schooling is included in the term "primary education" used in a statute).

However, discretionary powers are numerous – e.g., the power to transfer, promote, classify, dismiss, etc. I have dealt with the general principles relating to the control of such powers elsewhere.[3] Disciplinary powers are a very special example of discretionary powers. The reason for this is that in disciplining staff, administrations exercise a *quasi-judicial* power which is different from other discretionary powers, such as the power to promote or classify, etc. The quasi-judicial nature of the power was adverted to and emphasized for the first time by the United Nations Administrative Tribunal (UNAT) in a series of cases beginning in 1998.[4] I am not sure that any other tribunal has used this description specifically. In earlier cases, the

---

[1] See *Ballo*, ILOAT Decision No. 191 [1972] at p. 6 and *de Merode*, WBAT Decision No. 1 [1981] at p. 21. See also my Treatise, Vol. I, p. 272 ff. (C.F. Amerasinghe, *The Law of the International Civil Service*, second edition (1994)).

[2] See C.F. Amerasinghe, ibid. pp. 271–2.

[3] See C.F. Amerasinghe, ibid. pp. 229–40.

[4] See *Augustine*, UNAT Decision No. 890 [1998], *Jhuthi*, UNAT Decision No. 897 [1998], *Uggla*, UNAT Decision No. 898 [1998], *Shahrour*, UNAT Decision No. 939 [1999], *Kiwanuka*, UNAT Decision No. 941 [1999].

UNAT had in effect paid lip service to the powers of administrations by stating that "in disciplinary matters the Secretary-General has a broad power of discretion,"[5] although those powers are not broader than other powers and are subject to stricter control. But this was only lip service, as was demonstrated by what the UNAT actually did in such cases which was to control the discretion to discipline strictly. The Tribunal said in *Shahrour* that the exercise of the discretion, for such it is, to impose disciplinary measures "also involve[s] the exercise of a quasi-judicial power to impose sanctions for offences rather than the exercise of pure executive discretion."[6] The consequence of this is that the control exercised by tribunals (most of them, at any rate) to prevent what may generically be called "abuse of discretion" in disciplinary cases is stricter in many respects, though it may fall short of a substitution of judgment. The World Bank Administrative Tribunal (WBAT), I am happy to say, followed the above approach, starting with the decision in *Singh*.[7] The International Labour Organization Administrative Tribunal (ILOAT)'s approach has been similar.[8]

While it may require more than 5 to 10 minutes to elaborate on this thesis fully, it may be said briefly that the particular strictures are especially in the areas of the establishment of facts incriminating the staff member, the legality of the characterization of offences and the nature of the penalty imposed.

The ILOAT, the WBAT and the UNAT have in the actual exercise of control acted on the basis that the control is stricter in disciplinary cases.[9] In regard to the establishment of the facts against the staff members, tribunals have been so strict that they have almost substituted their own judgment as to whether the findings against the staff members should have been made or as to the nature of the findings against the staff members, though perhaps not quite. Facts are examined in great detail and the tribunals satisfy themselves that the evidence warrants the findings against the staff members.[10] What is the standard used in determining whether the administration has correctly established the facts against the staff member on the evidence? Is it manifest unreasonableness or simply unreasonableness that will upset the finding by the administration or does the tribunal

[5] See, e.g., *Djimbaye*, UNAT Decision No. 583 [1992], para. VI.

[6] *Shahrour*, UNAT Decision No. 939 [1999], para. IX.

[7] *Singh*, WBAT Decision No. 105 [1991]. See also *King*, WBAT Decision No. 131 [1993], *Carew*, WBAT Decision No. 142 [1995] and *Planthara*, WBAT Decision No. 143 [1995].

[8] See, e.g., *Connolly-Battisti (No. 2)*, ILOAT Decision No. 274 [1976].

[9] See *Connolly-Battisti (No. 2)*, ILOAT Decision No. 274 [1976], *Shahrour*, UNAT Decision No. 939 [1999], *Kiwanuka*, UNAT Decision No. 941 [1999], *Mustafa*, WBAT Decision No. 207 [1999].

[10] See cases referred to above in footnotes 4, 7 and 8.

go further and ask whether it agrees with the finding? The tribunal clearly examines the evidence *de novo* and, while using the test of reasonableness (not manifest unreasonableness), comes close to establishing whether it agrees with the finding against the staff member, so strict is its approach. The tribunals review the facts like an appeals court in a national jurisdiction. While they do not examine the evidence in order to come to a finding as a court of first instance, they do examine the evidence in order to satisfy themselves that the findings against the staff member were warranted, indeed, almost to the extent of determining whether they agree with the adverse finding or to what extent they do.

In the area of proportionality of sanctions, tribunals are very particular in protecting staff members from injustice – injustice in the tribunals' opinion. Similarly, tribunals will not hesitate to find that the administration erred in law in defining what was an offence subject to discipline, if they conclude that the characterization was improper in their opinion.

It may be appropriate to cite from *Kiwanuka* (UNAT) the statement of general principle relating to the control of disciplinary powers:

> The jurisprudence . . . has been developing and definitions have been refined. In reviewing this kind of quasi-judicial decision and in keeping with the relevant general principles of law, in disciplinary cases the Tribunal generally examines (i) whether the facts on which the disciplinary measures were based have been established; (ii) whether the established facts legally amount to misconduct or serious misconduct; (iii) whether there has been any substantive irregularity (e.g., omission of facts or consideration of irrelevant facts); (iv) whether there has been any procedural irregularity; (v) whether there was an improper motive or abuse of purpose; (vi) whether the sanction is legal; (vii) whether the sanction imposed was disproportionate to the offence; (viii) and, as in the case of discretionary powers in general, whether there has been arbitrariness. . . . Most recently in Judgment No. 898, *Uggla*, paragraph II (1998), the Tribunal made a similar general statement.
>
> Clearly the Tribunal takes the view that the imposition of disciplinary sanctions involves the exercise of a discretionary power by the Administration. It further recognizes that, unlike other discretionary powers, such as transferring and terminating services, it is also a special exercise of *quasi-judicial* power. For these reasons the process of review exercised by the Tribunal is of a particular nature. The Administration's interest in maintaining high standards of conduct and thus protecting itself must be reconciled with the interest of staff in being assured that they are not penalized unfairly or arbitrarily.[11]

The statement covers all that generally is pertinent to the control of discretionary powers, but what is of interest is the reference particularly to the areas of establishment of facts, characterization of the offence and pro-

[11] *Kiwanuka*, UNAT Decision No. 941 [1999] p. 11.

portionality of sanctions. I believe that the WBAT took a similar (but perhaps not identical) approach in *Carew*,[12] *Planthara*[13] and *Mustafa*.[14] The precedents show that tribunals take great pains to investigate these areas in disciplinary cases. Indeed, proportionality is rarely referred to in other areas.

The speakers here have described the judicial control of discretion in general but, as I said, I set out to draw your attention to the development of judicial control in the disciplinary area. It would seem that tribunals have been careful, and rightly so, to protect staff members from prejudice in this area because injustice could result in serious damage to their careers – even more so apparently than in the case of dismissal, e.g., for unsatisfactory service.

So important is this approach to the exercise of disciplinary powers that in a series of recent cases decided in 1998 and 1999 from UNRWA, where the administration had dismissed staff members under a regulation which permitted dismissal *in the interests of the agency* and where it appeared from the record that the staff members had been dismissed for disciplinary reasons (namely misconduct), the UNAT treated the dismissals as for disciplinary reasons and applied the standards and general principles relevant to the control of the discretion to discipline.

While the interest of the administration to maintain high standards of conduct is acknowledged and respected and cannot be ignored, tribunals are most concerned to protect the interests of staff members in not being punished improperly for disciplinary violations.

---

[12] *Carew*, WBAT Decision No. 142 [1995].
[13] *Planthara*, WBAT Decision No. 143 [1995].
[14] *Mustafa*, WBAT Decision No. 207 [1999].

COMMENTS

LE CONTRÔLE DU POUVOIR DISCRÉTIONNAIRE DE L'ADMINISTRATION PAR LES TRIBUNAUX ADMINISTRATIFS INTERNATIONAUX: OBSERVATIONS À LA LUMIÈRE DE LA PRATIQUE DU TRIBUNAL ADMINISTRATIF DE LA BANQUE MONDIALE

Francisco Orrego Vicuña*

Summary

Judges Gentot and Valticos have provided a most accurate discussion of the nature and limits of the review that international administrative tribunals can undertake in respect of managerial discretion. The following comments will address some relevant aspects of the practice of the World Bank Administrative Tribunal (WBAT) in this regard.

The WBAT requires that discretionary decisions be adopted in the genuine interests of the Organization, an element significantly underlined by Judge Gentot. It follows, as noted in both presentations, that discretionary powers must always be exercised in observance of the rules, general principles of law and the applicant's employment contract, and that the power of the administration is thereby limited. In this respect, the most common phrase appearing in the judgments of the WBAT is that the Tribunal will not interfere with the exercise of discretion unless the decision contested "constitutes an abuse of discretion, being arbitrary, discriminatory, improperly motivated or carried out in violation of a fair and reasonable procedure."

There are a number of recent developments in the case law of the WBAT which highlight both the nature and extent of the WBAT's competence to review discretionary decisions of the World Bank. Such developments fall under the categories of: (i) process; (ii) the Bank's organizational commitments; (iii) the Bank's quasi-judicial powers; (iv) the Tribunal's appellate jurisdiction; and (v) the Bank's internal legislation.

With respect to "process," the WBAT is concerned in many cases not so much with isolated decisions which standing alone might be unobjectionable, but rather with an aggregate of decisions which, taken as a whole, might amount to an abuse of discretion. Such a decision-making process may constitute "mismanagement of the Applicant's career" and reveal "errors of judgment which taken together amount to unreasonableness and arbitrariness." The Tribunal's broader approach

* Vice-Président au Tribunal administratif de la Banque mondiale; Professeur à l'Institut des études internationales, Université du Chili.

thus ensures the better protection of the rights of civil servants and helps the Administration to redress situations of continuing mismanagement.

As to "organizational commitments," the WBAT has emphasized the need for the Administration to honor its commitments to staff members, such as promises to convert fixed-term positions into permanent ones. It has thus been held, for example, that the "possibility exists also that there may be something in the surrounding circumstances which creates a right to the conversion of a fixed-term appointment to a permanent one." The Tribunal's approach in this respect helps to strengthen the trust upon which the Bank's relationship with its staff members must be built.

Regarding "the Bank's quasi-judicial powers," some discretionary powers amount in fact to the exercise of a quasi-judicial function by the Administration, as is typically the case with the imposition of disciplinary measures. Such powers are reviewed by the WBAT as if the WBAT had been requested to make the contested decision in the first instance. In one case, the WBAT described the various elements to be examined, namely: (a) the existence of the facts; (b) whether they legally amount to misconduct; (c) whether the sanction imposed is provided for in the law of the Bank; (d) whether the sanction is not significantly disproportionate to the offence; and (e) whether the requirements of due process were observed.

Concerning "the Tribunal's appellate jurisdiction," the WBAT has such jurisdiction over decisions of the Pension Benefits Administration Committee (PBAC) in pension matters. This jurisdiction is broader than that for the review of managerial discretion. In this context, the Tribunal examines the same elements as in cases involving the Bank's quasi-judicial powers, but also undertakes a broader examination of whether the conditions required by the Staff Retirement Plan for granting benefits were met, and whether the PBAC correctly interpreted the applicable law. A similar appellate function is performed by the WBAT in respect of the decisions of the Workers' Compensation Administrative Review Panel.

Lastly, with respect to "the Bank's internal legislation," the WBAT in the leading case of *de Merode* took a first step in reviewing administrative policies that might affect fundamental and essential elements of the rights and duties of staff members. The WBAT has since regularly reviewed legislation that may entail discrimination or other violations of law. Recently, the need arose to take this latter review a step further on account of the legislation enacted by the World Bank to provide pension reform. In *Crevier* and other subsequent pension cases, the Applicants and the Staff Association complained against the very objective pursued by the reform and its inspiring philosophy, independent of the manner in which it might affect an individual staff member. The WBAT examined each aspect of the contentions in order to determine whether the Bank's legislation had been reasonable and fair. In the end, the Tribunal upheld the Bank's legislation.

The Bank's enactment of legislation can be reviewed by the WBAT on a case-by-case basis in applications raised by staff members who claim to have been adversely impacted by decisions made on the basis of such legislation. However, it would be inappropriate for the WBAT, or any other administrative tribunal, to assume the role of a rule-reviewing body. Such a role could lead to the nullification of rules enacted by the governing bodies and result ultimately in the supremacy of one organ over another.

* * *

Les Juges Gentot et Valticos ont relevé les problèmes les plus importants relatifs à la nature et aux limites du contrôle du pouvoir discrétionnaire de l'Administration que peuvent exercer les tribunaux administratifs internationaux. J'ai tout particulièrement retenu une remarque du Juge Gentot: si les tribunaux ne peuvent pas substituer leur propre jugement à celui de l'auteur d'une décision contestée adoptée dans le cadre de l'exercice du pouvoir discrétionnaire de l'Administration, "pouvoir discrétionnaire n'est pas synonyme d'arbitraire". J'ai également noté l'observation du Juge Valticos: pareils pouvoirs de contrôle se situent en fait à la limite extérieure de la compétence des tribunaux internationaux, même si tous y ont recours dans une plus ou moins large mesure.

Les observations qui suivent porteront sur quelques aspects pertinents de la pratique du Tribunal administratif de la Banque mondiale. Il sera fait référence en particulier aux développements récents qui ont mis en évidence tant la nature que l'étendue de la compétence du Tribunal à cet égard.

Il convient de noter tout d'abord que la pratique du Tribunal administratif de la Banque mondiale est pleinement conforme au principe qui fonde cette instance de contrôle, à savoir que les décisions prises à titre discrétionnaire doivent être véritablement adoptées dans l'intérêt de l'organisation, élément abondamment souligné par le Juge Gentot. Il en résulte donc, comme l'indiquent également les deux exposés, que les décisions prises à titre discrétionnaire doivent toujours être prises dans le respect des règles, des principes généraux du droit et du contrat de travail. Il en résulte que le pouvoir de l'Administration est limité. Finalement, comme le note le Juge Valticos, il s'agit d'assurer que les fonctionnaires internationaux soient protégés par un régime de droit et que les décisions prises à leur égard soient pleinement transparentes.

Les motifs de recours devant le Tribunal administratif de la Banque mondiale sont bien expliqués dans l'ouvrage de Monsieur Amerasinghe, lequel couvre les concepts de détournement de pouvoir, irrégularités de fond ou irrégularités de procédure[1]. L'expression qui revient le plus souvent dans les décisions du Tribunal administratif de la Banque mondiale est que le Tribunal ne s'immiscera pas dans l'exercice du pouvoir discrétionnaire, à moins que la décision contestée ne "constitue un abus de pouvoir par son caractère arbitraire, discriminatoire, par l'absence de motifs propres ou par son exécution en violation d'une procédure équitable et raisonnable"[2].

---

[1] C.F. Amerasinghe, *The Law of the International Civil Service*, vol. 1, 1994, p. 277 et s.

[2] *Montasser*, Décision No. 156 [1997], paragraphe 10.

Dans ce cadre, la pratique du Tribunal administratif de la Banque mondiale met en lumière plusieurs tendances présentant un intérêt particulier pour la conception du contrôle du pouvoir discrétionnaire de l'Administration:

i) Processus: Il convient de noter, tout d'abord, que le Tribunal, dans bien des cas, ne s'intéresse pas tant aux décisions individuelles susceptibles d'affecter un agent qu'à un processus décisionnel dans son ensemble. Il se peut qu'une décision ne soit pas condamnable en soi mais que l'addition des décisions prises constitue un abus de pouvoir. Il a donc été conclu que pareil processus décisionnel pouvait parfois constituer "des irrégularités de gestion de la carrière du requérant" et attester d'"erreurs de jugement qui, prises dans leur ensemble, présentent un caractère déraisonnable et arbitraire"[3]. Cette optique plus large assure au mieux la protection des droits des fonctionnaires et aide l'Administration à remédier aux situations de mauvaise gestion persistante.

ii) Engagements: Les tribunaux en général, et le Tribunal administratif de la Banque mondiale en particulier, insistent toujours sur la nécessité du respect par l'Administration des engagements pris envers ses employés. Il a donc été jugé, par exemple, qu'"il est possible aussi que certains éléments dans les circonstances environnantes ouvrent droit à la transformation d'un contrat à durée déterminée en contrat permanent"[4]. Dans une affaire récente, le Tribunal a conclu qu'une promesse de conversion avait été faite de manière valide et que le requérant avait satisfait aux conditions requises de performance satisfaisante; la décision de ne pas transformer son statut a donc été jugée comme constituant un abus de pouvoir[5]. Cette optique contribue également à renforcer la confiance sur laquelle doit reposer la relation entre les membres du personnel et l'Administration.

iii) Pouvoir quasi-juridictionnel: Certains pouvoirs discrétionnaires équivalent en fait à l'exercice d'une fonction quasi-juridictionnelle par l'Administration, comme c'est généralement le cas en matière d'adoption de mesures disciplinaires. La norme de contrôle devient généralement plus stricte à cet égard, et, comme l'a noté Monsieur Amerasinghe, le Tribunal peut examiner la décision à nouveau, comme s'il lui avait été demandé de prendre lui-même la décision initialement[6]. Dans une affaire, le Tribunal administratif de la Banque mondiale a décrit les divers points à examiner: i) l'existence des faits; ii) la question de savoir si ces derniers constituent légalement une faute; iii) la question de savoir si la sanction imposée est

---

[3] *Chhabra*, Décision No. 139 [1994], paragraphe 57.
[4] *Mr. X*, Décision No. 16 [1984], paragraphe 38.
[5] *Bigman*, Décision No. 209 [1999].
[6] Amerasinghe, op. cit., p. 267.

prévue par le droit de la Banque; iv) celle de savoir si la sanction n'est pas sensiblement disproportionnée à l'infraction; et v) celle de savoir si les exigences d'une procédure régulière ont bien été respectées[7].

iv) Juridiction d'appel: Dans certains domaines, le Tribunal administratif de la Banque mondiale exerce une juridiction de recours spéciale, un véritable recours en appel, qu'il convient de distinguer aussi bien du rôle joué par le Comité d'appel (*Appeals Committee*) que du contrôle que le Tribunal lui-même exerce sur le pouvoir de l'Administration. Cette juridiction revêt à la fois un caractère exceptionnel et plus large que le contrôle du pouvoir discrétionnaire de l'Administration. Les décisions du Comité d'administration des prestations du système de pension (*Pension Benefits Administration Committee*) peuvent faire l'objet d'un appel direct devant le Tribunal car il n'existe pas d'autres voies de recours interne[8]. Dans ce contexte, le Tribunal examine les mêmes éléments que ceux qu'il examinerait en cas de contrôle quasi-juridictionnel, mais il entreprend également d'établir, plus largement, si les conditions d'octroi des prestations stipulées par le régime des pensions du personnel ont été respectées et si le Comité a correctement interprété les règles applicables[9]. Une fonction d'appel similaire existe concernant les décisions du Comité de révision en matière d'indemnités liées aux accidents de travail (*Review Panel for Workers' Compensation Benefits*)[10].

v) Législation: Dans l'affaire *de Merode* qui a fait jurisprudence, le Tribunal administratif de la Banque mondiale a entrepris pour la première fois d'examiner les politiques administratives susceptibles d'affecter des éléments fondamentaux et essentiels des droits et devoirs des employés[11]. À l'occasion de cette affaire, le Tribunal a introduit une limitation significative de l'exercice du pouvoir discrétionnaire dans ce contexte, statuant que ces éléments, à la différence d'autres moins fondamentaux, ne peuvent être modifiés sans l'assentiment de l'employé concerné. Une deuxième étape a trait à l'examen périodique par les tribunaux de textes juridiques impliquant une discrimination ou d'autres anomalies.

Dernièrement, toutefois, il s'est avéré nécessaire d'intensifier cet examen à propos de textes ayant force de législation promulgués par la Banque mondiale sur la réforme des pensions. Dans l'affaire *Crevier* et les autres affaires qui ont suivi, le requérant et l'association du personnel ont non seulement invoqué la discrimination et d'autres prétendues déficiences, mais ont émis une objection à l'encontre de l'objectif même de la réforme et

---

[7] *Planthara*, Décision No. 143 [1995], paragraphe 24.
[8] *Courtney (No. 2)*, Décision No. 153 [1996], paragraphe 30.
[9] *Shenouda*, Décision No. 177 [1997], paragraphe 12.
[10] *Chhabra (No. 2)*, Décision No. 193 [1998], paragraphe 7.
[11] *de Merode*, Décision No. 1 [1981], paragraphes 41 et 42.

de la philosophie qui l'inspire, indépendamment de la manière dont ces textes pouvaient affecter tel ou tel membre du personnel[12]. Après avoir examiné tous les arguments des requérants, le Tribunal administratif a établi le caractère raisonnable et équitable de la législation de la Banque, qu'il a confirmée. Il s'ensuit, par conséquent, que la promulgation d'une législation peut faire l'objet d'un examen sous l'angle des limitations dont fait l'objet le pouvoir discrétionnaire.

Le Juge Gentot, dans ses remarques de clôture, s'est inquiété du caractère prétendument souverain des pouvoirs des organes directeurs des organisations internationales. Pareille inquiétude doit être tempérée eu égard à la pratique du Tribunal administratif de la Banque mondiale qui rend possible l'examen de la législation. Toutefois, il faut opérer une distinction minutieuse à cet égard, bien mise en évidence par Sir Robert Jennings, entre le contrôle normalement exercé par les tribunaux administratifs au cas par cas, dans le cadre de leurs attributions normales, et l'institution d'une autorité institutionnelle de contrôle qui pourrait éventuellement annuler les règles promulguées par les organes directeurs et aboutir, à terme, à la suprématie d'une instance sur l'autre. Il me semble qu'il n'est pas opportun de conférer aux tribunaux administratifs ce deuxième type d'attribution institutionnelle qui pourrait dépasser les limites de leurs compétences.

Les discussions qui précèdent nous permettent de dégager une conclusion importante. Fondamentalement, le contrôle du pouvoir discrétionnaire a pour objet d'établir si une décision est raisonnable[13] et satisfait aux normes appropriées de la justice[14]. Cette fonction a pour unique objet de garantir pleinement le respect des droits individuels des employés conformément à la règle de droit et d'éviter toute décision arbitraire en même temps que d'aider l'institution à respecter une ligne de conduite conforme à son intérêt.

---

[12] *Crevier*, Décision No. 205 [1999].
[13] *Hammond*, Décision No. 86 [1989], paragraphe 34.
[14] *Salle*, Décision No. 10 [1982], paragraphe 30.

COMMENTS

CONSTRAINTS ON JUDICIAL REVIEW OF MANAGERIAL DISCRETION: SUBSTANTIVE AND PROCEDURAL

Raul C. Pangalangan*

Résumé

Plusieurs juges ont siégé à la fois au Tribunal administratif de la Banque asiatique de développement (TABAsD) et au Tribunal administratif de la Banque mondiale (TABM). Un des juges au TABAsD a siégé au Tribunal administratif de l'Organisation internationale du Travail (TAOIT) jusqu'à une époque récente.

Les Juges Gentot et Valticos soulignent que les limites au contrôle judiciaire du pouvoir discrétionnaire existent en droit interne et dans le droit des organisations internationales. Pour le Juge Gentot, ces limites sont dues aux règles générales édictées par les organisations internationales en vertu de leur pouvoir souverain. Pour le Juge Valticos, c'est historiquement le caractère délégué des pouvoirs des tribunaux administratifs qui dessine les limites de leur contrôle.

Le droit interne connaît aussi des domaines soustraits au contrôle judiciaire: il s'agit des "questions politiques" dont les tribunaux ne peuvent remettre en question la légalité mais uniquement le caractère arbitraire.

Il apparaît donc que la position d'une Cour suprême à l'intérieur d'un Etat est semblable à celle d'un tribunal administratif au sein d'une organisation internationale: pour les deux formations, le véritable critère de la possibilité d'un recours est l'existence de standards objectifs qui pourraient les guider à déterminer si une décision a été prise de manière valable. De tels standards peuvent aussi bien être formels que substantiels. De fait, les jugements du TABAsD se sont parfois basés sur des critères formels (*Lindsey*) et parfois sur des critères substantiels (*Amora*).

Le TABAsD a aussi contrôlé des décisions administratives réglementaires en se basant principalement sur des critères substantiels dans les affaires suivantes:

a – *Mesch et Siy* où le Tribunal a considéré, dans un premier temps, que le remboursement d'impôts était requis par le principe de l'égalité de traitement et, dans un second temps, que le remboursement d'impôts n'était pas une condition d'emploi fondamentale et essentielle

b – *Samuel* où le Tribunal a apprécié la conformité d'une circulaire relative à l'âge de la retraite avec les dispositions du Règlement intérieur du personnel

c – *Breckner* où le Tribunal a considéré que les conditions relatives à l'admission à un plan de retraite anticipée relevaient plus de la volonté de motiver cer-

* Executive Secretary, Asian Development Bank Administrative Tribunal; Dean and Associate Professor of Law, University of the Philippines.

tains employés à l'adopter que de celle de récompenser les employés pour leurs services rendus

d – *De Armas* relative à la non-application des bénéfices accordés aux expatriés à l'égard des ressortissants de l'Etat-hôte.

Dans ces affaires, le Tribunal était appelé à interpréter des règles générales qui exprimaient des préoccupations substantielles.

Un juge au TABAsD, le Professeur Martti Koskenniemi, a récemment relevé que le recours de plus en plus fréquent au critère flexible du "caractère raisonnable" d'une décision permet aux juges d'imposer leurs propres vues morales sous le couvert d'appliquer la loi. Un ancien juge au TABAsD, le Professeur Florentino P. Feliciano, a estimé que plus une règle est générale, plus elle requiert des dispositions détaillées d'application, sinon les juges se transformeraient en faiseurs de politiques sociales et économiques.

Pour empêcher cette dérive, il faudrait à la fois élaborer des standards procéduraux et clarifier les normes substantielles, même s'il est difficile pour ces dernières d'arriver à des conceptions communes aux différentes nations et cultures dont se compose la société internationale.

* * *

I thank the World Bank Administrative Tribunal (WBAT) for organizing this meeting. Each international administrative tribunal stands alone as if it were within an international organization, yet must draw wisdom from the case-law of other tribunals. Our meeting today brings those tribunals together to break bread and share precedents beyond what their published reports can offer.

The Asian Development Bank (AsDB) Administrative Tribunal's ties to the WBAT go back to the AsDB Tribunal's founding President, Professor Elihu Lauterpacht, QC, one of the original judges and later President of the WBAT, and continues today with "overlapping" memberships in the persons of Professor Robert Gorman and Dr. Thio Su Mien. (The AsDB Tribunal's other "overlap" is with the ILO Administrative Tribunal, with whom it shared until recently the current AsDB Tribunal President, Justice Mark Fernando.)

Both speakers have recognized that constraints on judicial review of discretionary decisions exist in both the law governing international organizations and in municipal law as well. Significantly, both speakers have identified the parallel underlying principles in both fields of law. Mr. Gentot proposes that judicial review is limited in regard to "general rules" derived from the sovereign character of the powers of an international organization. Mr. Valticos noted that, historically, what constrained international administrative tribunals (ATs) early in their existence was the delegated nature of their jurisdiction, i.e., that their power to judge was merely "assigned" by a higher authority.

Municipal law similarly immunizes "political questions" from judicial review, but its rationale has gone beyond this traditional distinction between sovereign and delegated powers. Under the political question doctrine, the true test of justiciability is the availability of *objective* standards by which a court can tell if a decision has been validly made. The Court is thus limited to determining not the *correctness* but the *arbitrariness* of a decision. Both speakers have noted a similar logic by international ATs. Mr. Gentot cites how the "power of appreciation," ordinarily beyond judicial review, becomes justiciable when subordinated to "strict rules." Mr. Valticos identified the objectifying mechanisms: competence to act; procedural regularity; formal validity; manifest errors of fact or law; and abuse of authority.

The political question doctrine emerged in domestic constitutional laws to limit judicial review over acts by the executive and legislative branches of government. The position of a national supreme court within a state can thus be seen as parallel to that of an international AT within an international organization: they are both organic agencies or internal tribunals. They differ, however, in that some domestic supreme courts are at least theoretically co-equal to the political branches in municipal law, whereas in international organizations ATs are invariably creatures of Management (i.e., the executive) and the governing boards (i.e., the legislature consisting of representatives of the Member States).

I propose that the political question doctrine is useful in examining the exercise of judicial review by ATs. I propose further that the objective standards that render cases justiciable are not just *procedural/formal*, but *substantive/normative* as well.

As regards acts of an executive character, for instance, the AsDB Tribunal, in *Lindsey*, Decision No. 1, 1 ADBAT Reports 1 (1992), has reviewed the non-renewal of a fixed-term appointment, a matter ordinarily discretionary and thus non-justiciable. The Tribunal applied *procedural* tests and found a lack of due process in the performance evaluation leading to the decision not to renew. On the other hand, in *Amora*, Decision No. 24, 3 ADBAT Reports 1 (1997), the Tribunal inquired *substantively* into a succession of one-year contracts, set them aside as "a pure fiction," and held that an employer-employee relationship existed for the full period of his service. These contracts were set aside – not on the *formal* grounds that consent was vitiated, or that form was defective, or that solemnities were wanting, but – on the *substantive* ground that the successive one-year contracts did not embody the true relationship between the parties.

The AsDB Tribunal has also reviewed acts of a rule-making, legislative character in the following cases, relying largely on *substantive* grounds in adjudicating the cases:

(a) whether there is a right to tax reimbursement for staff whose national governments have opted to tax their Bank-paid income (*Mesch and Siy*, Decision No. 2, 1 ADBAT Reports 21 (1994), holding that tax reimbursement was required by the principle of equal treatment), and whether the Bank may unilaterally amend or revoke that right (*Mesch and Siy* (*No. 4*), Decision No. 35, 3 ADBAT Reports 71 (1997), holding that tax reimbursement is not a fundamental and essential condition of employment, and that the Bank may legislate that the principle of equal pay for equal work be applied to *before*-tax salaries);

(b) whether the age of retirement is 65 with optional retirement at 60 (at the option of either Management or the staff member), as provided in the Staff Regulations enacted by the Bank's Board of Directors, or 60, as embodied in an administrative order issued by Management (*Samuel*, Decision No. 15, 2 ADBAT Reports 51 (1996), holding that the administrative order was consistent with Management's option allowed under the Staff Regulations);

(c) whether the eligibility clauses of an early/optional retirement program unfairly excluded staff members who had high performance ratings (*Breckner*, Decision No. 25, 3 ADBAT Reports 17 (1997), holding that the eligibility requirements were consistent with the legislative purposes, and the principle of equal remuneration for comparable work did not apply to the benefits under the program, which were not a reward for past service but an inducement for staff whom the Bank wished to retire); and

(d) whether the exclusion of host country (i.e., Philippine) nationals from certain employment ("expatriate") benefits constitutes an impermissible discrimination (*De Armas*, Decision No. 39, 4 ADBAT Reports 9 (1998), holding that the exclusion was not based on nationality but on the place of service and the functional advantages of serving in one's home country, *except* for third-country tertiary education and *force majeure* protection, as to which both expatriate and non-expatriate staff were similarly situated).

In these cases, the Tribunal was called upon to interpret substantive purposes which have been codified and enacted into rules, including an administrative order containing the Bank's Personnel Policy Statement. (Note too that the norm of equality has been most frequently cited in these cases, and yet international ATs have not adopted doctrinal techniques, highly developed in municipal jurisdictions, for applying "strict scrutiny" when the discrimination is based on "suspect" criteria, typically race- or gender-based.)

A judge of the AsDB Tribunal, Professor Martti Koskenniemi, recently wrote a book review on the use of the test of reasonableness by international judges.[1] He noted the increasing recourse to broad tests of "rea-

[1] Koskenniemi, Book Review of O. Corten, L'utilisation du "raisonnable" par le juge international: discours juridique, raison et contradictions (1997), 94 *AJIL* 198 (2000).

sonableness," to "general and evaluative language" which, while purporting to limit judges' discretion – recall Mr. Valticos' call for "guard rails" to discretion – actually allows judges increased subjectivity, thereby "transfer[ring] social power from the legislators to the law appliers, thus creating the danger of administrative or judicial abuse." This enables judges to impose their own moral choices under the guise of merely applying the law, and without having openly to confess to having made a subjective call. He concludes that this de-formalization of law is the liberal lawyer's technique for reconciling formal rules with the intuitive claims of justice.

On the other hand, a former judge of the AsDB Tribunal, Philippine Supreme Court Justice Florentino P. Feliciano, has warned in the context of a Philippine case that broad directive or normative clauses (such as, in that case, a right to health) may require more detailed implementing legislation ("specific, operable norms and standards"), lest the courts be forced to rely on broad procedural standards such as "grave abuse of discretion" to render them judicially enforceable.

> Where *substantive* standards as general as . . . "the right to health" are combined with *remedial* standards as broad ranging as "a grave abuse of discretion", the result will be . . . to propel the courts into the uncharted ocean of social and economy policy making.[2] (emphases supplied)

The ocean-ward drift is caused as much by the de-formalization of procedural law (toward broad tests of reasonableness) as by the formalization of substantive values (in directive clauses) through which otherwise unenforceable norms are enacted into positive rules and institutional obligations are made directly enforceable through courts.

Conversely, to restrain that drift, we need both to elaborate procedural standards and to clarify substantive norms as well. Normative clarification serves the goal of predictability in decision-making and the preservation of rights against abuse of discretion. Yet perhaps it is precisely because international organizations and their administrative tribunals are global in character that such normative clarification is more difficult. They thus prefer procedural standards, which appear to be more susceptible to a core of meaning shared by a more easily identifiable group of international lawyers and judges, to substantive norms, which are open to a wider range of symbols and meanings that are rarely shared across nations and cultures.

---

[2] *Minors Oposa v. Factoran*, G.R. No. 101083, 30 July 1993, 224 SCRA 792 (Feliciano, J., concurring).

COMMENTS

REMARQUES RELATIVES AUX RAPPORTS DES PRÉSIDENTS GENTOT ET VALTICOS

David Ruzié*

Summary

When reviewing the methodology applied by organizations for salary adjustment, the position adopted by a number of tribunals is sometimes questionable. This is illustrated by a dissenting opinion in the International Labour Organization Administrative Tribunal (ILOAT) judgment in *Berthet (No. 2) et al.*, where the dissenting judge criticized the majority's "blessing on a staff regulation which leaves the adjustment of salaries to the 'sovereign' appreciation of the employer." From an academic point of view, it is regrettable that budgetary policy sometimes prevails over purely legal considerations.

With respect to the assessment of qualifications of staff members who have applied for a vacant position, the approach taken by the Council of Europe Administrative Tribunal (CEAT or the Tribunal) is different from the one adopted by the Court of First Instance of the European Communities. The CEAT makes a distinction between objective and subjective qualifications. The determination of whether a qualification is objective or subjective is, however, itself subjective, even though objective qualifications certainly exist (e.g. age, diplomas). The CEAT considered in its *Sixto* judgment that the Administration's discretionary power to assess the subjective qualifications of staff members is not as extensive as it might believe, and that the Tribunal would review the subjective assessments made by the Administration. The Tribunal then, however, attempted unconvincingly to avoid the issue by stating that it "does not consider it necessary in this case to settle the question of whether the disputed qualifications are of an objective or a subjective nature." The Tribunal instead found that "it emerges from an examination of the record of the meeting of the Panel [examining the applications] that the Panel did conduct a conscientious examination of the respective qualifications of all the applicants."

By contrast, the Court of First Instance of the European Communities does not restrict itself to observing whether there has been a thorough evaluation of the candidates' qualifications. The Court instead concluded in its judgment of *Cantoreggi v. European Parliament* that there had been an obvious error of evaluation, in that the Administration had considered the budgetary and financial qualifications of the contested candidate as determinative while completely overlooking the specific requirements concerning knowledge and professional experience included in the

* Juge, Tribunal administratif de la Banque des règlements internationaux; Professeur émérite à l'Université René-Descartes (Paris V).

vacancy announcement. The Court thus did not hesitate to review the assessment made by the Administration even though the scope of the Court's review was limited.

* * *

J'aimerais indiquer au préalable que je ne m'exprime pas ici en tant que juge, mais en tant qu'universitaire et praticien du contentieux de la fonction publique internationale, depuis plus de quarante ans. Je voudrais faire deux séries de brèves remarques sur un passage figurant dans chacun des deux rapports que nous avons entendus.

A propos du rapport du Président Gentot

Tout d'abord, s'agissant du rapport fort intéressant et instructif du Président Gentot, j'aimerais dire que, même s'il s'agit d'une jurisprudence concordante, la position adoptée par un certain nombre de juridictions, dont le Tribunal administratif de l'OIT, est parfois discutable en ce qui concerne précisément la méthodologie de l'ajustement des rémunérations. En effet, sur la base d'un jugement récent, à savoir le jugement 1912 (*Berthet (No. 2), Lampinen, Leberman et Schechinger*) du Tribunal administratif de l'OIT, un membre du Tribunal a développé une opinion dissidente très ferme, en regrettant qu'après avoir posé l'année précédente, dans le jugement 1821 (*Allaert et Warmels (No. 3)*), un certain nombre de principes devant être respectés dans l'intérêt des agents, s'agissant de la méthodologie de l'adaptation des rénumérations:

> "le jugement rendu par la majorité, bien que semblant admettre ces principes [évoqués dans le jugement 1821], les vide en fait de leur substance en en faisant de vaines paroles. On y souscrit à un statut du personnel qui laisse l'ajustement des traitements à l'appréciation 'souveraine' de l'employeur. Comment peut-on parler dans ces conditions de 'méthodologie', de 'système' ou de 'norme'? Il ne s'agit de rien de cela" (§ 3).

Cette affaire soulève un problème également rencontré dans d'autres juridictions administratives, notamment dans le cadre des juridictions administratives des organisations européennes coordonnées. C'est le problème des implications budgétaires des problématiques portées devant le tribunal. En tant qu'universitaire, je regrette que parfois des considérations politiques, pour ne pas dire de politique budgétaire, l'emportent sur des considérations purement juridiques.

A propos du rapport du Président Valticos

Le Président Valticos a fort justement rappelé que le Tribunal administratif du Conseil de l'Europe avait précisé qu'en matière d'appréciation des qualifications requises des fonctionnaires, il fallait distinguer les qualifications objectives et les qualifications subjectives, en sous-entendant que s'agissant des premières, le Tribunal pouvait avoir un pouvoir de contrôle plus poussé. A cet égard, je soulignerai que savoir si une qualification est subjective ou objective est elle-même une question subjective, même s'il est certain qu'il existe des conditions objectives (âge, diplôme . . .).

Monsieur Valticos a dit "qu'en matière d'appréciation des qualifications subjectives des fonctionnaires, l'exercice du pouvoir discrétionnaire de l'autorité chargée de leur appréciation ne saurait être aussi étendu que semble le penser l'Administration, qui revendique une très large marge d'appréciation". Dans les jugements *Sixto* (Recours No. 210/1995) et *Palmieri* (Recours No. 221/1996), on a vu le Tribunal administratif du Conseil de l'Europe dire que, même s'agissant de qualifications subjectives, l'Administration est tenue de se soumettre au contrôle du Tribunal. Malheureusement, dans l'affaire *Sixto* le Tribunal a dit qu'il

> "n'estime pas nécessaire en l'espèce de trancher la question de savoir si les qualifications litigieuses revêtent un caractère objectif ou subjectif" (§ 25–2).
>
> "En effet, il résulte de l'examen du procès-verbal de la réunion du Jury que celui-ci s'est livré à un examen consciencieux des qualifications respectives de tous les candidats. . . ." (§ 26).
>
> "Même si le requérant conteste que M. F. possédait les qualifications requises, le Jury est arrivé à la conclusion contraire" (§ 27).

Autrement dit, c'est une fausse fenêtre, comme disent parfois les universitaires lorsqu'ils commentent une décision.

Le Tribunal de première instance des communautés européennes à Luxembourg ne se contente pas, pour sa part, de constater qu'il y a eu une appréciation poussée des qualifications et, dans une affaire jugée le 15 décembre 1999 (Affaire T-144/98, *Cantoreggi c. Parlement européen*) à propos d'un recrutement sur base de promotion, le Tribunal a considéré qu'il y avait eu une erreur manifeste d'appréciation. En effet, l'Administration avait retenu "comme déterminantes les qualifications budgétaires et financières de M. N et en faisant totalement abstraction des exigences spécifiques concernant les connaissances et l'expérience professionnelle en matière de gestion technique des bâtiments que contenaient les deux avis [de vacance]" (Recueil Fonction publique II 1325 point 37). Autrement dit, le Tribunal de première instance de Luxembourg n'hésite pas à reprendre l'examen dans un cadre de contrôle limité, et – pour reprendre la formulation que le Tribunal administratif de l'OIT utilise à différentes reprises pour qualifier les hypothèses dans lesquelles il peut y avoir un contrôle restreint ou limité – lorsque des conclusions erronées ont été tirées du dossier, il considère que cela aboutit à "une erreur manifeste d'appréciation".

OPEN DISCUSSION

A. Kamal Abul-Magd, Session Chair
Distinguished participants, I ask your indulgence in limiting yourselves to five minutes, unless the issue is exceptionally important, in which case the limit may be extended to seven minutes.

Jean-Didier Sicault, Avocat à la Cour d'appel de Paris
Thank you, Mr. Chairman. I would like to address a question raised by President Gentot in his speech. The question is very simple, but there may be no answer to it.

Pourrions-nous préciser les rapports qu'entretiennent le concept de restrictions financières ou restrictions budgétaires (financial constraints or budgetary constraints) avec le concept de pouvoir discrétionnaire? J'envisage ici deux hypothèses: non seulement celle des questions salariales, où le lien est évident, mais également celle d'un contingent budgétaire fixé pour les promotions. Une institution pourrait par exemple fixer un contingent de X milliers ou millions de dollars pour les promotions pour l'exercice N. Peut-on pousser plus avant l'analyse du rapport qu'entretiennent ces deux notions?

Christian Tomuschat, Juge au Tribunal administratif de la Banque africaine de développement
Je ferai deux commentaires très brefs. Premièrement, si l'on se livre à une étude du pouvoir discrétionnaire des administrations, il faut également prendre en considération l'expérience de la Cour de Justice des communautés européennes. Monsieur Ruzié en a d'ailleurs déjà parlé. Il faut, à cet égard, se référer aux propos de Maurice Lagrange, grand juriste français, qui était membre du Conseil d'Etat et était devenu l'un des premiers avocats généraux à la Cour de Justice des communautés européennes. Maurice Lagrange s'était livré à une étude de la notion de détournement de pouvoir sur la base des droits nationaux des six pays membres faisant alors partie de la Communauté économique européenne. Il avait bien défini cette notion de détournement de pouvoir et je crois que ses conclusions sont toujours valables.

Deuxièmement, j'aimerais évoquer le problème des contrats à durée limitée qui est, à mon avis, l'un des plus grands défis pour les tribunaux administratifs dans toutes les organisations internationales. On note, en effet, une tendance forte à n'accorder que des contrats à durée limitée. A cet égard, il faut se demander si les autorités compétentes sont tout à fait libres dans leur décision de renouveler ou non le contrat ou si elles sont tenues de prendre en considération les intérêts des personnes concernées. Deux situations sont possibles. Une personne peut être "nue": ses droits et ses intérêts ne sont pas protégés. Mais une personne au service d'une institution internationale n'est pas "nue": elle dispose d'une confiance légitime. Je crois que l'exercice du pouvoir discrétionnaire doit être apprécié de manière différente selon l'un ou l'autre de ces cas. Dans la mesure où il existe une certaine confiance légitime, l'exercice du pouvoir discrétionnaire doit être plus serré, plus concret et plus poussé. Lorsqu'une personne est demandeuse d'emploi, l'administration est plus libre. Mais lorsqu'il s'agit d'une personne ayant été au service d'une institution internationale pendant dix, quinze ou vingt ans avec des contrats à durée limitée, une confiance s'est instaurée. Le pouvoir discrétionnaire peut alors se rétrécir et les juges peuvent devenir plus exigeants dans leur appréciation de la décision de renouveler ou non le contrat.

Seydou Ba, Juge au Tribunal administratif de l'Organisation internationale du Travail
J'aimerais réagir au commentaire de Monsieur le Professeur Ruzié sur les jugements 1821 et 1912 du Tribunal administratif de l'OIT. Je précise au préalable que, contrairement à ce que laisse croire ce commentaire, ce ne sont pas des considérations uniquement d'ordre budgétaire qui ont poussé le Tribunal administratif de l'OIT à adopter des solutions apparemment différentes dans ses jugements 1821 et 1912. Pour bien comprendre la situation, il faut se référer aux modifications intervenues dans la procédure d'ajustement des salaires au niveau des organisations coordonnées. Ce problème de l'ajustement des salaires, au cœur des jugements en question, a été traité à plusieurs reprises par le Tribunal de l'OIT. Les organisations qui ont fait l'objet de ces jugements appliquaient les décisions adoptées par les organisations coordonnées en matière d'ajustement de salaires. Le Tribunal administratif de l'OIT a toujours estimé qu'à partir du moment où ces organisations avaient décidé de se soumettre aux décisions des organisations coordonnées, elles ne pouvaient pas s'en écarter tant qu'elles n'avaient pas modifié leurs réglementations. Le Tribunal a soutenu ce point de vue dans la décision 1419 relative à l'affaire *Meylan.*

L'organisation concernée par le jugement 1821 avait décidé de modifier les textes se référant aux décisions des organisations coordonnées. Le jugement 1821 est intervenu après la modification de ces textes. Il a rappelé le principe suivant: une organisation a la possibilité de modifier ses règles, à la condition qu'elle reste dans le cadre des principes généraux dégagés et de la jurisprudence. Dans le jugement 1821, le Tribunal a estimé que l'organisation n'avait pas respecté ces principes. C'est la justification de l'annulation de la décision attaquée. Dans le jugement 1912, le Tribunal a estimé, en revanche, que l'organisation lui avait donné suffisamment d'indications pour lui permettre de considérer que la décision avait été prise sur des critères objectifs, dans le respect des principes généraux et de la jurisprudence.

D'autres jugements ont été rendus par la suite après le jugement 1912 et ont sanctionné les organisations qui ne s'étaient pas référées objectivement aux principes dégagés par le jugement 1821. Dans ces cas, il a été décidé d'annuler les décisions des organisations qui ne s'étaient pas conformées aux critères dégagés dans les principes suffisamment et clairement indiqués dans le jugement 1821. De fait, commenter le jugement 1912 en disant que l'on s'est fondé sur des considérations budgétaires me paraît réducteur.

Bola A. Ajibola, Judge, World Bank Administrative Tribunal
Thank you, Mr. Chairman. We have heard a variety of viewpoints this morning from two speakers and four commentators. The focus has been on the exercise of discretion and the abuse or non-abuse of it by the employers or administrative powers. I think that we should now turn our focus on ourselves, the judges. Who will judge us as to what we are doing and whether we are doing our job properly? I would like to turn to one particular area. Supposing you are seized with a matter and must interpret a particular rule, regulation, constitution or law and you take a decision interpreting the rule or regulation. Who will decide whether such a decision is right or wrong? What yardstick should be used?

There are so many possible units of measure. As indicated in the 1969 Vienna Convention on the Law of Treaties, one might take the objective, subjective or intentional approach. One might also choose to examine the existing *travaux préparatoires* as well. What have you done in coming to a decision as to whether a power has been properly exercised within the rules and regulations? I often find myself in that difficulty. The only effective yardstick I have been able to use is the following: if I make a decision and can sleep with only one eye closed, it is likely that something is wrong with the judgment. Let me raise a question: Does there exist any appellate body above the international administrative tribunals? Who will judge the judges? Thank you.

Laurence Boisson de Chazournes, Professeur à l'Université de Genève
Je ferai deux commentaires qui porteront essentiellement sur les propos de Francisco Orrego Vicuña. Celui-ci a dressé un panorama intéressant des différentes possibilités de contrôle de la légalité exercée ou pouvant être exercée par les tribunaux administratifs.

Mon premier propos s'inscrit dans une logique de politique juridique animée par un souci de sécurité juridique et d'égalité devant le droit. Il porte sur le contrôle de la législation, c'est-à-dire le contrôle du respect de la norme générale et, par exemple, le rôle joué par le Tribunal administratif, notamment de la Banque mondiale, en matière de respect de la règle de droit à l'intérieur du système de la Banque mondiale.

En appréhendant cette possibilité de contrôle, Francisco Orrego Vicuña a utilisé une typologie axée sur un contrôle au cas par cas ou sur une autorité institutionnelle de contrôle susceptible d'annuler les règles promulguées par les organes directeurs de l'organisation. Il s'est prononcé contre cette seconde solution. Je remarque que ces deux hypothèses s'inscrivent dans une logique de contrôle *a posteriori*: l'autorité de la Banque mondiale a pris ses décisions et le Tribunal administratif a le pouvoir de les annuler ou de les corriger.

J'ai lu et beaucoup bénéficié du rapport qu'avait préparé Francisco Orrego Vicuña pour le centenaire de la Conférence de La Haye en mai 1999. Cela m'a donné à penser que l'on pourrait maintenant réfléchir à la mise en place d'un contrôle *a priori* et à la possibilité éventuellement donnée aux tribunaux administratifs et, en particulier, à celui de la Banque mondiale d'intervenir au stade de la formulation des politiques juridiques afin d'indiquer ce qu'est le respect de la règle de droit ou ce que seraient les principes généraux de droit, par exemple lorsqu'une organisation modifie le système de pensions, comme la Banque mondiale l'a fait il y a quelques années.

Ma seconde remarque a trait au droit applicable. Le principe est celui selon lequel le pouvoir discrétionnaire doit se différencier d'un pouvoir arbitraire. Quand on identifie le droit applicable en ce domaine, on voit que l'on y adjoint les principes généraux de droit. Or ceux-ci sont une source du droit international, qui est nourrie par une pratique conventionnelle, institutionnelle et coutumière, notamment par les décisions rendues par les instances européennes et universelles ayant compétence en matière de protection internationale des droits de l'homme. Nous pourrions imaginer, dans le sens indiqué par le Juge Ajibola, qu'il devrait y avoir une contamination plus fertile entre les juridictions internationales et, ce faisant, que les juridictions administratives fassent aussi référence aux principes et à la jurisprudence des organes de protection des droits de l'homme.

Ibrahim F.I. Shihata, former General Counsel, World Bank

Mr. Chairman, I would like to come back to the very fine line between the review of the exercise of discretionary power and the Tribunal substituting itself for management in the exercise of that power. Of course, this is a classic subject that has been dealt with extensively in the literature. However, for practical purposes, it must be recognized that there is an element of personal judgment in every exercise of discretionary power and that there is an element of personal judgment in the review of that exercise. Yet, when a decision-maker reaches a decision, he or she has to take into account the underlying policies and values of the staff rules and the role of management. Meanwhile, the Tribunal may not be fully cognizant of these policies and values. Therefore, its evaluation, based on its own sense of justice, might be quite different from the sense of justice exercised in the light of the policies and values in place.

Allow me to provide an example. There was a case in the World Bank where two staff members within the Bank's printing services consistently overstated their overtime work. A decision was taken to fire them both. The Tribunal (*Carew v. IBRD*, Decision No. 142 [1995]; *Planthara v. IBRD*, Decision No. 143 [1995]) found, on the basis of the principle of proportionality, that this was an excessive sanction. Yet an institution that preaches the fight against corruption to the rest of the world cannot itself afford anything other than zero tolerance for corruption. Any petty corruption is just as serious as grand corruption, and termination of service consequently seemed to be the right answer. A tribunal that looks at the issue without regard to that background, and only "objectively" or "subjectively," is likely to find it excessive. In this particular case, the Tribunal asked the Bank to reinstate or compensate these two individuals. The Bank chose compensation, and then changed the rules so as to make this sanction mandatory for any fraudulent or corrupt act, no matter how great or small it might be. Otherwise, we could not have fulfilled our role as preachers of anti-corruption throughout the world.

I would hope that, when evaluating the proportionality of discretionary measures and when reviewing the exercise of discretionary power, tribunals do not make their decisions by isolating the cases from the underlying policies and values of each institution.

Eva-Maria Gröniger-Voss, adjointe du conseiller juridique de l'Organisation européenne pour la recherche nucléaire (CERN)

J'aimerais poser une question au Président Gentot qui s'ajoute aux remarques du Professeur Ruzié et du Juge Seydou Ba concernant les jugements relatifs à nos organisations sœurs: l'Organisation européenne pour des recherches astronomiques dans l'hémisphère austral (ESO) et le Laboratoire européen de biologie moléculaire (LEBM). Le CERN a suivi avec beaucoup d'intérêt la précision apportée par le Tribunal administratif de l'OIT à propos de la discrétion dont disposent les organisations internationales pour les décisions et l'établissement des méthodes d'ajustement des salaires. Il a été question de deux jugements: le jugement 1821 concernant l'ESO et le jugement 1912 concernant le LEBM. A mon avis, ces deux jugements ne sont pas, à leur lecture, aussi compatibles que ce qui a été dit. Le Tribunal considère-t-il que ces jugements forment une évolution? Sinon, comment faut-il comprendre le fait que, malgré la similitude des situations dans les deux Organisations, dans le cas du jugement de l'ESO, la méthode ait été sévèrement critiquée et dans le cas du LEBM, cette critique n'apparaît plus?

Gilbert Guillaume, Président, Cour internationale de Justice
J'aimerais simplement faire une observation. La question de l'étendue du contrôle exercé par le juge sur les décisions qui lui sont déférées est une question de nature très générale. Elle ne concerne pas seulement les tribunaux administratifs internationaux. Elle va beaucoup plus loin. J'en veux pour preuve l'exemple suivant. Il a été porté devant la Cour internationale de Justice une affaire dans laquelle une des parties conteste la licéité de décisions prises par le Conseil de sécurité. Dans l'hypothèse où nous nous reconnaîtrions compétents pour contrôler cette licéité, la question de l'étendue du contrôle du juge se poserait. C'est une question qui entrerait dans la problématique que nous abordons aujourd'hui.

Francisco Orrego Vicuña, Vice-Président, Tribunal administratif de la Banque mondiale
Je pense qu'il faut distinguer ce qui est strictement administratif de ce qui dépasse ce cadre. La révision du pouvoir discrétionnaire au cas par cas dans le parcours des travaux de quelques tribunaux est un processus tout à fait normal. Les choses seraient différentes si une espèce d'autorité institutionnelle avait le pouvoir de contrôler et éventuellement d'annuler les décisions. Elle se placerait de fait à un niveau supérieur aux autres organes. La fonction de contrôle relève à mon avis bien davantage d'un tribunal de type constitutionnel et pas tellement d'un tribunal administratif. Deux solutions sont dès lors possibles. Premièrement, les statuts de l'organisation pourraient demander au tribunal d'exercer un contrôle *a priori*. Le tribunal donnerait alors une sorte d'avis consultatif sur des questions qui lui seraient soumises par l'Administration. Mais pour cela, il aurait besoin d'un mandat spécifique. La deuxième voie (celle de l'interprétation) me paraît dangereuse car elle va trop loin. Selon la deuxième voie, il faudrait interpréter les statuts comme donnant au tribunal le pouvoir de contrôle. Mais si l'autre organe n'est pas d'accord avec cette interprétation, la collision est inévitable. De tels cas ont été vus dans d'autres contextes nationaux.

L'année passée, nous avons eu un débat très intéressant à propos de la Cour internationale de Justice dans le cadre du centenaire de la Conférence de paix. J'ai soutenu que la Cour internationale avait une fonction constitutionnelle en plus de son rôle dans le règlement des différends. Le Président Guillaume a évoqué dans ces conditions la nécessité d'un amendement éventuel de la charte et des statuts. Ce sont des questions valables qu'il est légitime de poser. En tout cas, il est utile de distinguer les aspects administratifs et les aspects constitutionnels.

A. Kamal Abul-Magd, Session Chair

I would like to make a comment with reference to the important issues raised by Dr. Shihata and Judge Ajibola. I think that, in administrative tribunals, we have all felt the problem of trying first to understand the culture of an institution to the best of our ability. This problem is part of the dynamics of the judicial process anywhere. In the World Bank, we have greatly benefited from certain meetings that used to be held during lunch and which brought together the President of the Bank, the General Counsel and representatives of the Staff Association. These meetings enabled issues to come to light that would not otherwise have surfaced through written memoranda. In this way, they could be appreciated and understood. No administrative tribunal wants to make decisions in isolation from the real needs of both the staff and the institution. Presently, our means of educating ourselves on these issues are very limited.

Secondly, I would like to take up the subject of corrective measures. Every reviewing body finds it necessary, at some point or another, to modify existing law. The U.S. Supreme Court sometimes invalidates certain legislation. Beyond a certain point, the only way for a country to remedy the situation is to create new legislation that is free from problems of unconstitutionality, while continuing to address the needs of the country. This problem is eternal and cannot be resolved very decisively.

Within every reviewing tribunal, there are usually two schools: the activists and those who encourage restraint. Judges choose positions on the basis of their sense of the lack of balance of power between the two parties. This is precisely why French administrative law, which was invented to protect the administration, gradually moved towards defending the weaker part – the individuals or staff members.

We do err. Management is a human institution; courts are also human institutions. Both are bound to make mistakes. If I were to choose between making mistakes in possible violation of the rule of law or mistakes that leave individuals vulnerable and without legal protection, I would definitely side with the weaker, with the individuals. I would leave it to the other side to correct my mistakes.

One issue that must be discussed is how to create an interaction between tribunals and institutions that does not violate the independence and integrity of the administrative tribunal. This would make us more aware. France solved this problem very early by giving the members of the *Conseil d'Etat* access to the active administration. We need to take some similar action. This is why it is always said that civil courts are unqualified to judge an administrative act: they do not grasp the culture, needs and particularities of managerial and administrative situations.

Lastly, as regards Judge Ajibola's suggestion, I do not think that we need an appellate court. The finality of decisions is a very legitimate consideration. Thank you.

Stephen M. Schwebel, Former President, International Court of Justice
Thank you, Mr. Chairman. I would like to make a brief comment on the remarks made by President Guillaume and Professor Orrego Vicuña. I am clearly not speaking here in my capacity as a member of the International Monetary Fund Administrative Tribunal, but as a former member of the International Court of Justice. Administrative tribunals are set up to review the legality of acts of the administration: that is inherent and express. There are limits to the power of review and deference to managerial discretion. Yet, the very point of an administrative tribunal is to review the legality of administrative acts. In my view, it is extraordinary to maintain that the International Court of Justice was set up to review the legality of the judgments of the Security Council as to whether a situation was or is a threat to or a breach of peace. There is nothing in the Charter of the United Nations or the Statute of the Court that so indicates. Similarly, neither the *travaux préparatoires* of either document nor the practice of the Court to date suggest that this is possible. In my view, if the Court were to arrogate to itself such a power, there would be an unprecedented crisis in the functioning of the United Nations.

A. Kamal Abul-Magd, Session Chair
This session is meant to be a time for brainstorming and I am glad to see that we are moving in this direction.

Gilbert Guillaume, Président, Cour internationale de Justice
Je me suis bien gardé de prendre position sur la question évoquée par le juge Schwebel. Savoir si la Cour internationale de Justice a ou n'a pas compétence pour contrôler les décisions du Conseil de sécurité est une question actuellement soumise à la Cour à laquelle j'appartiens et, par conséquent, je me garderai bien d'exprimer le moindre sentiment à ce sujet.

Dans l'hypothèse où la Cour se reconnaîtrait compétente, et seulement dans cette hypothèse, se poserait la question de l'étendue du contrôle qu'elle pourrait exercer sur les décisions du Conseil de sécurité. Il faudrait alors se demander si ce contrôle devrait être complet ou s'il ne pourrait pas être ce qu'on appelle en droit administratif français un contrôle restreint, c'est-à-dire un contrôle dans lequel on rechercherait si la décision du Conseil a été prise selon les règles de procédure applicables et s'il n'y a pas eu d'erreur manifeste d'appréciation, sans entrer dans la qualification juridique des faits.

Elizabeth Evatt, Judge, World Bank Administrative Tribunal
Thank you, Mr. Chairman. Seeing as this is a brainstorming session, I thought I might respond briefly to the learned Professor Laurence Boisson de Chazournes. She put forward the question as to whether tribunals should refer to decisions of bodies that deal with human rights issues. I thought it was an important issue to raise in this discussion. To me, it seems an anomaly of growing dimensions that neither the UN nor other international bodies are subject to the very covenants and conventions that they drafted for the observance by the State parties. While I do not presume to suggest that this should apply to the Security Council, I do think that one ought to encourage thinking about how tribunals could bring into their work some greater reference to the covenants and conventions on human rights. Thank you.

Celia Goldman, Registrar, International Monetary Fund Administrative Tribunal
Thank you. As an American-trained lawyer, one of the developments in the law of the international administrative tribunals that I find most interesting is that to which Judge Gentot referred: the *Barnes* case which was decided by the World Bank Administrative Tribunal. In that and other similar cases (including the case of *Ms. "C"* in the International Monetary Fund Administrative Tribunal), the challenged administrative act was sustained, but compensation was awarded for procedural irregularity. Might some of the commentators provide us with a roadmap to situations where the degree of procedural irregularity rises to the level of an abuse of discretion that would warrant a rescinding of the decision? This differs from situations where the degree of irregularity would warrant a sustaining of the decision and awarding of compensation.

Ranjan (C.F.) Amerasinghe, Judge, United Nations Administrative Tribunal
Thank you very much. I would like to address the human rights issue raised by Laurence Boisson de Chazournes. In an early case decided by the Council of Europe Appeals Board, the Appeals Board specifically stated that they were bound by the European Convention and Charter because the Council was responsible for them. From the outset, the Tribunal stated that it would abide by the provisions of the Human Rights Convention

and apply the appropriate laws. The UN would have no problem with this stance, seeing that the Charter includes a provision requiring that human rights be observed. The UN Tribunal has regarded the general principles of human rights to be binding. These are general principles of law and would be applied anyway. Indeed, there are some principles of human rights law, such as non-discrimination, which are *ius cogens*, so to speak, and take precedence over the written law, just as there are other fundamental principles of international administrative law which are also *ius cogens*, so to speak.

A. Kamal Abul-Magd, Session Chair

I would like to thank the speakers, commentators and members of the conference who took part and who made our discussion most informative. This is indeed a brainstorming session. Perhaps we will entertain new ideas after this. I would make one request of the afternoon session and its chair, Sir Eli Lauterpacht: that the topic of the afternoon, the practical issues arising in international administrative tribunals, be expanded to include the issue raised by Dr. Shihata and Judge Ajibola, namely the nature of the relationship between the tribunals and the institutions. We need to render justice within the context of the general interest of the institution. It follows that we must understand how matters are perceived by both the management and the Staff Association. This issue remains difficult because it brings the independence and integrity of the tribunal into question. Nonetheless, justice has to be rendered within the framework of the realities of the society.

PRACTICAL ISSUES ARISING IN INTERNATIONAL ADMINISTRATIVE TRIBUNALS

Sir Elihu Lauterpacht, QC*
Session Chair

Mr. Ziadé will open this session and will be followed by Professor Flogaitis. After hearing their presentations, we will be in a position to assess the kind of topics that we would like to discuss. Our commentators will then speak. We will hear from those commentators who are members of tribunals, then from representatives of respondent institutions, and then from counsel for applicants.

* Former President, World Bank Administrative Tribunal; former President, Asian Development Bank Administrative Tribunal.

SOME PRACTICAL ISSUES ARISING IN INTERNATIONAL ADMINISTRATIVE TRIBUNALS

Nassib G. Ziadé*

Résumé

L'exposé se basera sur la comparaison des statuts et règlements ainsi que de la pratique récente de douze tribunaux administratifs internationaux, à savoir le Tribunal administratif de la Banque mondiale (TABM), le Tribunal administratif de la Banque asiatique de développement (TABAsD), le Tribunal administratif du Fonds monétaire international (TAFMI), le Tribunal administratif de la Banque africaine de développement (TABAfD), le Tribunal administratif de l'Organisation de coopération et de développement économiques (TAOCDE), le Tribunal administratif du Conseil de l'Europe (TACE), la Commission de recours de l'Organisation du traité de l'Atlantique Nord (OTAN), le Tribunal administratif de l'Organisation des Etats américains (TAOEA), la Commission de recours de l'Agence spatiale européenne, le Tribunal administratif de la Banque inter-américaine pour le développement (TABID), le Tribunal administratif des Nations Unies (TANU) et le Tribunal administratif de l'Organisation internationale du Travail (TAOIT).

I. *La composition des tribunaux administratifs internationaux*

a) La méthode de désignation des membres du tribunal: Le Président et les membres du TAFMI sont désignés par le Directeur général du Fonds monétaire international. Le Président (et le Président suppléant) du TACE sont désignés par la Cour européenne des Droits de l'Homme alors que les autres membres du TACE sont désignés par le Comité des Ministres du Conseil de l'Europe. Au TABM, au TABAsD, au TABAfD et au TABID, les membres du Tribunal sont désignés par le Conseil des Administrateurs ou le Conseil des Gouverneurs de chaque institution. Au TANU et au TAOEA, les membres du Tribunal sont désignés par l'Assemblée générale de l'institution et au TAOIT par la Conférence de l'Organisation internationale du Travail (qui est équivalente à l'Assemblée générale des Nations Unies).

Si l'autorité qui désigne les membres des différents tribunaux administratifs peut varier, les méthodes de désignation, quant à elles, se ramènent à deux: l'une à caractère politique permet aux Etats-membres de proposer le nom des candidats et exclut normalement toute consultation aussi bien de l'administration de l'institution que de l'association du personnel, alors que l'autre préserve le caractère

* Executive Secretary, World Bank Administrative Tribunal; former Counsel, International Centre for Settlement of Investment Disputes (ICSID).

interne du processus de désignation en y faisant contribuer l'association du personnel de l'institution considérée. Des exemples du premier mode de désignation sont fournis par la Commission de recours de l'OTAN, le TACE (pour les membres autres que le Président et le Président suppléant), la Commission de recours de l'Agence spatiale européenne, le TANU et le TAOEA. Le TABM, le TABAsD, le TABAFD et le TAFMI constituent des illustrations du second mode de désignation. Il est bon de noter une particularité relative au TABID, selon laquelle le Conseil des Administrateurs nomme trois juges d'une liste présentée par l'Association du personnel et quatre juges d'une liste présentée par le Président de la Banque.

b) Le nombre de membres: Généralement, les tribunaux administratifs internationaux se composent de cinq à sept membres. Le statut des juges peut néanmoins varier selon les tribunaux. Alors que dans la plupart des tribunaux les juges ont un statut uniforme, leur statut est différent au sein d'autres tribunaux. Ainsi, on retrouve au TAOCDE, au TACE, à la Commission de recours de l'OTAN et au TAFMI à côté des juges titulaires, des juges suppléants et des remplaçants.

c) La nationalité des membres: Les textes, dans leur quasi-totalité, posent l'exigence que les juges doivent être de nationalités diverses. Les textes régissant la plupart des tribunaux (TABM, TABAsD, TABID, TACE, Commission de recours de l'OTAN, TAOEA, TAFMI et TABAfD) y ajoutent l'exigence que les juges doivent être des ressortissants d'Etats-membres de l'organisation considérée. Le TAFMI et le TABAfD tempèrent cette règle en prévoyant que les juges doivent être des ressortissants d'Etats-membres au moment de leur nomination, ce qui leur permettrait le cas échéant de se maintenir dans leur fonction en cas de changement ultérieur de nationalité.

d) Le mandat des membres: La majorité des statuts penche vers une durée de trois ans. La plupart des statuts ne posent pas de limites au nombre de mandats.

e) Les qualifications des membres: Les statuts peuvent sembler divergents mais reflètent en réalité une certaine uniformité. Les principales qualités exigées des juges sont la moralité et la compétence.

Divers textes exigent des juges d'être de "haute moralité", d'une "intégrité reconnue", d'une "impartialité prouvée", de posséder les qualifications requises pour être nommés à de hautes fonctions judiciaires ou bien d'être des jurisconsultes d'une compétence reconnue. Toutes ces formules sont empruntées à l'article 2 du Statut de la Cour internationale de Justice (CIJ) qui régit les qualifications des juges.

Certains textes se veulent plus spécifiques et requièrent une compétence particulière en matière de droit du travail ou de la fonction publique (TAOCDE et Commission de recours de l'Agence spatiale européenne) ou de droit administratif (TACE). Certains exigent un équilibre entre la tradition des pays de droit civil et des pays de la *common law* (TAOEA) ou encore la "représentation des principaux systèmes juridiques des pays Membres de l'Organisation" (TAOCDE). Dans le silence des autres textes, il semble que les dispositions du TAOEA et du TAOCDE reflètent une pratique concordante. Une autre pratique de ces divers tribunaux consiste à préserver les équilibres géographique et régional. L'ensemble de ces pratiques rejoint le but fixé par le Statut de la CIJ, à savoir que "dans l'ensemble la représentation des grandes formes de civilisation et des principaux systèmes juridiques du monde" soit assurée.

Cette uniformité en matière de qualifications requises des membres des tribunaux administratifs internationaux est à l'origine des désignations répétées de certains membres dans plus d'un tribunal. De telles désignations contribuent à un rapprochement entre les divers tribunaux, rapprochement dont le premier jugement du TABM dans l'affaire *de Merode* s'est fait l'écho.

f) Les incompatibilités: Pour plusieurs textes (TACE, TAOCDE, Commission de recours de l'OTAN, Commission de recours de l'Agence spatiale européenne et TAOEA), les membres du personnel sont exclus de la fonction de juge aux tribunaux administratifs. D'autres textes (TABAsD, TAFMI, TABAfD, TABID et TABM) se montrent plus exigeants puisqu'ils étendent l'interdiction aux anciens membres du personnel. Les Statuts du TABAsD et du TABAfD interdisent aux juges de devenir des membres du personnel pendant une durée de cinq ans après l'expiration de leur mandat, et le Statut du TABID introduit la même restriction pour une durée plus courte de trois ans. Le Statut du TABM interdit aux juges tout emploi ultérieur auprès de la Banque. Il est rare cependant qu'une limite d'âge soit précisée, comme le prévoit le Règlement de procédure du TAOEA.

II. *Le fonctionnement des tribunaux administratifs internationaux*

a) Le nombre de sessions et de cas: Il revient au président du tribunal de fixer le nombre de sessions annuelles. Celles-ci, ainsi que le nombre d'affaires décidées lors de chaque session, peuvent varier selon les tribunaux. C'est ainsi que le TAOIT tient deux sessions par an comportant chacune cinquante à soixante affaires. En revanche, la Commission de recours de l'OTAN tient cinq sessions par an comportant chacune deux affaires. Depuis 1997, le TABM, quant à lui, tient deux à trois sessions et tranche en moyenne vingt-deux cas par an.

b) Les langues utilisées: Le Règlement de procédure du TAFMI prévoit expressément que la langue de procédure du Tribunal est l'anglais. Dans le silence de leurs Règlements de procédure, le TABM et le TABAsD considèrent l'anglais comme étant la langue officielle. En revanche, dans la plupart des tribunaux administratifs internationaux, il existe plus d'une langue officielle. Certains tribunaux (TAOCDE, TACE, TABAfD, TAOIT et Commission de recours de l'OTAN) admettent les requêtes aussi bien en anglais qu'en français. D'autres tribunaux admettent les requêtes dans les langues officielles de leurs Etats-membres (Commission de recours de l'Agence spatiale européenne) ou dans celles de l'institution défenderesse (TAOEA, TABID et TANU).

La langue choisie par la partie requérante au TAOCDE, au TACE et au TAOIT sera suivie tout au long de la procédure écrite devant le Tribunal. En revanche, aux TABAfD, TABID et TAOEA, la partie défenderesse n'est pas limitée dans son choix à la langue choisie par la partie requérante.

Dans la plupart des tribunaux où plus d'une langue officielle est pratiquée (Commission de recours de l'OTAN, TANU, TACE, TAOIT et TAOCDE), le jugement rendu dans l'une des langues officielles fera foi et sera ensuite traduit vers une autre langue officielle. Pour d'autres tribunaux, la pratique oscillera entre utiliser une seule langue officielle (TABAfD) ou considérer deux langues comme faisant également foi (TAOEA).

c) Panels ou tribunaux en sessions plénières?: La plus grande diversité règne quant à cette question. Il est utile d'observer en premier lieu que certains tribunaux ne peuvent fonctionner, vu leur composition, que par panels de trois membres. C'est ainsi que le TAOCDE, le TACE et la Commission de recours de l'OTAN sont formés de trois membres titulaires et de trois membres suppléants.

De même, le TAFMI est composé d'un Président, de deux membres associés et de deux membres suppléants qui interviennent en l'absence des membres associés.

Dans les autres tribunaux où tous les membres ont le même statut, la question se pose de savoir si c'est le tribunal dans sa formation élargie ou plutôt des panels nommés par le tribunal qui devront trancher. Certains statuts ne donnent pas de choix quant à la formation appelée à trancher. Ainsi, le Statut du TABID exige que toutes les affaires soient tranchées par le Tribunal en session plénière. Par contre, le TANU exige que toutes les affaires soumises au Tribunal soient tranchées par des panels de trois membres.

Les Statuts du TAOIT, du TAOEA ainsi que du TABAsD permettent les deux formes de formation. Cependant, l'option accordée semble théorique tant les textes régissant le TAOIT et le TAOEA ne permettent la réunion de ces deux Tribunaux dans leur formation élargie qu'en cas de "circonstances exceptionnelles". Le TABAsD, quant à lui, pourra juger une affaire qui lui est soumise dans sa formation élargie lorsque le Tribunal considère un tel choix justifié ou lorsque l'une des parties présente au Tribunal une requête raisonnée à cet effet à laquelle ce dernier accède.

Le Statut et les Règles de procédure du TABM sont, en pratique, les seuls textes qui n'imposent pas de conditions quant au choix du Tribunal d'opter pour la formation plénière ou le panel. Durant les dix-sept premières années de son existence, ce Tribunal a choisi délibérément de trancher toutes les affaires en session plénière. Depuis l'année 1997, toutefois, suite à l'augmentation du nombre d'affaires portées devant ce Tribunal, le recours au panel est devenu la règle.

Dans tous les cas où un panel est appelé à trancher des affaires soumises à un tribunal, le panel devrait être présidé par le président du tribunal ou son vice-président. A cet égard, les critères de constitution des panels sont variés: dans certains cas, c'est la nature de l'affaire qui la détermine; dans d'autres, les critères linguistiques sont prépondérants. Parfois, le choix est purement fortuit: ainsi le Règlement du personnel de la Commission de recours de l'Agence spatiale européenne prévoit que les membres du panel (autres que le Président ou le Président suppléant) seront désignés par rotation alphabétique, et le Règlement de procédure du TAOEA prévoit la désignation des membres du panel par tirage au sort. Dans cette dernière hypothèse, le Règlement de procédure prévoit néanmoins que les membres choisis par tirage au sort devraient être préparés à céder leur place à d'autres membres du Tribunal afin d'assurer que la composition du panel reflète d'abord l'équilibre juridique entre la tradition de droit civil et celle de la *common law*, permette ensuite la conduite de la procédure dans la langue utilisée pour décider l'affaire, et réponde enfin à toutes autres raisons pratiques. Quoi qu'il en soit, une similitude se dégage de tous les exemples précédents, à savoir que la sélection des membres des panels est une question qui relève du seul tribunal et sur laquelle les parties n'ont pas à être consultées.

d) Les opinions dissidentes: Les tribunaux administratifs internationaux tentent souvent d'arriver à des décisions consensuelles. Un tel résultat peut toutefois s'avérer illusoire. La question qui se pose dans ce genre d'hypothèses consiste à savoir si l'émission d'une opinion dissidente ou séparée est possible.

Il est des cas où le statut et les règles de procédure du tribunal permettent expressément l'émission d'opinions dissidentes. C'est le cas du TAFMI, du TABM, du TAOEA, du TABAsD et du TABID. Dans le cas des trois derniers Tribunaux, des opinions dissidentes ont en fait été émises de manière occasionnelle. Par contre, le Règlement de procédure du TACE semble exclure la possibilité de l'émission d'une opinion dissidente; en effet, il prévoit en son article 35(2) que les jugements n'indiqueront pas s'ils ont été rendus à l'unanimité ou à la majorité, ce qu'une opinion dissidente ne manquerait pas de révéler.

La majorité des textes applicables sont cependant silencieux en ce qui concerne la question de savoir si les opinions dissidentes sont permises. Les textes disposent laconiquement que le tribunal peut rendre son jugement à la majorité. En l'absence de dispositions prohibitives, les juges du TANU et du TAOIT ont considéré qu'il était de leur droit d'émettre des opinions dissidentes quoique de manière exceptionnelle, alors que de telles opinions n'ont jamais été émises par les juges du TABAfD, du TAOCDE, de la Commission de recours de l'OTAN, ou de la Commission de recours de l'Agence spatiale européenne.

III. *Les moyens d'éviter les procédures vexatoires*

La question s'est posée aux tribunaux administratifs internationaux de trouver la parade aux requêtes abusives, et plus particulièrement à celles répétitives et infondées. De telles requêtes surchargent inutilement les tribunaux et les détournent de l'examen de cas plus méritoires. En outre, elles entraînent des procédures longues et coûteuses notamment pour l'institution défenderesse qui est partie au procès d'une part et qui supporte les frais et coûts de fonctionnement du tribunal d'autre part.

Une des solutions retenues par certains statuts (tels celui du TAFMI, du TABAfD, du TACE, de la Commission de recours de l'OTAN et du TAOEA) est de condamner la partie demanderesse dont la requête est manifestement abusive à rembourser à l'organisation défenderesse les frais encourus. A titre illustratif, le Statut du TACE permet au Tribunal d'ordonner à la partie requérante le remboursement de tout ou partie des dépenses s'il estime que le recours est "abusif". De même, reprenant les formulations du Statut du TAFMI, le Statut du TABAfD permet au Tribunal d'ordonner à la partie requérante de verser à la Banque africaine une compensation raisonnable au titre de tout ou partie des frais de procédure lorsqu'il constate que la requête n'a "manifestement aucun fondement en fait ou en droit" ou que la partie requérante "entendait retarder le règlement du litige ou harceler la Banque ou ses fonctionnaires et employés".

En pratique, cette faculté n'a jamais été mise en œuvre au TAFMI, au TABAfD ou à la Commission de recours de l'OTAN. Bien que le Secrétaire Général du Conseil de l'Europe ait demandé dans certains cas au TACE de condamner la partie requérante au paiement des dépens, le TACE n'a pas donné suite à de telles demandes. Au TAOEA, bien que le Tribunal ait condamné la partie demanderesse au paiement des frais et dépens de l'organisation pour certaines requêtes manifestement infondées, l'organisation s'est abstenue de réclamer à la partie demanderesse les sommes qui lui étaient dues.

Devant les tribunaux dont les statuts ne prévoient pas l'imposition de pénalités pour la présentation de cas abusifs, à l'exception d'un cas isolé à la fin des années 70 et au début des années 80 à la Commission de recours de l'Organisation de coopération et de développement économiques (devenue depuis lors le TAOCDE), aucun requérant n'a jamais été condamné à rembourser les frais et dépens, et ce, quand bien même la requête aurait été abusive ou vexatoire.

Bien que son Statut soit silencieux sur la question, le TAOIT a déclaré "sans équivoque" pour l'avenir dans un jugement rendu en 1999 dans l'affaire *Vollering*

(No. 15) qu'il était en droit de condamner un requérant à assumer les dépens dans des cas appropriés, et ce, dans le cadre du pouvoir qui est le sien de "contrôler sa propre procédure". Le TAOIT a justifié cette mesure eu égard au fait que "des requêtes futiles, abusives et répétées devant le Tribunal absorbent ses ressources et l'empêchent de traiter de manière rapide et complète les nombreuses requêtes méritoires qui sont portées devant lui" et que les requêtes futiles sont "coûteuses et synonymes d'une perte de temps pour l'organisation défenderesse". Le TAOIT a néanmoins souligné que l'imposition de pénalités pour présentation de cas abusifs doit être exercée "avec la plus grande précaution et uniquement dans les situations les plus exceptionnelles étant donné qu'il est essentiel que le Tribunal soit ouvert et accessible aux fonctionnaires internationaux sans qu'ils aient à subir l'effet dissuasif et rédhibitoire d'une éventuelle condamnation à assumer les dépens".

En définitive, cette faculté d'imposer une pénalité pour présentation d'un cas abusif demeure très rare dans la pratique. Elle a, aux yeux des tribunaux, le double inconvénient d'être trop dissuasive vis-à-vis de certains plaignants timorés quoique dans leur droit et de ne pas l'être assez vis-à-vis d'autres plaignants plus rompus à la chicane judiciaire.

Certains statuts (tels celui du TABM, du TABAsD, du TAOCDE, du TAOIT, du TACE et du TAFMI) mettent à la disposition des tribunaux administratifs internationaux un moyen plus sûr et en tout cas plus efficace de remédier aux requêtes abusives. Confronté à une requête qu'il considère "manifestement irrecevable ou dénuée de fondement", le Président du TABM, du TABAsD et du TAOCDE invitera le Greffier ou le Secrétaire exécutif à surseoir à tout acte de procédure jusqu'à la session prochaine du Tribunal. Ce dernier devra, après examen de la requête, soit la rejeter sans autre procédure, soit décider de l'instruire suivant la procédure ordinaire. Le même processus s'appliquera au TAOIT, à la seule différence que le Président, au lieu d'inviter le Greffier à surseoir à tout acte de procédure, pourra le charger d'envoyer copie de la requête à l'organisation défenderesse "à seule fin d'information". Au TACE, si le Président considère qu'un recours est "manifestement irrecevable", il adressera aux juges du Tribunal un rapport motivé à cet effet. Si les juges du Tribunal ne soulèvent pas d'objections dans un délai de deux mois, le recours sera déclaré irrecevable et une copie du rapport du Président sera communiquée à la partie requérante.

Il est bon d'observer que le TABM et le TAOIT ont eu recours durant les dernières années aux dispositions relatives à la procédure sommaire dans un certain nombre d'hypothèses. La procédure sommaire telle que décrite plus haut est bénéfique aussi bien au tribunal qu'aux deux parties. Pour la partie demanderesse, cette procédure permet d'être rapidement fixée sur le point de savoir si sa requête est irrecevable ou dénuée de fondement et, par conséquent, de faire l'économie d'un procès. En rejetant de manière sommaire la demande, le tribunal économisera aussi du temps et de l'argent et évitera d'exposer la partie requérante au paiement d'une pénalité. L'intérêt bien compris de toutes les parties concernées par la procédure commanderait en dernière analyse de recourir à la procédure sommaire de rejet mais uniquement dans des situations extrêmes.

IV. *Le caractère irrévocable des jugements des tribunaux administratifs internationaux*

a) Généralités: Les jugements de tous les tribunaux administratifs internationaux sont irrévocables. Les textes des divers statuts prévoient, dans une variété de formules, que les jugements sont "obligatoires", "definitifs", et "sans appel". En même temps, la plupart des textes prévoient des exceptions limitées au principe général de l'irrévocabilité des jugements sous la forme de recours en révision, en interprétation, ou en rectification et posent des conditions strictes à l'admissibilité de tels recours. A cet égard, deux difficultés peuvent se présenter.

La première difficulté peut apparaître quand une partie tente d'utiliser ces recours à des fins abusives. Dans ces cas, les tribunaux ne devraient pas hésiter à faire preuve d'une grande fermeté.

La seconde difficulté peut apparaître dans les situations où le statut et le règlement de procédure applicables au tribunal sont silencieux quant à la possibilité qu'un jugement puisse faire l'objet de l'un ou de l'autre des recours envisagés. Il est heureux de constater que la solution dominante adoptée par les tribunaux administratifs internationaux consiste à admettre ces recours même en l'absence de textes les réglementant. Ainsi, le TABM, se référant à l'article 82 de la Convention de La Haye de 1907 sur le règlement pacifique des conflits, a décidé dans son jugement *Agodo* rendu en 1989 que le TABM en tant que tribunal international possède le pouvoir inhérent d'interpréter ses propres jugements en cas de différend entre les parties quant à leur sens ou à leur portée, et ce, quand bien même son Statut ne contiendrait pas de dispositions à cet effet. Et le TABM de décider subséquemment en 1994 dans son jugement *Moses (No. 2)* qu'il possède à lui seul le pouvoir de donner une interprétation définitive et obligatoire de ses jugements. De même, le TANU – dont le Statut et le Règlement sont également silencieux concernant la question de la recevabilité des requêtes d'interprétation – a observé dès 1955 dans son jugement *Crawford et autres* que "la compétence pour interpréter leurs jugements est généralement reconnue aux tribunaux nationaux et internationaux". Le TANU a ensuite admis dans le même jugement qu'il serait guidé par les principes généraux relatifs à l'interprétation des jugements posés par la CIJ en 1950 dans l'affaire du *Droit d'asile*, à savoir qu'une demande d'interprétation d'un jugement n'est recevable que si elle vise à éclaircir le sens et la portée de ce que le Tribunal a décidé avec force obligatoire et non à obtenir la solution de questions qui n'ont pas été ainsi décidées, et qu'en outre il faut qu'existe une contestation sur le sens et la portée du jugement. Enfin, le TAOIT – dont le Statut aussi bien que le Règlement ne contiennent pas de dispositions relatives à la révision, l'interprétation et la rectification des jugements – examine cependant de tels recours conformément à des conditions strictement limitées. S'agissant du recours en révision d'un jugement, le TAOIT a décidé qu'il ne pouvait être déclaré recevable que dans des cas tout à fait exceptionnels, notamment "lorsque le requérant invoque des faits ou des moyens de preuve que, sans sa faute, il n'aurait pas été en mesure de faire valoir au cours de la précédente procédure" (jugement *Smith (No. 2)* rendu en 1973) ou "lorsque des faits nouveaux d'importance décisive auraient été découverts depuis le jugement" (jugement *Verdrager (No. 2)* rendu en 1978). De même, le TAOIT admet les recours en interprétation de manière restrictive. En effet, dans son jugement *Bonneau (No. 3)* rendu en 1987, le TAOIT, reprenant les termes de son jugement *Hopkirk (No. 2)* rendu treize ans plus tôt, a considéré que le recours en interprétation d'un jugement rendu par le Tribunal n'est recevable "que si ce jugement présente dans son dispositif une incertitude ou une ambiguïté sur son sens ou sa portée".

b) La révision des jugements: La plupart des textes régissant les tribunaux administratifs internationaux (TANU, TABM, TAFMI, TABAsD, TABAfD, TABID, TAOEA, TAOCDE, Commission de recours de l'OTAN et Commission de recours de l'Agence spatiale européenne) s'inspirent de l'article 61 du Statut de la CIJ et admettent le recours en révision d'un jugement si les trois conditions suivantes sont remplies:

1– la découverte par l'une des parties, après le prononcé du jugement, d'un fait qui, de par sa nature, aurait pu exercer une influence décisive sur ledit jugement;
2– la preuve qu'au moment du prononcé du jugement ce fait n'était connu ni du tribunal ni de la partie l'ayant découvert; et
3– la présentation du recours en révision durant un délai limité courant du jour de la découverte du fait nouveau.

Certains textes (TAFMI, TABAfD, TABID, TAOEA et TANU) imposent une condition supplémentaire, à savoir que l'ignorance du fait nouveau ne soit pas imputée à la faute ou à la négligence de la partie l'ayant découvert.

La question s'est posée de savoir si la procédure de révision d'un jugement était compatible avec l'exclusion de l'appel prévue par les textes applicables aux tribunaux administratifs internationaux, et la CIJ y a répondu par l'affirmative. En effet, la CIJ a décidé dans un avis consultatif du 13 juillet 1954 intitulé *Effet de jugements du Tribunal administratif des Nations Unies accordant indemnité* que la disposition du Statut du TANU conférant à ce dernier le pouvoir de prononcer des jugements définitifs et sans appel "ne peut toutefois être considérée comme interdisant au tribunal de réviser lui-même un jugement, dans des circonstances particulières, lorsque des faits nouveaux d'importance décisive ont été découverts; et le tribunal a déjà exercé ce pouvoir. Pareille révision strictement limitée, faite par le tribunal lui-même, ne peut être considérée comme un 'appel'. . . ." Comme corollaire à ce principe, le TABM a décidé dans son jugement *van Gent* rendu en 1983 que la procédure limitée de révision d'un jugement prévue par le Statut du TABM ne saurait être utilisée par une partie pour camoufler une procédure d'appel d'un jugement qui lui serait défavorable.

c) L'interprétation des jugements: Les textes régissant le TAFMI, le TABAfD, le TAOCDE, le TAOEA et la Commission de recours de l'Agence spatiale européenne leur donnent le pouvoir d'interpréter les jugements "dont les termes semblent obscurs ou incomplets" (TABAfD) ou lorsque "le dispositif d'un jugement est peu clair ou incomplet ou que ses éléments sont contradictoires entre eux ou avec les motifs" (TAOCDE). Alors que les textes régissant le TAFMI et la Commission de recours de l'Agence spatiale européenne ne fixent pas un délai pour la présentation du recours en interprétation, les autres textes fixent un délai relativement court (trente jours (TAOEA), soixante jours (TABAfD) et trois mois (TAOCDE)) à compter de la notification du jugement. Le nombre de conclusions devant être échangées au cours de la procédure d'interprétation varie selon les tribunaux. Alors que les règles de procédure du TABAfD et du TAFMI présentent une certaine flexibilité en ce qu'elles requièrent des deux Tribunaux seulement de laisser à l'autre partie "l'opportunité raisonnable" de présenter ses observations sur la question, le Règlement de procédure du TAOCDE étend aux recours en interprétation les règles applicables aux requêtes ordinaires présentées devant le Tribunal.

Un recours en interprétation doit uniquement tendre à préciser le sens et la portée d'un jugement. Tout recours tendant sous couvert de l'interprétation à réformer un jugement clair sera rejeté.

d) La rectification des jugements: Les textes régissant le TANU, le TAFMI, le TABAfD, le TABID, le TAOCDE, le TAOEA, la Commission de recours de l'OTAN, la Commission de recours de l'Agence spatiale européenne et le TACE prévoient que leurs jugements peuvent être corrigés ou rectifiés par le Tribunal (ou par son Président dans le cas du TACE) soit d'office soit sur requête de l'une ou des deux parties. La nature des erreurs pouvant donner lieu à un recours en rectification varie selon les textes: il peut s'agir d'une erreur matérielle, typographique ou dactylographique, d'une erreur arithmétique ou de calcul, ou encore d'une erreur résultant d'une inadvertance ou d'une omission. A l'exception du TABID et du TAOCDE, les textes ne fixent pas de délais durant lesquels les recours en rectification peuvent être admis.

La plupart des textes passent sous silence les questions relatives au nombre des conclusions et à l'ordre dans lequel elles devraient être échangées entre les parties lors de la procédure de rectification, laissant ainsi aux tribunaux respectifs le soin de prendre les décisions adéquates dans chaque cas. En revanche, les Règlements de procédure du TAOCDE, du TAOEA et de la Commission de recours de l'OTAN étendent aux procédures de rectification les règles applicables aux nouvelles affaires qui leur sont soumises.

* * *

The occasion of the 20th anniversary of the establishment of the World Bank Administrative Tribunal (WBAT) presents itself both as a challenge and as an opportunity to consider some of the practical issues arising in the operations of the WBAT and other international administrative tribunals. Though not exhaustive, the list of such other tribunals covered in this paper consists of: the Asian Development Bank Administrative Tribunal (AsDBAT); the International Monetary Fund Administrative Tribunal (IMFAT); the African Development Bank Administrative Tribunal (AfDBAT); the Organisation for Economic Co-operation and Development Administrative Tribunal (OECDAT); the Council of Europe Administrative Tribunal (CEAT); the North Atlantic Treaty Organisation Appeals Board (NATOAB); the Organization of American States Administrative Tribunal (OASAT); the European Space Agency Appeals Board (ESAAB); the Inter-American Development Bank Administrative Tribunal (IDBAT); the United Nations Administrative Tribunal (UNAT); and the International Labour Organization Administrative Tribunal (ILOAT).

At the time of the establishment of the World Bank Administrative Tribunal, many of the above-mentioned tribunals had not yet been established. There certainly exists today a body of law richer and more developed than the one that existed prior to the proliferation of international administrative tribunals. Additional Statutes and Rules of Procedure were enacted when the new international administrative tribunals were established and additional practices started emerging when the new tribunals began to operate.

Given the proliferation of international administrative tribunals and the large number of questions raised by the texts applicable to them as well as by their practices, it would be unrealistic to present in a paper a full account of all practical issues pertaining to such tribunals. Accordingly, this paper will focus on the following topics: (1) the composition of administrative tribunals; (2) their internal functioning; (3) the handling by tribunals of frivolous and abusive requests; and (4) the extent to which judgments of such tribunals are final.

I. *Composition of Tribunals*

(a) *Method of appointment of Tribunal members*

The appointment of Tribunal members varies among different institutions. The President and the members of the IMFAT are appointed by the Managing Director of the IMF.[1] The Chair (and Deputy Chair) of the CEAT are selected by the European Court of Human Rights[2] while its other members are selected by the Committee of Ministers of the Council of Europe.[3] In the WBAT, the AsDBAT, the AfDBAT and the IDBAT, Tribunal members are appointed by the Executive Directors or the Board of Directors of each institution.[4] With respect to the NATOAB, the OECDAT and the ESAAB, the Tribunal members are appointed by the Council of each institution.[5] In the UNAT and the OASAT, Tribunal members are appointed by the General Assembly of the institution[6] and in the ILOAT by the Conference of the International Labour Organization[7] (which is the equivalent of the General Assembly of the United Nations).

[1] IMFAT, Statute, Art. VII. In appointing the President of the Tribunal, the Managing Director shall seek the approval of the Executive Board.

[2] CEAT, Statute, Art. 1(2) and (3) and Art. 2.

[3] *Id.* at Art. 1(2) and (3).

[4] WBAT, Statute, Art. IV(2); AsDBAT, Statute, Art. IV(2); AfDBAT, Statute, Art. VI(2); IDBAT, Statute, Art. III(2).

[5] NATOAB, Statute, Art. 4.11; OECDAT, Staff Regulation 22(d); ESAAB, Staff Regulation 34.1.

[6] UNAT, Statute, Art. 3(2); OASAT, Statute, Art. III(1), Rules of Procedure, Art. 1(3).

[7] ILOAT, Statute, Art. III(2).

More significant than the identity of the appointing authority is the method by which lists of names are proposed to that authority. In some cases, the method seems to be rather political in nature because the actual proposals are made by member States of the institution. This is the situation in the NATOAB, the CEAT (for judges other than the Chair and Deputy Chair), the ESAAB,[8] the UNAT and the OASAT. There, neither the management of the institution nor its Staff Association is normally consulted in the process. In other cases, the proposal process is internal to the institution and is carried out after appropriate consultation[9] within the institution. The consultation process will then include, either by statutory requirement[10] or by practice,[11] the Staff Association.

In the IDBAT, although the proposal process is internal to the institution, the management and the Staff Association do not necessarily engage in consultations since each side is responsible for proposing its own list of names. From the list drawn up by the Staff Association, the Board of Executive Directors will appoint three judges; from the list drawn up by the President of the Bank, the Board of Executive Directors will appoint four judges.[12] The situation in the IDBAT clearly represents a sharing arrangement between the Staff Association and the Bank rather than a process that requires consultation on each and every name.

(b) *Number of members*

Though the number of members in some international administrative tribunals has fluctuated in recent years,[13] tribunals today commonly have five (AsDBAT[14] and IMFAT),[15] six (AfDBAT,[16] OECDAT,[17] CEAT,[18]

---

[8] ESAAB, Staff Rule 34/1. It may be noted that the Director-General of the European Space Agency (ESA) may also propose candidates to the Council after taking into account proposals from the Staff Association. (*Id.*)

[9] WBAT, Statute, Art. IV(2); AsDBAT, Statute, Art. IV(2); AfDBAT, Statute, Art. VI(2); IMFAT, Statute, Art. VII(1).

[10] AsDBAT, Statute, Art. IV(2); AfDBAT, Statute, Art. VI(2); IMFAT, Statute, Art. VII(1)(a).

[11] This is the case with the WBAT and the OECDAT.

[12] IDBAT, Statute, Art. III(2).

[13] The Statute of the AsDBAT (effective 1 April 1991) provided that the Tribunal is composed of three members. Amendments made to the Statute of the AsDBAT on 22 December 1994 (effective 1 January 1995) increased the number of members of the Tribunal to five. At one time, there were three judges and four deputies in the ILOAT; there are now seven judges.

[14] AsDBAT, Statute, Art. IV(1).

[15] IMFAT, Statute, Art. VII.

[16] AfDBAT, Statute, Art. VI(1).

[17] OECDAT, Staff Regulation 22(d).

[18] CEAT, Statute, Art. 1(1) and (3).

NATOAB,[19] OASAT[20] and ESAAB)[21] or seven (WBAT,[22] IDBAT,[23] UNAT,[24] and ILOAT)[25] members. There are, however, variations with respect to the status of the judges. While in most tribunals, the judges have the same status, their status is different in other tribunals. In the OECDAT and the CEAT, out of the six members, three are judges and three are deputies who act in the absence of the judges.[26] The same applies in the NATOAB where out of the six members, there are one President, two full members, an alternate President, and alternates for the two full members.[27] In the IMFAT, there are one President, two associate members and two alternates.[28] Cases will ordinarily be decided by the President and the two associate members.[29] In the event that an associate member is unable to hear a case, the President will replace him with an alternate.[30] In the event that the President is unable to hear a case, he will be replaced by the elder of the two associate members, who will in turn be replaced by an alternate.[31]

(c) *Nationality of members*

Almost all the texts governing Administrative Tribunals require Tribunal members to be of different nationalities.[32] Most of the texts also require Tribunal members to be nationals of Member States of the Organization.[33] The IMFAT and the AfDBAT qualify the latter requirement by providing that members of the Tribunal should be nationals of Member States at the time of their appointments,[34] thus allowing them to remain in their

---

19 NATOAB, Statute, Art. 4.11–12.
20 OASAT, Statute, Art. III(1), Rules of Procedure, Art. 1(1).
21 ESAAB, Staff Regulation 34.1.
22 WBAT, Statute, Art. IV(1).
23 IDBAT, Statute, Art. III(1), Rules of Procedure, Art. 1(1).
24 UNAT, Statute, Art. 3(1).
25 ILOAT, Statute, Art. III(1).
26 OECDAT, Staff Regulation 22(d); CEAT, Statute, Art. 1.
27 NATOAB, Statute, Art. 4.11–12.
28 IMFAT, Statute, Art. VII.
29 *Id.*, Art. VII(4).
30 *Id.*
31 *Id.*
32 UNAT, Statute, Art. 3(1); OECDAT, Staff Regulation 22(d); ILOAT, Statute, Art. III(1); ESAAB, Staff Regulation 34.1; AfDBAT, Statute, Art. VI(1); WBAT, Statute, Art. IV(1); AsDBAT, Statute, Art. IV(1); IDBAT, Statute, Art. III(1), Rules of Procedure, Art. 1(1); CEAT, Statute, Art. 1(4); NATOAB, Statute, Art. 4.11; OASAT, Statute, Art. III(2), Rules of Procedure, Art. 1(2)(a).
33 WBAT, Statute, Art. IV(1); AsDBAT, Statute, Art. IV(1); IDBAT, Statute, Art. III(1), Rules of Procedure, Art. 1(1); CEAT, Statute, Art. 1(5); NATOAB, Statute, Art. 4.11; OASAT, Statute, Art. III(2), Rules of Procedure, Art. 1(2)(a); IMFAT, Statute, Art. VII(1)(c); AfDBAT, Statute, Art. VI(1).
34 IMFAT, Statute, Art. VII(1)(c); AfDBAT, Statute, Art. VI(1).

positions should there be subsequent changes of their nationality or changes in the membership status of their country of nationality.

(d) *Length of appointment*

Most of the Statutes provide that members of the Tribunal are appointed for three years.[35] One Statute provides for a two-year appointment;[36] another provides for a five-year appointment;[37] and two provide for a six-year appointment.[38]

Three Statutes (OECDAT, ILOAT and NATOAB) are silent on the question of reappointment of Tribunal members.[39] It seems to be the practice, however, to consider their appointment renewable. Four Statutes (IDBAT, OASAT, UNAT and WBAT) allow members of the Tribunal to be reappointed only once.[40] The majority of the Statutes provide, however, that Tribunal members may be reappointed without a limit as to the number of times.[41]

(e) *Qualifications*

Though the qualifications that would enable a person to be considered for appointment as a member of a Tribunal vary among the Statutes, a certain uniformity emerges from the otherwise divergent texts. As a general rule, Tribunal members are held to high moral standards and must be demonstrably competent to handle cases that come before them.

---

[35] AsDBAT, Statute, Art. IV(3); AfDBAT, Statute, Art. VI(4); CEAT, Statute, Art. 1(2); IDBAT, Statute, Art. III(3); OECDAT, Staff Regulation 22(d); ILOAT, Statute, Art. III(2); NATOAB, Statute, Art. 4.11. This was also the situation at the WBAT prior to July 31, 2001.

[36] IMFAT, Statute, Art. VII(1).

[37] WBAT, Statute, Art. IV(3).

[38] ESAAB, Staff Regulation 34.3; OASAT, Statute, Art. III(1), Rules of Procedure, Art. 1(4). It is interesting to note that while in the ESAAB, the six-year terms of the six members start together and end together, in the OASAT the six-year terms of the six members are staggered so that each year the term of one member expires.

[39] OECDAT, Staff Regulation 22(d); ILOAT, Statute, Art. III(2); NATOAB, Statute, Art. 4.11.

[40] IDBAT, Statute, Art. III(3); OASAT, Statute, Art. III(4), Rules of Procedure, Art. 1(6); UNAT, Statute, Art. 3(2); WBAT, Statute, Art. IV(3). It may be noted, however, that the Statutes of the OASAT and the WBAT provide for a longer term of appointment of Tribunal members (six and five years, respectively, and not three years as is the case with most other tribunals). (See *supra* notes 37–38 and accompanying text.)

[41] AsDBAT, Statute, Art. IV(3); AfDBAT, Statute, Art. VI(4); CEAT, Statute, Art. 1(2); IMFAT, Statute, Art. VII(2); ESAAB, Staff Regulation 34.3. This was also the situation at the WBAT prior to July 31, 2001.

In this respect, Tribunal members are required by the various texts to be "persons of high moral character,"[42] "persons of recognized . . . integrity,"[43] "persons of proven impartiality,"[44] or "eminent persons."[45]

Moreover, many Statutes provide in general terms that Tribunal members "must possess the qualifications required for appointment to high judicial office or be jurisconsults of recognized competence."[46] Other Statutes are more specific in their requirements: Tribunal members shall be "experienced lawyers, law professors or judges by profession,"[47] "jurists or otherwise highly qualified in labour law or civil service law or in the field of labour relations at the national or international level,"[48] "persons with particular competence in labour legislation and in staff relations, preferably from the international field,"[49] or persons with great experience in administrative law.[50] The WBAT today combines these general and specific requirements.[51]

The OASAT Statute requires in addition that the composition of the Tribunal, as a whole, reflect both the common law tradition and the civil law tradition.[52] Similarly, the OECDAT requires that the Tribunal's composition "ensure that the main legal systems of the Member countries of

[42] WBAT, Statute, Art. IV(1); AsDBAT, Statute, Art. IV(1); AfDBAT, Statute, Art. VI(1).

[43] IDBAT, Statute, Art. III(1), Rules of Procedure, Art. 1(1).

[44] OECDAT, Staff Regulation 22(d).

[45] ESAAB, Staff Rule 34/1(iii).

[46] AsDBAT, Statute, Art. IV(1); AfDBAT, Statute, Art. VI(1); IMFAT, Statute, Art. VII(1)(c). This was also the situation at the WBAT prior to July 31, 2001. Similarly, Article III(1) of the Statute and Article 1(1) of the Rules of Procedure of the IDBAT provide that members of the Tribunal must be persons "who have the necessary qualifications to occupy a similar position in the highest judicial courts of their countries or who are jurisconsults of recognized competence." All of these formulations are reminiscent of the qualifications of the judges of the International Court of Justice who, according to Article 2 of its Statute, must "possess the qualifications required in their respective countries for appointment to the highest judicial offices, or [be] jurisconsults of recognized competence in international law."

[47] OASAT, Statute, Art. III(2), Rules of Procedure, Art. 1(2)(a). In the past, the President of the CEAT had to be a judge on the European Court of Human Rights. As of April 1, 2000, he or she may no longer be an active judge on the European Court, but should, however, be a judge on an international tribunal, a national court of a member State of the Council of Europe, or a former judge on the European Court of Human Rights (CEAT, Statute, Art. 1(2)).

[48] OECDAT, Staff Regulation 22(d).

[49] ESAAB, Staff Rule 34/1(iii).

[50] CEAT, Statute, Art. 1(2).

[51] Article IV(1) of the Statute of the WBAT provides in relevant part that "[t]he members of the Tribunal shall be persons of high moral character and must possess the qualifications required for appointment to high judicial office or be jurisconsults of recognized competence in relevant fields such as employment relations, international civil service and international organization administration."

[52] OASAT, Statute, Art. III(7).

the Organization [be] represented."[53] Though the other texts are silent on this question, it is believed that the OAS and OECD provisions reflect a general practice among international administrative tribunals. Another emerging general practice in most of these tribunals is to maintain a geographical balance and a regional distribution in the composition of the tribunals. These practices might be said to be aiming for the goal set for the International Court of Justice in its Statute that "in the body as a whole the representation of the main forms of civilization and of the principal legal systems" should be assured.[54]

The existence of similar requirements for Tribunal membership among the various international administrative tribunals has resulted in appointments of certain individuals to more than one tribunal. Thus, it is significant to reflect on the WBAT's first decision in *de Merode*, where it was emphasized that "the judgments of one tribunal may refer to the jurisprudence of another" and where it was noted that there is a tendency towards a certain *rapprochement* among international administrative tribunals.[55] In this respect, the appointment of the same individuals to different tribunals will further contribute to the *rapprochement* among the various tribunals.

(f) *Ineligibility to serve*

Several texts codify the well-accepted principle that members of the Organization's staff (and representatives of member-States to the Organization) may not be Tribunal members.[56] Other texts go even further by precluding present as well as former staff members of the Organization from serving as Tribunal members.[57]

Two Statutes provide that Tribunal members will be ineligible from becoming staff members of the Organization for a period of five years after the expiry of their appointment.[58] One Statute introduces a similar restriction for a shorter period of two years.[59] Another Statute prohibits Tribunal members from ever obtaining employment with the Organization.[60]

[53] OECDAT, Staff Regulation 22(d).

[54] ICJ, Statute, Art. 9.

[55] *de Merode*, WBAT Decision No. 1 [1981], para. 28.

[56] CEAT, Statute, Art. 1(1); OECDAT, Staff Regulation 22(d); NATOAB, Statute, Art. 4.11; ESAAB, Staff Regulation 34.2; OASAT, Statute, Art. III(6)(c), Rules of Procedure, Art. 1(2)(b).

[57] AsDBAT, Statute, Art. IV(1); IMFAT, Statute, Art. VII(1); AfDBAT, Statute, Art. VI(1); IDBAT, Statute, Art. III(1), Rules of Procedure, Art. 1(1). The WBAT adopted a similar restriction as of July 31, 2001. WBAT, Statute, Art. IV(1).

[58] AsDBAT, Statute, Art. IV(1); AfDBAT, Statute, Art. VI(1).

[59] IDBAT, Statute, Art. III(1), Rules of Procedure, Art. 1(1).

[60] This restriction was adopted by the WBAT as of July 31, 2001. WBAT, Statute, Art. IV(1).

Only the Rules of one Tribunal provide for an age limitation: individuals who have reached the age of 65 before being nominated for election are ineligible to serve as members of the OASAT.[61]

II. *Functioning of Tribunals*

(a) *Number of sessions and cases*

All of the texts give the President or the Chair of the Tribunal the power to fix as many sessions as needed per year for the purpose of deciding cases and dealing with matters affecting the administration or operation of the Tribunal.[62] There are, however, divergent practices among the different tribunals with respect to the number of sessions held per year as well as to the number of cases decided during each session. The figures compiled reveal divergences such as the following: on the one hand, the ILOAT holds two sessions per year, with 50 to 60 cases decided per session, and the UNAT holds two sessions per year, with 20 to 25 cases decided per session; on the other hand, tribunals such as the NATOAB generally hold five sessions per year, with two cases decided per session. Over the past years, the approach taken by the WBAT has fallen somewhere in the middle; it has since 1997 held two to three sessions per year, with an average of 22 cases decided per year.

(b) *Working languages*

Rule II of the Rules of Procedure of the IMFAT provides that "[t]he working language of the Tribunal shall be English." Though the Rules of Procedure of the WBAT and the AsDBAT are silent on the matter, the practice has been to consider English as the official language in both jurisdictions.

In most of the Tribunals, however, there is more than one working or official language, and an application (or an appeal or a complaint, depending on the terminology used in the texts) may be brought in any one of these languages. English and French are the official or working languages

---

[61] OASAT, Rules of Procedure, Art. 1(2)(b).

[62] WBAT, Rules of Procedure, Rule 5(1) and (2); AfDBAT, Rules of Procedure, Rule VII; OECDAT, Statute, Art. 7; UNAT, Statute, Art. 4, Rules of Procedure, Art. 5; ILOAT, Statute, Art. IV, Rules, Art. 3; IDBAT, Statute, Art. IV(2), Rules of Procedure, Art. 6; OASAT, Statute, Art. IV, Rules of Procedure, Arts. 5 and 6; CEAT, Statute, Art. 9(2), Rules of Procedure, Rule 8; AsDBAT, Rules of Procedure, Rule 5; ESAAB, Staff Regulation 41.1, Staff Rule 41.1/1; NATOAB, Statute, Arts. 4.51 and 4.53.

at the OECDAT,[63] the CEAT[64] and the AfDBAT;[65] applications (or appeals in the case of the CEAT) may be filed in either of these two languages.[66] Similarly, complaints in the ILOAT[67] and appeals in the NATOAB[68] may be filed either in English or in French. There are other Tribunals where there are even more than two languages in which applications may be submitted. Thus, in the ESAAB, the appeal may not only be submitted in French or English but also "in the official language, or one of the official languages of the Member State of which the claimant is a national."[69] In the OASAT, complaints may be filed in any one of the four official languages of the Organization of American States,[70] i.e., English, Spanish, Portuguese and French. In the IDBAT, though Spanish and English are the working languages of the Tribunal,[71] the Tribunal may agree to the complainant's request that written and oral proceedings be conducted in one of the other official languages of the Bank,[72] i.e., French or Portuguese.[73] In the UNAT, applications may be filed in any of the official languages of the United Nations,[74] i.e., Arabic, Chinese, English, French, Russian and Spanish.[75]

The language chosen at the outset by the applicant in the OECDAT, the appellant in the CEAT and the complainant in the ILOAT will be used in any subsequent written pleadings in these tribunals.[76] In other tribunals, such as the AfDBAT, the IDBAT and the OASAT, the respondent, in its choice of a language in which to file its pleadings, is not restricted to the language chosen by the applicant.

Finally, it may be noted that in most of the tribunals where there is more than one official language, judgments are delivered in one of the

---

[63] OECDAT, Rules of Procedure, Rule 1(a).

[64] CEAT, Statute, Art. 6, Rules of Procedure, Rule 11.

[65] AfDBAT, Rules of Procedure, Rule II.

[66] OECDAT, Rules of Procedure, Rule 1(b); CEAT, Rules of Procedure, Rule 16(2); AfDBAT, Statute, Art. III(5).

[67] ILOAT, Rules, Art. 6(1)(a).

[68] NATOAB, Rules of Procedure, Art. 1(c).

[69] ESAAB, Staff Rule 41.6/1(iii).

[70] OASAT, Statute, Art. VI(6), Rules of Procedure, Art. 26(1).

[71] IDBAT, Rules of Procedure, Art. 31(1).

[72] *Id.*

[73] In practice, there has only been in the IDBAT one case in which the proceedings were conducted in French and one case in which the proceedings were conducted in Portuguese, both at the request of the complainant. (Information provided by the IDBAT Secretariat.)

[74] UNAT, Statute, Art. 7(7).

[75] In practice, however, 80–85% of the cases are submitted to the UNAT in English and 10–15% of the cases are submitted in French. (Information provided by the UNAT Secretariat.)

[76] OECDAT, Rules of Procedure, Rule 1(b); ILOAT, Rules, Art. 6(4).

official languages (generally the language chosen by the member of the tribunal drafting the judgment or the language of the proceedings), which will be the authentic text, and are then translated into another official language.[77] In other tribunals, the practice regarding the language of the judgments varies between using one language (AfDBAT) or treating two languages as equally authentic (OASAT).

(c) *Panels v. Tribunals*

Some of the Tribunals are composed in such a way that they can only function in panels of three members. As already noted, in the OECDAT, the CEAT and the NATOAB, out of the six members, three are full members and three are deputies or alternates who act only in the absence of the full members.[78] In the IMFAT, where there are one President, two associate members and two alternates, cases are ordinarily decided by the President and the two associate members.[79]

In all of the other Tribunals, where all the members have the same status, the question arises whether cases should be decided by the full Tribunal or by panels formed by the Tribunal. There are some Tribunals in which the Statutes do not afford the Tribunal the option of having its cases decided either by the full Tribunal or by panels formed by the Tribunal. Thus, the Statute of the IDBAT requires that applications submitted to the Tribunal "be reviewed and decided upon by all of its members."[80] By contrast, the Statute of the UNAT provides that all cases must be decided by panels of three members.[81] This also seems to be the situation in the ESAAB.[82]

In the ILOAT, the OASAT and the AsDBAT, there seems to be an option to have cases decided either by panels or by full Tribunals. But the question is, however, to what extent that option is real in these three Tribunals when there are serious restrictions imposed on the Tribunals by their Statutes and Rules. Pursuant to these texts, cases are normally decided by panels of three members.[83] In the ILOAT, it is only "in exceptional

[77] This is the practice in the NATOAB, the UNAT, the CEAT, the ILOAT and the OECDAT. (Rule 1(a) and (d) of the Rules of Procedure of the OECDAT states that judgments shall be provided in French or English and then translated into the other language, the original version being the authentic text.)

[78] See *supra* notes 26 and 27 and accompanying text.

[79] See *supra* notes 28 to 31 and accompanying text.

[80] IDBAT, Statute, Art. III(4).

[81] UNAT, Statute, Art. 3(1). The UNAT's Statute was amended in recent years to allow the whole Tribunal to consider a case which "raises a significant question of law" (Art. 8). This possibility remains, however, exceptional.

[82] ESAAB, Staff Regulation 41.2.

[83] ILOAT, Statute, Art. III(3); OASAT, Statute, Art. III(6), Rules of Procedure, Art. 2(2); AsDBAT, Statute, Art. V(4).

circumstances" designated by the President of the Tribunal that cases will be decided by five or seven members.[84] In the OASAT, the President may convene a plenary session of the six members of the Tribunal "[u]nder exceptional circumstances, for cases involving particular importance or difficulty, or to deal with cases that a three judge panel is unable to resolve."[85] Interestingly, in the AsDBAT, cases will be decided by the full Tribunal, not only in cases where the Tribunal believes that a full Tribunal is warranted, but also in cases where a party itself makes a reasoned request to that effect and the Tribunal agrees with the request.[86]

The Statute and the Rules of Procedure of the WBAT are, in practice, the only texts that do not impose limitations on the option of the Tribunal of deciding a case in plenary session or in a panel. Although the texts allow the Tribunal to form panels of not less than three of its members to deal with a particular case or group of cases,[87] the WBAT deliberately chose in the first 17 years of its operations to decide all cases submitted to it in plenary sessions. Since 1997, however, as a result of an increased caseload in the work of the Tribunal, practical necessities (and not any requirement in its Statute or Rules) dictated a shift in its 17-year policy. Since 1997, the date when the panel system was used for the first time by the WBAT, recourse to the panel system has become the rule rather than the exception. (In 1998, for instance, out of the 21 cases decided by the Tribunal, 17 were by panels.)

When panels are constituted, each panel should normally be chaired by either a President or a Vice President.[88] As to the criteria for the constitution of the panels, they vary. In some instances, panels are chosen depending on the nature of the cases submitted to the Tribunal. In other instances, the actual composition of the panels will depend on linguistic criteria and on the members' fluency with the language of the proceedings. There may also be cases where the composition of panels is purely coincidental. Thus, Staff Regulation 41.2 of the ESAAB provides that the two members of a panel, other than the presiding Chairman or Deputy Chairman, "will be selected in rotation, in alphabetical order." In the OASAT, the composition of the panels is determined by lot.[89] The Rules, however, provide that in the interests of the effective operation of the Tribunal, members selected

[84] ILOAT, Statute, Art. III(3).

[85] OASAT, Rules of Procedure, Rule 2(3). In practice, Presidents of the OASAT have not in the last years convened a plenary session of the Tribunal to decide a case.

[86] AsDBAT, Statute, Art. V(5), Rules, Rule 5A(1) and (2).

[87] WBAT, Statute, Art. V(2), Rules, Rule 6(1).

[88] UNAT, Rules, Art. 3(3); ESAAB, Staff Regulation 41.2; OASAT, Rules of Procedure, Art. 2(5); AsDBAT, Rules, Rule 5A(3); WBAT, Rules, Rule 6(2).

[89] OASAT, Statute, Art. III(6)(a), Rules of Procedure, Art. 2(5).

by lot to serve on panels should be prepared to exchange places with other members of the Tribunal "to ensure that the composition of each panel: a) reasonably reflects the two major legal traditions of the Hemisphere (the common-law tradition and the civil-law tradition), b) has a reasonable ability to conduct work in the language used for hearing particular cases, and c) responds to other practical reasons."[90] It is clear from these examples that the selection of panel members is purely internal to the Tribunal and is not a matter on which parties to pending cases should be consulted.

(d) *Dissenting opinions*

Tribunals or panels constituted by them always attempt to reach a consensus in their decisions and to draft language which reflects the consensus and is acceptable to all members. There are situations where Tribunal members are, however, unable to agree on the dispositive part of a judgment or on the legal reasoning of the judgment. The question arises whether the texts allow for the filing of dissenting or separate opinions in such situations.

There are instances where the texts allow expressly for the filing of dissenting or separate opinions. Thus, Rule XVIII(3) of the IMFAT Rules of Procedure provides that "[a]ny member differing as to the grounds upon which the judgment was based or some of its conclusions, or dissenting from the judgment, may append a separate or dissenting opinion." Similar provisions are provided for in the OASAT Rules of Procedure and in the AsDBAT Statute.[91] Article 26(2) of the IDBAT Rules of Procedure, and Article XI(2) of the WBAT Statute, for their part provide that "[d]issenting and concurring opinions, as well as clarifications," can "be set out in the judgment."[92] No dissenting opinions have ever been filed in the IMFAT or the WBAT, but dissenting opinions have been filed occasionally in the OASAT, the AsDBAT and the IDBAT. In the IDBAT, where the Tribunal is comprised of three members appointed by the Executive Directors from lists submitted by the Staff Association and four members from lists submitted by the President of the Bank, a noteworthy feature is that dissenting opinions do not necessarily reflect the views of the party who submitted the name of the dissenting member for appointment.

The majority of the texts are, however, silent on the question whether dissenting opinions are permissible. They merely provide that the Tribunal shall reach its decisions by a majority of the members present at a

[90] OASAT, Rules of Procedure, Art. 2(6).
[91] OASAT, Rules of Procedure, Art. 50(4); AsDBAT, Statute, Art. IX.
[92] The WBAT's provision in this respect was adopted as of July 31, 2001.

session.[93] In the absence of a specific directive in the texts, some members of the UNAT and the ILOAT have availed themselves, though exceptionally, of the right to file dissenting opinions. No such opinions, however, have been filed in the AfDBAT, the OECDAT, the NATOAB and the ESAAB.

It may finally be noted in this respect that Rule 35(2) of the CEAT Rules of Procedure provides that the judgments of the Tribunal "shall not indicate if they have been taken by a unanimous or by a majority decision." Such a provision certainly seems to preclude the possibility of a Tribunal member filing a dissenting opinion as this would unequivocally reveal that the judgment was reached by a majority of the members present and not on a unanimous basis.

III. *Avoidance of vexatious proceedings*

Many international administrative tribunals have been confronted with the difficult problem of how to respond to the filing of applications that are found to be abusive or frivolous and, more particularly, to the filing of repeated applications that are baseless. Such applications certainly add to the workload of the tribunals, take up time that could be devoted to meritorious cases, can involve lengthy proceedings and are costly to the respondent institution that has to defend the cases in addition to bearing the expenses of the Tribunal.

An award by the Tribunal of compensation to the respondent institution may be an option in such cases. The Statutes of the IMFAT,[94] the AfDBAT,[95] the CEAT,[96] the NATOAB,[97] and the OASAT[98] allow for the imposition of penalties on applicants. The IMFAT and the AfDBAT may order an applicant to reimburse the institution for all or part of the reasonable costs it incurred in defending the case if the application was patently without factual basis or legal merit or if the applicant "intended to delay the resolution of the case or to harass the [institution] or any of its officers or employees." The CEAT may order the appellant to pay all or part of

---

[93] AfDBAT, Statute, Art. XI(6), Rules of Procedure, Rule XXI(1); ILOAT, Statute, Art. VI(1); OECDAT, Statute, Art. 12(a); UNAT, Statute, Art. 11(1); NATOAB, Statute, Art. 4.81; ESAAB, Staff Regulation 41.15. Such was also the situation in the WBAT prior to July 31, 2001.

[94] IMFAT, Statute, Art. XV.

[95] AfDBAT, Statute, Art. X.

[96] CEAT, Statute, Art. 11(1).

[97] NATOAB, Statute, Art. 4.82.

[98] OASAT, Statute, Art. IX(5), Rules of Procedure, Art. 50(7).

the costs incurred if it considers that the appeal constituted "an abuse of procedure," and the NATOAB may decide not to reimburse to an appellant the security deposited if it considers that the appeal was "an abuse of process." The OASAT may order an applicant to pay to the respondent an indemnity for attorney's fees and costs when an applicant "has brought a clearly frivolous claim or objection."

In practice, neither the IMFAT nor the AfDBAT has ever imposed a penalty on an applicant. The NATOAB, in its decisions, has always ordered the repayment of the security deposited by the appellant. Although the Secretary-General of the Council of Europe has asked the CEAT in some cases to order appellants to pay costs, the CEAT has refrained from making such orders. Indeed, in other instances where the appellants lost their cases, the CEAT ordered, in accordance with Article 11(3) of its Statute, that they be reimbursed for certain legal fees. In the OASAT, though the Tribunal has ordered the applicant in some instances[99] to reimburse the organization for its expenses and attorney's fees, it is not the usual practice for the organization to seek such reimbursement from the applicant.[100]

In the tribunals that do not have provisions allowing for the imposition of penalties on applicants for the submission of frivolous cases (i.e., the UNAT, WBAT, AsDBAT, ILOAT, OECDAT, IDBAT and ESAAB), with the exception of an isolated incident in the late 1970s/early 1980s at the OECD Appeals Board[101] – which became in 1991 the OECDAT – applicants have never been asked to reimburse costs or expenses, even where the cases brought by them were abusive or vexatious.

Though the ILOAT has thus far not imposed penalties on applicants who brought requests that were found to be abusive, frivolous or vexatious, it indicated in a recent decision[102] that it was ready to reconsider its position:

---

[99] See, e.g., *José Luis Pardo v. Director General of the Inter-American Institute for Cooperation on Agriculture*, OASAT Decision No. 120 [1993], where the applicant was ordered to pay costs of the proceedings in the amount of $1,000 for "submitting a patently baseless case," and *Janet Ector v. Secretary General of the Organization of American States*, OASAT Decision No. 121 [1993], where the applicant was ordered to pay costs in the amount of $1,000 as "the penalty for reasserting an unfounded claim" in the form of an application for revision.

[100] It may be noted that, pursuant to Article XV(2) of the Statute of the IMFAT, the Managing Director of the Fund "may, in particular cases, waive the claim of the Fund against the applicant."

[101] An applicant, Mr. Angelopoulos, brought twenty-two consecutive cases, six of which, the Appeals Board felt, were abusive. The Board decided that the filing of such abusive cases did not warrant the reimbursement of the applicant's caution (OECD Appeals Board's Decisions No. 67 of April 6, 1979; No. 83 of March 19, 1981; No. 84 of March 19, 1981; No. 91 of January 15, 1982; No. 96 of July 6, 1982; and No. 97 of March 3, 1983).

[102] *Vollering (No. 15)*, ILOAT Decision No. 1884 [1999].

> The Tribunal has never heretofore imposed a costs penalty upon a complainant. However, it asserts unequivocally that it possesses the inherent power to do so as part of the necessary power to control its own process. Clearly, such power must be exercised with the greatest care and only in the most exceptional situations since it is essential that the Tribunal should be open and accessible to international civil servants without the dissuasive and chilling effect of possible adverse awards of costs. That said, however, there is another side to the coin: frivolous, vexatious and repeated complaints to the Tribunal absorb the latter's resources and impede its ability to deal expeditiously and fully with the many meritorious complaints which come before it. They are also, of course, costly and time-wasting for the defendant organisation.
>
> In the present case the Organisation has not asked for an award of costs but has simply sought a declaration that the complaint is an abuse of process. The Tribunal makes such a declaration and further declares that in future it will award costs against complainants in appropriate cases if they are sought.[103]

This first option of imposing a penalty on an applicant who has brought a frivolous claim is not without risk. On the one hand, the threat of a penalty may result in discouraging applicants who have meritorious cases from submitting them to the Tribunal. On the other hand, it is not certain that such a threat would have a deterrent effect on the submission of frivolous claims. In the isolated incident at the OECD Appeals Board referred to earlier, where an applicant brought twenty-two consecutive cases, that applicant kept bringing new cases despite the fact that the Appeals Board decided not to reimburse his caution in earlier ones. These drawbacks of the first option could explain its lack of popularity among Tribunals and their reluctance to use it.

The texts governing the WBAT,[104] the AsDBAT,[105] the IMFAT,[106] the OECDAT,[107] the ILOAT[108] and the CEAT[109] put at the disposal of the tribunals a more efficient and certainly safer device to deal with applications that are "clearly inadmissible" (IMFAT), "manifestly inadmissible" (CEAT), "clearly inadmissible or devoid of merit" (OECDAT), "clearly irreceivable or devoid of merit" (ILOAT), or "clearly irreceivable or devoid of all merit" (WBAT and AsDBAT). If it appears that an application falls within one of these categories, the President of the WBAT or the AsDBAT, or the Chairman of the OECDAT, will instruct the Executive Secretary

[103] *Id.* at paras. 8 and 9 of the "Consideration" section.
[104] WBAT, Rules of Procedure, Rule 7(11).
[105] AsDBAT, Rules of Procedure, Rule 6(11).
[106] IMFAT, Statute, Art. X(2)(d), Rules of Procedure, Rule XII.
[107] OECDAT, Statute, Art. 6(d).
[108] ILOAT, Rules, Art. 7.
[109] CEAT, Statute, Art. 5(2), Rules of Procedure, Art. 19(2).

or Registrar to take no further action until the next session of the Tribunal. The Tribunal will, after considering the application, either adjudge that it be summarily dismissed or order that it be proceeded with in the ordinary way. The same will apply at the ILOAT, except that the President of the Tribunal, rather than instructing the Executive Secretary to take no further action until the next session of the Tribunal, "may instruct the Registrar to forward [the complaint] to the defendant organization for information only." In the CEAT, if the Chair considers an appeal to be manifestly inadmissible, he or she shall provide a report to that effect to the judges of the Tribunal. In the absence of any objection from the judges within two months, the appeal will be declared inadmissible and a copy of the report will be communicated to the appellant.

The WBAT has in the recent years made use of the rule allowing for summary dismissal of cases on the sole basis of the application in many instances.[110] The ILOAT has also resorted to the same procedure.[111]

---

[110] In two cases (*Witter*, Order, 1997 *WBAT Reports* 243; and *Romain (No. 2)*, Order, 1997 *WBAT Reports* 245), the Tribunal held that the applications were devoid of all merit as they were essentially repetitive of earlier applications and as the issues raised in them had already been addressed in earlier judgments. In a third case (*Verdier*, Order, 1998 *WBAT Reports* 177), the Applicant submitted a request to "reinstate" an earlier application that had been withdrawn seven years earlier after the Applicant's French legal guardian had accepted a settlement offer from the Bank. The Tribunal held that the request was clearly irreceivable as the Tribunal did not have jurisdiction to review the procedures followed and the decisions made by the French judicial authorities in accordance with French law. In two other cases (*Baartz*, Order, 1999 *WBAT Reports* 147; and *Baartz*, Order, 2000 *WBAT Reports* 197), the Applicant submitted petitions to reconsider an earlier judgment rendered in his case. The Tribunal found that both petitions were devoid of all merit. In the first of these two cases, the Applicant submitted the statement of a new witness and the Tribunal held that the availability of a new witness was not in itself a new fact and that there was no supporting evidence that the only new facts submitted by the Applicant might have had a decisive influence on the judgment of the Tribunal. In the second case, the Applicant submitted the statement of a witness who had earlier testified before the Appeals Committee and the Tribunal held that the production of such a witness was not in itself "a discovery of a fact" and that the information presented by the witness did not constitute new evidence. In a further case (*Yasmin*, Order, 2000 *WBAT Reports* 199), the widow of an applicant submitted a request for revision of the judgment rendered in her husband's case. The Tribunal found that the request was devoid of all merit, in that most of the information presented in it was not newly discovered and was known to the Tribunal at the time of its judgment, and any information in the request that might have been considered new would not have had a decisive influence on the judgment of the Tribunal.

[111] To cite a few examples, the ILOAT has summarily dismissed applications for review on the basis that: (a) the evidence tendered by the complainant was "incredible" (*Mendiratta (No. 5)*, ILOAT Decision No. 1377 [1995]); (b) the Applicant failed to cite any "circumstance that the Tribunal ha[d] not already taken account of in its [earlier] judgments on the merits" (*Carretti (Nos. 6 and 7)*, ILOAT Decision No. 1387 [1995]); and (c) "an alleged mistake of law [was] an inadmissible plea for review" (*Saunders (No. 17)*, ILOAT Decision No. 1529 [1996]). With respect to a request for interpretation that was submitted to it, the ILOAT summarily dismissed the request on the basis that the judgment was "quite clear and [left] no room for interpretation about the Tribunal's ruling on the dispute." (*Diotallevi (No. 4)*, ILOAT Decision No. 1521 [1996]).

It may be noted that a proper use of the summary dismissal mechanism is beneficial to the Tribunal as well as to both parties. In the case of the Applicant, he or she is made aware at a very early stage that the case is irreceivable or has no merit and is, therefore, spared time and expense. By dismissing a case at this early stage, the Tribunal will also save time and money and will obviate the need to resort to the drastic measure of imposing a penalty on the Applicant for what will otherwise be considered a vexatious or frivolous case. It may be submitted that while a Tribunal should resort to summary dismissal only in extreme cases, the interests of all those involved in the process clearly warrant this in such extreme cases.

IV. *Finality*

(a) *General*

All of the texts provide in rather similar formulations for the finality of the judgments rendered by international administrative tribunals. In many cases, the texts emphasize that the judgments shall be final and without appeal;[112] in other cases, that they shall be final and binding;[113] in some other cases that they shall be binding, final and without appeal.[114] Other texts merely state that the judgments shall not be subject to appeal.[115]

In one of its early judgments, the WBAT elaborated on the implications of the principle of finality:

> No party to a dispute before the Tribunal may, therefore, bring his case back to the Tribunal for a second round of litigation, no matter how dissatisfied he may be with the pronouncement of the Tribunal or its considerations. The Tribunal's judgment is meant to be the last step along the path of settling disputes arising between the Bank and the members of its staff.[116]

Most of the texts allow for limited exceptions to the general principle of finality in the form of revision, interpretation or rectification. Other texts are silent as to whether any or all of these exceptions to the principle of finality may be invoked. These questions will be discussed below.

[112] WBAT, Statute, Art. XI(1); IMFAT, Statute, Art. XIII(2); ILOAT, Statute, Art. VI(1); UNAT, Statute, Art. 11(2); IDBAT, Statute, Art. VIII(2); OASAT, Statute, Art. X(2).

[113] AsDBAT, Statute, Art. IX(1); OASAT, Rules of Procedure, Art. 51(1).

[114] AfDBAT, Statute, Art. XII(1); ESAAB, Staff Regulation 41.17(i).

[115] OECDAT, Statute, Art. 12(b); CEAT, Statute, Art. 12(2); NATOAB, Statute, Art. 4.84, Rules of Procedure, Art. 5(c).

[116] *van Gent (No. 2)*, WBAT Decision No. 13 [1983], para. 21.

(b) *Revision*

The texts of the UNAT,[117] the WBAT,[118] the IMFAT,[119] the AsDBAT,[120] the AfDBAT,[121] the IDBAT,[122] the OASAT,[123] the OECDAT,[124] the NATOAB[125] and the ESAAB[126] provide for the revision of judgments.

The provisions governing revision of judgments are inspired by Article 61 of the Statute of the International Court of Justice and follow its language in some instances almost verbatim. In this respect, the texts of the above-mentioned tribunals lay down three conditions for the admissibility of a request for revision of a judgment:

1. the discovery by a party to a case in which a judgment has been delivered of a fact[127] which by its nature might have had a decisive influence on the judgment of the Tribunal;
2. the showing that at the time the judgment was delivered such fact was unknown both to the Tribunal and to the party having discovered the fact; and
3. the submission by that party of a request for revision within a limited period of time[128] after it acquired knowledge of such fact.

Some texts impose a further condition, namely that the ignorance of the fact "was not the responsibility"[129] of the party making the request for revi-

[117] UNAT, Statute, Art. 12.
[118] WBAT, Statute, Art. XIII.
[119] IMFAT, Statute, Art. XVI, Rules of Procedure, Rule XIX.
[120] AsDBAT, Statute, Art. XI.
[121] AfDBAT, Statute, Art. XII(4), Rules of Procedure, Rule XXII.
[122] IDBAT, Statute, Art. VII(2)(f), Rules of Procedure, Art. 27.
[123] OASAT, Statute, Art. XI(1), Rules of Procedure, Art. 51(2) and (4).
[124] OECDAT, Statute, Art. 12(b), Rules of Procedure, Rules 11 and 13.
[125] NATOAB, Statute, Art. 4.84, Rules of Procedure, Art. 5(c) and (d).
[126] ESAAB, Staff Regulation 41.17(iii) and (iv).
[127] While most of the texts speak of the discovery of a "fact," some texts (IMFAT, Rules of Procedure, Rule XIX(1); AfDBAT, Rules of Procedure, Rule XXII(1); IDBAT, Rules of Procedure, Art. 27(1); OASAT, Statute, Art. XI(1), Rules of Procedure, Art. 51(2)) mention the discovery of "a fact or a document" and one text (OECDAT, Rules of Procedure, Rule 11(a)) the discovery of "a fact or evidence."
[128] The request for revision should be submitted before certain tribunals within a period of six months after the party acquired knowledge of the fact (WBAT, Statute, Art. XIII(1); IMFAT, Statute, Art. XVI; AsDBAT, Statute, Art. XI(1); AfDBAT, Statute, Art. XII(4)), before other tribunals within thirty days after the party requesting the revision acquired knowledge of the fact and, in any event, within one year from the date on which that party was notified of the judgment (IDBAT, Rules of Procedure, Art. 27(2); OASAT, Statute, Art. XI(1), Rules of Procedure, Art. 51(2); UNAT, Statute, Art. 12), and before other tribunals within three months from the date of discovery of the fact and within five years from the date of the notification of the judgment (OECDAT, Rules of Procedure, Rule 11(b); NATOAB, Statute, Art. 4.84, Rules of Procedure, Art. 5(c); ESAAB, Staff Regulation 41.17(iii)).
[129] IMFAT, Rules of Procedure, Rule XIX(1); AfDBAT, Rules of Procedure, Rule XXII(1).

sion, "was not due to fault or deceit by that party,"[130] "was not due to negligence,"[131] or "is not attributable to the party's own negligence or fraud."[132]

Since the process of revision of a judgment may result in a reversal or reformation of the judgment based on the decisive facts discovered, the question arises as to whether revision is compatible with the exclusion of appeal set forth in the various texts applicable to international administrative tribunals. The International Court of Justice answered this question in the affirmative when it examined the possibility for the UNAT to revise its judgments:

> This rule [providing that the judgments of the UNAT shall be final and without appeal] contained in Article 10, paragraph 2 [of the Statute of the UNAT], cannot however be considered as excluding the Tribunal from itself revising a judgment in special circumstances when new facts of decisive importance have been discovered; and the Tribunal has already exercised this power. Such a strictly limited revision by the Tribunal itself cannot be considered as an 'appeal' within the meaning of that Article. . . .[133]

Inasmuch as the exercise by an international administrative tribunal of its strictly limited power of *revision* of one of its prior judgments cannot be considered an appeal, a request for *review* of a judgment would, according to most international administrative tribunals, be considered an appeal and defeat the principle of finality of judgments. In this respect, the WBAT stated:

> The limited powers of revision of a judgment authorized by Article XIII of the Statute cannot be used as a cover for a party to appeal what it considers an unfavorable or unsatisfying decision by the Tribunal.[134]

(c) *Interpretation*

The texts of the IMFAT,[135] the AfDBAT,[136] the OECDAT,[137] the OASAT[138] and the ESAAB[139] empower these tribunals to interpret their judgments

[130] IDBAT, Rules of Procedure, Art. 27(1); OASAT, Statute, Art. XI(1).

[131] UNAT, Statute, Art. 12.

[132] OASAT, Rules of Procedure, Art. 51(2).

[133] Effect of awards of compensation made by the U.N. Administrative Tribunal, Advisory Opinion of July 13th, 1954: I.C.J. Reports 1954, p. 55.

[134] *van Gent (No. 2)*, WBAT Decision No. 13 [1983], para. 29.

[135] IMFAT, Statute, Art. XVII, Rules of Procedure, Rule XX.

[136] AfDBAT, Statute, Art. XII(3), Rules of Procedure, Rule XXIII.

[137] OECDAT, Statute, Art. 12(b), Rules of Procedure, Rules 12 and 13.

[138] OASAT, Rules of Procedure, Art. 50(8). It may be noted that in the context of the OASAT, parties may request a "clarification" of a judgment.

[139] ESAAB, Staff Regulation 41.17(ii) and (iv).

upon the request of one or both parties if the operative provisions of the judgment "appear obscure or incomplete,"[140] "are ambiguous or incomplete or . . . inconsistent either with each other or with the *ratio decidendi* (reasons in point of law),"[141] or if "difficulties arise as to [its] meaning or scope."[142] While the texts governing the IMFAT and the ESAAB do not provide for a time limit within which a request for interpretation may be submitted, other texts do impose such a time limit. Such a request should be submitted within thirty days (OASAT),[143] sixty days (AfDBAT)[144] or three months (OECDAT)[145] from the date of the notification of the judgment.

The extent of the exchange of pleadings during interpretation proceedings varies among international administrative tribunals. The Rules of Procedure of the IMFAT and the AfDBAT[146] require both Tribunals to give the other party or parties "a reasonable opportunity to present its or their views on the matter." This language is flexible in that it allows the Tribunals to determine on a case-by-case basis the number of pleadings and their sequence.[147] By contrast, the Rules of Procedure of the OECDAT[148] indicate that the procedure followed with respect to normal cases brought before the Tribunal will apply *mutatis mutandis* to requests for interpretation.

It is a recognized principle that interpretation neither impairs the finality nor involves a review of a judgment, but is only a determination of its meaning and scope. The rules applicable to interpretation give expression to this principle. According to the Rules of Procedure of the OASAT, the Tribunal shall decide a request for clarification of a judgment "without reconsidering the merits of the case."[149] In the ESAAB, if the Chairman considers that a request for interpretation "clearly amounts to an appeal against a decision of the Board," and the other members of the Board do not object to this determination, the Chairman may "deliver a reasoned decision stating the request to be inadmissible."[150] In the IMFAT and the

---

[140] IMFAT, Statute, Art. XVII; AfDBAT, Statute, Art. XII(3).
[141] OECDAT, Rules of Procedure, Rule 12.
[142] ESAAB, Staff Regulation 41.17(ii).
[143] OASAT, Rules of Procedure, Art. 50(8).
[144] AfDBAT, Rules of Procedure, Rule XXIII(1).
[145] OECDAT, Rules of Procedure, Rule 12.
[146] IMFAT, Rules of Procedure, Rule XX(3); AfDBAT, Rules of Procedure, Rule XXIII(3).
[147] In the two requests for interpretation submitted so far by the International Monetary Fund to the IMFAT (*Ms. C v. International Monetary Fund*, Order No. 1997–1, and *Ms. Y v. International Monetary Fund*, Order No. 1999–1), the Tribunal requested a single exchange of pleadings. The IMFAT may, however, require a more extensive exchange of pleadings in future cases. (Information provided by Ms. Celia Goldman, Registrar, IMFAT.)
[148] OECDAT, Rules of Procedure, Rule 13.
[149] OASAT, Rules of Procedure, Art. 50(8).
[150] ESAAB, Staff Regulation 41.17(iv).

AfDBAT, the Tribunal shall, in the light of the views presented by the parties, decide whether the application for interpretation is admissible. Only in such cases will the Tribunal issue its interpretation.[151]

(d) *Rectification*

The texts governing the UNAT,[152] the IMFAT,[153] the AfDBAT,[154] the IDBAT,[155] the OECDAT,[156] the OASAT,[157] the NATOAB,[158] the ESAAB[159] and the CEAT[160] provide that their judgments may be corrected or rectified by the Tribunal (in the case of the CEAT, by its Chair) either *ex officio* or on the application of one or both parties. The nature of the errors that are subject to rectification varies from text to text: they range from clerical, arithmetical and typographical errors to errors arising from oversight, slip or omission and accidental errors. With the exception of the IDBAT and the OECDAT, the texts do not set time limits within which requests for correction may be submitted.[161]

While most of the texts are silent on the number and sequence of pleadings that are to be exchanged between the parties during rectification proceedings – thus giving the Tribunals flexibility to decide what would be appropriate for each case – the Rules of Procedure of the OECDAT,[162] the OASAT[163] and the NATOAB[164] extend to rectification proceedings the procedures applicable to new cases brought before them.

---

[151] IMFAT, Rules of Procedure, Rule XX(3); AfDBAT, Rules of Procedure, Rule XXIII(3). In *Ms. C v. International Monetary Fund, op. cit.*, the IMFAT admitted the application for interpretation before issuing its interpretation. In *Ms. Y v. International Monetary Fund, op. cit.*, though the IMFAT decided not to admit the Fund's application for interpretation on the ground that the term whose interpretation was requested was "neither obscure nor incomplete," it also indicated that it did not concur with the interpretation provided by the requesting party.

[152] UNAT, Statute, Art. 12.

[153] IMFAT, Statute, Art. XVII, Rules of Procedure, Rule XVIII(5).

[154] AfDBAT, Statute, Art. XII(3), Rules of Procedure, Rule XXI(4).

[155] IDBAT, Rules of Procedure, Art. 26(5).

[156] OECDAT, Statute, Art. 12(b), Rules of Procedure, Rules 10 and 13.

[157] OASAT, Statute, Art. XI(2), Rules of Procedure, Art. 51(3) and (4).

[158] NATOAB, Statute, Art. 4.84, Rules of Procedure, Art. 5(c) and (d).

[159] ESAAB, Staff Regulation 41.17(v).

[160] CEAT, Statute, Art. 12(2), Rules of Procedure, Rule 37.

[161] The parties may submit their requests for correction within thirty calendar days (in the case of the IDBAT, Rules of Procedure, Art. 26(5)) and three months (in the case of the OECDAT, Rules of Procedure, Rule 10) from the date of notification of the judgment.

[162] OECDAT, Rules of Procedure, Rule 13.

[163] OASAT, Rules of Procedure, Art. 51(4).

[164] NATOAB, Rules of Procedure, Art. 5(d).

(e) *Absence of provisions*

There are situations where the Statute as well as the rules and regulations applicable to a tribunal are silent as to whether a judgment may be subject to any or all of the three possible remedies of rectification, interpretation and revision. In such cases, one possible solution would be to deny the remedy in the absence of a text providing for it. This is the solution adopted in one case by the IDBAT, whose Rules of Procedure allow for the possibility of submitting requests for revision and for correction of errors but are silent on the possibility of submitting requests for interpretation or clarification of judgments. When a request for clarification of a judgment was made in one case before the IDBAT, the request was dismissed in a ruling issued by the President *pro tempore* of the Tribunal on the basis that it was "neither a request for the correction of errors nor a petition for the revision of the judgment."

A second solution would allow the Tribunal to admit the remedy notwithstanding the absence of a provision to that effect in its Statute. Fortunately, this seems to be the prevailing solution adopted by international administrative tribunals. With respect to requests for interpretation brought to Tribunals in the silence of the texts, many Tribunals have not hesitated to rule that they have an inherent power to interpret their own decisions in disputes between the parties as to the meaning and scope of these decisions. Thus, the WBAT, whose Statute and Rules of Procedure are silent with respect to the question of admissibility of requests for interpretation, decided:

> The Tribunal, as an international tribunal, has the inherent power to interpret its own decisions in case of dispute between the parties as to their meaning or scope, even if its Statute contains no provision to that effect. The Hague Convention on Pacific Settlement of Disputes of 1907 gives expression to this general principle, when it provides in Article 82 that:
>
> > 'Any dispute arising between the parties as to the interpretation and execution of the award shall, in the absence of an agreement to the contrary, be submitted to the decision of the tribunal which pronounced it.'[165]

The WBAT further decided in a subsequent judgment:

> The Tribunal has an inherent right, even, indeed, an obligation, to ensure that problems relating to the interpretation of a decision are swiftly resolved.... [I]t is the Tribunal, and the Tribunal alone, that has the power to give a final and binding interpretation of its decision.[166]

---

[165] *Agodo*, WBAT Decision No. 76 [1989], para. 30.
[166] *Moses (No. 2)*, WBAT Decision No. 138 [1994], para. 24.

The UNAT, whose Statute and Rules of Procedure are similarly silent on the question of admissibility of requests for interpretation, decided as early as in 1955[167] that

> [a]lthough the Statute of the Administrative Tribunal does not contain an express provision relating to the interpretation of judgements, both Parties agreed during the oral proceedings to admit that competence to interpret was inherent in the judicial function which the International Court of Justice, in its advisory opinion of 13 July 1954, declared the Tribunal to possess.
>
> . . .
>
> The Tribunal finds that the competence of national and international courts to interpret their own judgements is generally recognized.

The UNAT further held in the same judgment that it should be guided by the general principles regarding interpretation of judgments set out by the International Court of Justice in the *Asylum* case, namely that a request for interpretation of a judgment should be receivable only if its object is to obtain clarification of the meaning and scope of what the Tribunal decided with binding force (rather than to obtain an answer to questions not so decided) and if there existed a dispute as to the meaning or scope of the judgment.[168]

The ILOAT, whose Statute and Rules of Procedure do not contain provisions on rectification, interpretation or revision of judgments, examines such requests under strictly limited conditions that are, in essence, similar to the conditions set forth in the texts governing other international administrative tribunals. With respect to the revision of judgments, the ILOAT stated:

> There is no provision in the Statute or Rules of Court of the Administrative Tribunal for the revision of its judgments.
>
> Such a complaint could therefore be considered by the Tribunal only in quite exceptional circumstances, in particular if the complainant adduces facts or evidence which he was unable, through no fault of his own, to produce during the earlier proceedings; it would in any event not provide an opportunity for the parties to repair an omission or correct an error made by them during the original hearing of the case.[169]

---

[167] *Crawford and others*, UNAT Decision No. 61 [1955].

[168] The UNAT relied in subsequent judgments (*Carson*, UNAT Decision No. 87 [1963]; *Khederian*, UNAT Decision No. 137 [1970]; *Sabatier*, UNAT Decision No. 366 [1986]; *Al-Ali*, UNAT Decision No. 434 [1988]) on the criteria for interpretation of judgments set out by *Crawford and others*.

[169] *Smith (No. 2)*, ILOAT Decision No. 201 [1973]. This decision is in sharp contrast to a much earlier one (*Tranter*, ILOAT Decision No. 37 [1958]), which ruled that requests for revision were irreceivable "by reason of the absence of a procedure for the revision of the judgements delivered by the Tribunal."

The ILOAT stated in another judgment:

> Neither the Statute nor the Rules of Court permit an application for review of a judgment of the Administrative Tribunal. The Tribunal may therefore declare such an application receivable only in quite exceptional circumstances, for example when new facts of decisive importance have come to light since the date of the judgment.[170]

Similarly, the ILOAT considered in a few cases requests for interpretation brought by either party. It ruled in this respect in one of its judgments:

> A request for interpretation of a judgment by the Administrative Tribunal is receivable only if the operative part of the judgment gives rise to uncertainty or ambiguity about its meaning or purport.[171]

The ILOAT decided in another judgment:

> The Tribunal will entertain an application for interpretation of a judgment only if the operative part is unclear or ambiguous.[172]

---

[170] *Verdrager (No. 2)*, ILOAT Decision No. 350 [1978].
[171] *Hopkirk (No. 2)*, ILOAT Decision No. 240 [1974].
[172] *Bonneau (No. 3)*, ILOAT Decision No. 815 [1987].

ASPECTS OF JUDICIAL REVIEW OF ADMINISTRATIVE ACTION BY THE WORLD BANK ADMINISTRATIVE TRIBUNAL WITH RELEVANT COMPARISONS

Spyridon Flogaitis*

Résumé

Cette étude traite de certains aspects du contrôle judiciaire par le Tribunal administratif de la Banque mondiale (TABM ou Tribunal) de l'action de l'Administration. Le but de cette étude est de comparer les tribunaux administratifs internationaux de différentes organisations internationales. Une telle approche contribuera à l'amélioration des pratiques actuelles.

I. *La mise en œuvre du contrôle du TABM*

La Banque mondiale n'a pas élaboré un système général de contrôle judiciaire de son action administrative. L'initiative du contrôle judiciaire de l'action de l'Administration est réservée aux membres du personnel qui auraient à se plaindre de leurs rapports avec leur employeur. Ceux-ci peuvent demander l'annulation de la décision contestée, l'exécution de l'obligation invoquée, des dommages-intérêts ou une combinaison de ces trois modes de réparation. L'action est initiée par une requête adressée au Secrétaire exécutif du Tribunal.

Les conditions d'admissibilité sont laissées à l'appréciation discrétionnaire du Tribunal.

II. *Les conditions d'admissibilité*

Les conditions d'admissibilité tiennent à la nature de l'acte critiqué, à la qualité pour agir, au délai de l'action ainsi qu'à l'épuisement de tous les autres recours.

Quant à la nature de l'acte, la question se pose, dans le silence du Statut, de savoir si les décisions réglementaires peuvent être contestées à l'instar des décisions individuelles. Contrairement à la pratique du Tribunal administratif du Fonds monétaire international (TAFMI), le TABM a décidé que seules relevaient de sa compétence les décisions administratives individuelles. Tous les membres du personnel du groupe de la Banque mondiale ont qualité pour agir devant le TABM.

* President, United Nations Administrative Tribunal; Professor of Administrative Law, Faculty of Law, National and Capodistrian University of Athens.

Avoir qualité pour agir suppose que le requérant excipe d'une inobservation des termes du contrat d'emploi ou des conditions d'emploi: il doit être excipé d'une atteinte à un droit légitimement protégé. La qualité devra perdurer jusqu'au jour du prononcé du jugement.

Une autre condition d'admissibilité du recours devant le TABM consiste en l'épuisement de toutes les autres voies de recours internes disponibles. Les voies de recours à épuiser sont celles qui sont susceptibles de procurer le même effet que celui auquel vise la requête devant le TABM. Le Statut prévoit toutefois que les parties peuvent convenir de soumettre directement leur litige au Tribunal. De même, le fait pour la Banque de ne pas soulever l'exception relative à l'épuisement des voies de recours internes est considéré comme une renonciation valable à cette dernière.

Le délai pour agir devant le Tribunal est de cent-vingt jours courant à partir de la réalisation de l'événement donnant lieu au recours ou de la notification de cet événement. Deux situations particulières y dérogent, prévoyant que le point de départ du délai est le jour de la réception par le requérant d'une notification: lorsque la réparation demandée par le requérant antérieurement à la soumission de l'affaire au Tribunal lui a été refusée et lorsque la réparation, acceptée en son principe, n'est pas effectivement accordée après l'écoulement d'un délai de trente jours suivant la notification de l'acceptation.

L'usage des voies de recours internes est suspensif du délai de l'action, alors que la requête elle-même ne suspend pas l'exécution de la décision administrative contestée.

Un autre point de départ du délai est prévu lorsque le requérant et le Président de la Banque conviennent de soumettre directement le cas au Tribunal. Dans cette hypothèse, un délai de quatre-vingt-dix jours court à partir du jour où le requérant est notifié par le Président de sa réponse à la demande de soumission directe.

Il convient de signaler à cet égard que les délais de recours sont considérés d'ordre public.

III. *La procédure*

La requête est divisée en trois parties: une première partie expose les faits et les fondements juridiques de la demande. Une deuxième précise la décision contestée ainsi que les réparations demandées (exécution en nature ou par équivalent). Le requérant peut également demander toute mesure provisoire qu'il juge nécessaire. Les documents à l'appui de la requête se retrouvent dans une troisième partie appelée annexe. La requête est adressée au Secrétaire exécutif du Tribunal qui a des pouvoirs étendus pour s'assurer que les conditions d'admissibilité sont vérifiées. Ce dernier est autorisé à prendre les mesures nécessaires qui s'imposent pour éviter que la requête ne soit rejetée pour vice de forme.

Une fois que les conditions formelles de recevabilité lui semblent vérifiées, le Secrétaire exécutif veillera à assurer le caractère contradictoire de la procédure en transmettant une copie de la requête au défendeur. Si par contre, il estime que la requête est irrecevable ou dénuée de fondement, il en appellera au Président du Tribunal. Ce dernier effectuera un examen préliminaire de la requête. S'il la trouve clairement irrecevable ou dénuée de fondement, il peut demander au

Tribunal de suivre la voie de la procédure abrégée suivant laquelle ce dernier peut rejeter sommairement la requête ou décider de lui faire suivre la procédure normale. Dans le cadre de l'exercice de la compétence sus-indiquée, le Président du Tribunal peut charger le requérant de présenter des documents additionnels.

La même procédure s'applique à la réponse du défendeur qui doit être remise au Secrétaire exécutif dans un délai de soixante jours suivant la notification de la requête. La réponse sera notifiée au requérant par l'entremise du Secrétaire exécutif qui aura a son égard le même pouvoir de vérification de ses conditions d'admissibilité. Une réplique sera permise au requérant dans un délai de quarante-cinq jours à laquelle le défendeur pourra opposer une duplique dans un délai de trente jours.

Le dossier personnel du requérant devra lui être communiqué le plus tôt possible pour lui permettre de prendre connaissance des informations qui y sont contenues.

Le Président du Tribunal jouit de pouvoirs d'investigation étendus: il a un rôle indépendant dans la collecte des informations qui s'étend aux parties, aux témoins ainsi qu'aux experts. C'est seulement lorsqu'il estime que l'affaire est prête à être jugée que le Président charge le Secrétaire exécutif de l'inscrire au rôle des affaires à plaider.

La procédure orale

La procédure orale demeure facultative: elle n'est pas obligatoire pour le Tribunal même lorsque l'une des parties la demande. Cette procédure pourra inclure l'audition de témoins et d'experts ainsi que les plaidoiries. L'assistance d'un avocat n'est pas obligatoire; le requérant pourra assurer sa défense personnellement ou par l'intermédiaire d'un membre du personnel du groupe de la Banque.

Les interventions

L'intervention auprès du Tribunal est permise à toute personne ayant qualité pour agir devant le Tribunal et dont les intérêts pourraient être affectés par le jugement à venir. L'Association du personnel de l'institution défenderesse ou toute personne ou entité ayant un intérêt substantiel dans une affaire peut être autorisée par le Tribunal à participer aux débats en tant qu'"amicus curiae".

IV. *Les bases juridiques du contrôle*

Le Tribunal appréciera la valeur de la décision contestée au regard des dispositions du contrat d'emploi et des conditions d'emploi: le contrat est la loi des parties. Les dispositions pertinentes des règlements en vigueur, y compris celles du règlement de pension du personnel, au moment de l'inobservation invoquée font partie du contrat et des conditions d'emploi.

Dans l'affaire *de Merode*, le TABM a été confronté à la question de savoir si les relations entre la Banque et ses employés sont de nature contractuelle ou statutaire. Quoiqu'ayant retenu la première réponse, le Tribunal a aussi décidé que les conditions d'emploi pouvaient être amendées par la Banque de manière unilatérale. Ce pouvoir discrétionnaire est limité par les considérations suivantes: les changements doivent être raisonnablement liés à l'objectif qu'ils poursuivent, ainsi qu'au devoir de la Banque d'avoir des employés possédant "les plus hauts standards d'efficacité et de compétence technique"; les changements doivent être effectués de bonne foi et être adéquatement motivés; ils doivent éviter toute discrimination ainsi que tout dommage excessif causé aux membres du personnel; enfin, ils doivent avoir été étudiés avec grand soin.

Le Tribunal a également opéré une distinction entre les éléments essentiels et les éléments non essentiels du contrat d'emploi. Alors que les seconds peuvent être amendés sans l'accord de l'employé, les premiers ne le peuvent pas. Cette distinction a entraîné le Tribunal vers une tâche difficile consistant à adopter un critère de distinction entre ce qui est essentiel et ce qui ne l'est pas.

Enfin, une vue simplifiée des bases du contrôle permet de les classer, à l'instar du droit administratif français, en deux catégories: celle de l'illégalité externe et celle de l'illégalité interne. L'illégalité externe couvre toutes les questions de compétence et de procédure, alors que l'illégalité interne s'entend de la violation de la loi, de l'erreur de fait et de droit ainsi que du détournement et de l'abus de pouvoir.

V. *Le jugement*

Les jugements du Tribunal sont rendus à la majorité des membres présents, le Président ayant une voix prépondérante. Ils doivent être motivés.

Les délibérations du TABM ont lieu en deux phases. Tout d'abord, le Tribunal doit s'assurer que les règles de procédure ont été respectées. Ensuite, il examinera le fond de l'affaire. Le jugement du Tribunal sera rendu sur base des faits tels que présentés par les parties et de leur conformité au droit applicable. Le Statut du TABM dispose que le Tribunal peut ordonner soit l'annulation de la décision contestée soit l'exécution de l'obligation invoquée. Il peut donc décider de faire réintégrer son poste au demandeur. Le Tribunal devra néanmoins fixer, dans le cas où la partie défenderesse démontre de manière raisonnable qu'une telle solution est impraticable ou non conforme à l'intérêt de l'institution, la valeur de la compensation à payer au demandeur en réparation du dommage subi. Mais le Tribunal ne pourra pas modifier lui-même une décision administrative: lorsqu'un tel besoin se fait sentir, le Tribunal ordonnera à l'Administration de le faire en se conformant aux prescriptions énoncées dans le jugement. C'est là l'un des enseignements de l'affaire *de Merode* ainsi que de la jurisprudence subséquente. Par ailleurs, le jugement du Tribunal peut avoir un effet déclaratif.

Il est à noter qu'il n'est pas prévu de procédure pour l'exécution des jugements et que, pour obliger la Banque à s'y conformer, une nouvelle requête devant le Tribunal serait à prévoir.

Le jugement du Tribunal est rendu en dernier ressort. La révision est possible uniquement dans le cas où, postérieurement au jugement, l'une des parties découvre un fait qui aurait pu avoir une influence décisive sur le cours du procès: elle aura alors six mois pour introduire la requête en révision.

VI. *Les frais et dépens*

Le TABM, en rendant des décisions raisonnables sur la répartition des frais et dépens, entend faciliter le droit des employés à être représentés par un conseiller juridique. Une nouvelle pratique exige même du requérant qu'il présente une liste détaillée des frais et dépens encourus.

Le principe général en droit administratif international, pour reprendre la disposition du Statut du Tribunal administratif de la Banque inter-américaine pour le développement, est que "chacune des parties supporte les frais inhérents à la présentation de son cas au Tribunal". Certains textes applicables aux tribunaux administratifs internationaux prévoient que le requérant aura à indemniser l'institution des frais encourus au cas où la requête s'avère manifestement dénuée de fondement. D'autres prévoient que la partie perdante aura à payer tout ou partie des frais raisonnablement encourus par son adversaire.

VII. *Les mesures provisoires*

Quoique le Statut du TABM ne l'autorise pas à ordonner des mesures provisoires, la jurisprudence de ce dernier a établi qu'il lui appartenait de décider des mesures provisoires tendant à préserver les droits litigieux durant le cours de la procédure. Le Règlement de procédure du TABM en vigueur depuis le 1er janvier 2002 contient désormais une disposition expresse à cet effet.

VIII. *Conclusion*

A comparer le TABM avec d'autres institutions similaires, l'on peut en déduire que le premier n'a pas besoin d'améliorations majeures. On pourrait uniquement souhaiter que le Tribunal utilise plus largement ses pouvoirs et adopte certains des principes reconnus par d'autres institutions comme l'admission des recours contre les actes réglementaires ou l'imposition de pénalités pour les requêtes manifestement abusives.

* * *

Two years ago, the World Bank honored me by asking me to write a report on its grievance system. On that occasion, I praised the high standards of the World Bank Administrative Tribunal ("Tribunal" or "WBAT") and made some suggestions as to what changes should, in my opinion, be introduced to its procedures and working methods. I am honored once again today to take part in this high-level discussion among the most distinguished members of international academia and practice on the subject of international administrative tribunals.[1]

[1] I would like to take this opportunity to thank Ms. Sofia Chatzikonstanti for her invaluable help during the preparation of this paper. I would also like to thank Mr. Howard Dean and Mr. Peter C. Hansen for their assistance in preparing it for publication.

I would like to examine remedies, costs, interim relief and judgments. Please note that in English, the term "remedies" refers to the outcome of an action. In Continental Europe, however, the French term "actions" prevails. I would like to retain both meanings, if I may.

This study will compare administrative tribunals from similar international organizations. Such a comparative approach will generate examples that may be useful for stimulating suggestions for the improvement of existing practices. It is my belief that almost all of my initial suggestions can find answers in the existing Statute and Rules of the WBAT, if these are adequately interpreted, and also if some ideas are borrowed from similar tribunals.

I. *Initiating an Action before the WBAT*

As is perhaps the case with all international organizations, the World Bank Group has not introduced a general system of judicial review of its administrative actions. The system is instead one of fragmented or *ad hoc* jurisdiction, with judicial review of administrative action allowed only with respect to staff member complaints that arise in the course of the staff member's relationship with his or her employer.

As in all administrative tribunals, a case is instituted by a writ brought before the World Bank Administrative Tribunal. This writ is termed by the Statute an "application," and is submitted through the Executive Secretary of the Tribunal.[2] An applicant can request rescission of the contested decision, performance by the administration of the obligation invoked, damages, or all in combination.[3] When a number of applications relate to the same subject-matter, the Tribunal may decide to consolidate them and render a single decision.[4] If any of the parties objects to a request by the other party for consolidation, a decision is taken by the President of the Tribunal.[5] Applications should be detailed documents, divided into four parts: information about the applicant's personal and official status; pleas; the applicant's explanatory statement; and annexes generally containing documentary evidence.[6]

While all administrative tribunals define a number of requirements for admissibility, these are discretionary. This is because the Tribunal has the

---

[2] Statute of the Tribunal (hereinafter "Statute"), Article II; Rules of the Tribunal (hereinafter "Rules"), Rule 7.

[3] Statute, Article XII.

[4] See, e.g., *Gregorio*, Decision No. 14 [1983], para. 1.

[5] See, e.g., *The World Bank Staff Association*, Decision No. 40 [1987], para. 2.

[6] Rules, Rule 7, para. 1.

power to decide upon a case in the absence of one or more required conditions if there are exceptional circumstances. The definition of "exceptional circumstances" is, furthermore, left entirely to the Tribunal's discretion.[7] In this way, the Tribunal's proceedings subscribe to the best Anglo-Saxon traditions.

II. *Conditions of Admissibility*

The World Bank Administrative Tribunal's requirements for admissibility relate to the nature of the challenged act, *locus standi*, time limits, and the prior exhaustion of all other remedies.

The *legal nature of the act* in question is the first condition pertinent to admissibility, although this is not explicitly emphasized in the Statute. The Statute does not in fact specify whether general rules formulated by the Bank may be contested, or whether a challenge is instead restricted in scope only to administrative acts of an individual character (e.g., administrative decisions as in the English legal tradition, or administrative acts as in the German legal tradition).

The Tribunal has stated, however, that it has no jurisdiction to decide on the legality of rules of general character, even if such rules are administrative. It has indicated instead that only staff members directly affected by a Bank decision may legitimately apply under its jurisdictional rules. Otherwise, the Tribunal would be involved in the provision of advisory opinions concerning the validity of general rules. The Tribunal, therefore, does not exercise jurisdiction for the purpose of ordering rescission, specific performance or compensation where a staff member is not directly affected by an administrative decision.[8]

A notable counterexample among international administrative tribunals is to be found at the International Monetary Fund (IMF), where the legality of an administrative act may be challenged before the Administrative Tribunal (i.e., the IMFAT). For the purposes of the IMFAT Statute, the expression "administrative act" means any individual *or regulatory* act taken in the management of the Fund staff. The only difference in procedure between those challenges undertaken against individual acts and those leveled against general regulatory acts lies in the fact that if the administrative

---

[7] Statute, Article II, para. 2. The Tribunal applies that discretion very restrictively, however. See, e.g., *Setia*, Decision No. 134 [1993], paras. 30–32.

[8] *Agodo*, Decision No. 41 [1987], paras. 20, 25–27, 30–31, 33; *K. Berg*, Decision No. 51 [1987], para. 27; *Vandenheede*, Decision No. 52 [1987], para. 24; *Knox*, Decision No. 54 [1987], para. 24.

act challenged before the IMFAT is of an individual character, the staff member will be admitted before the IMFAT only after he or she has unsuccessfully followed the channels established for administrative review, including recourse to the IMF's Grievance Committee.[9]

Any Bank Group staff member can have *locus standi* before the WBAT,[10] and may file an application with the Tribunal. By contrast, persons who have a connection with the Bank Group not amounting to staff-member status are not qualified to apply. The applicant can be either a current or former staff member, or the representative of a staff member. The latter type of applicant may be a person claiming entitlement to the right of a staff member by reason of the staff member's death, or as one who receives payments under the Staff Retirement Plan. In the Statute of the Tribunal, the term "Bank Group" is understood to include the International Bank for Reconstruction and Development (IBRD), the International Development Association (IDA) and the International Finance Corporation (IFC).[11]

For a member of the staff to have *locus standi*, he or she must allege non-observance of his or her contract of employment or terms of appointment. This violation is established in relation to the pertinent regulations and rules, including the provisions of the Staff Retirement Plan in force at the time of the alleged non-observance. Although nothing is said in the Statute of the Tribunal about the required duration of *locus standi*, such status must exist until the final judgment is reached by the Tribunal, as the admissibility of applications or claims in non-jurisdictional cases is ruled upon either explicitly or implicitly in conjunction with the merits.

With respect to the admissibility of an application, a question arises as to whether there must be an infringement of a legally protected right, or whether the infringement of a mere interest is sufficient. The wording of the Statute avoids the problem, although it is true to say that in cases of "non-observance of the contract" a specific and personal right is in question. This interpretation is reinforced by the fact that interventions by third

---

[9] Statute of the International Monetary Fund Administrative Tribunal (IMFAT), Articles II and V.

[10] Statute of the WBAT, Article II, paras. 1, 3. As for the *locus standi* of the Staff Association, see *The World Bank Staff Association*, op. cit., paras. 78–79, 81–86, in which *locus standi* was denied on the basis that members of the Staff Association may apply directly to the Tribunal pursuant to the terms of the Statute if they are personally affected by a decision of the Bank.

[11] It should be noted that today, in addition to the International Bank for Reconstruction and Development (IBRD), the International Development Association (IDA) and the International Finance Corporation (IFC), which are expressly referred to in the Statute as the "Bank Group," the World Bank Group includes the International Centre for Settlement of Investment Disputes (ICSID) and the Multilateral Investment Guarantee Agency (MIGA). Although the Statute has not been amended to include these agencies, the staff of these two agencies have *locus standi* to appear before the Tribunal.

parties are explicitly allowed only on the ground that the third party's right will be affected by the judgment to be delivered by the Tribunal.

That a case be ripe or that *all other remedies* available within the Bank Group first be *exhausted* is a requirement of the WBAT's jurisdiction.[12] This condition makes an application to the Tribunal the ultimate remedy offered to staff members, who are first obliged to try all existing alternatives.[13] We should, however, understand alternative remedies as being only those having at least the same effect as the one sought by the application. In other words, a petition made by an applicant before the competent administrative authority of the Bank must be explicit as to what is being requested, and this remedy must be one of those available from the Tribunal. The Tribunal so decided when an applicant had addressed himself to the Appeals Committee but had failed to ask there for the rescission of the redundancy decision, thereby failing to exhaust all of the internal remedies available to him.[14]

The Statute nevertheless offers an alternative route of admissibility, this being if the applicant and the respondent (i.e., the Bank) agree to submit the case directly to the Tribunal.[15] This approach makes it possible to save time, which could be important in cases likely to result in important precedents. Equivalent to this is the possibility of the respondent simply not raising the question of prior exhaustion of internal remedies, despite the failure of the applicant to fulfill this requirement. Under the rules of procedure as interpreted by the Tribunal, the non-objection of the respondent corresponds to a waiver of this admissibility condition.[16] The Tribunal's case law gives the impression that admissibility conditions can be set aside by the parties, whereas in all legal systems, admissibility conditions are in principle questions of public order.

The *time limit* for filing an application before the Tribunal is one hundred and twenty days.[17] This deadline is measured from the latest of a

---

[12] Statute, Article II, para. 2.

[13] *K. Berg*, op. cit., paras. 30–33, 35–36; *Vandenheede*, op. cit., para. 27; *Knox*, op. cit., paras. 26–27; *Dhillon*, Decision No. 75 [1989], paras. 22, 25; *Steinke*, Decision No. 79 [1989], paras. 16–17; *de Jong*, Decision No. 89 [1990], paras. 29–31, 36–37, 44–46; *Ramorasoavina*, Decision No. 95 [1990], paras. 24–28, 33; *Kassab*, Decision No. 97 [1987], para. 47; *Bredero*, Decision No. 129 [1993], paras. 20–23; *Rae (No. 2)*, Decision No. 132 [1993], paras. 42–45; *Setia*, op. cit., paras. 24–26; *Romain*, Decision No. 136 [1994], paras. 27–30; *Bori*, Decision No. 137 [1994], paras. 28–31; *Abadian*, Decision No. 141 [1995], paras. 23, 25–26, 29–32; *Addy*, Decision No. 146 [1995], paras. 46–49; *Shaffer*, Decision No. 117 [1992], para. 29; *Courtney*, Decision No. 144 [1995], paras. 44–47.

[14] *Kassab*, op. cit., para. 47.

[15] Statute, Article II, para. 2(i).

[16] "It should be noted that the Respondent has explicitly waived any objection to the Applicant's failure to exhaust internal remedies, as otherwise required." (*Justin*, Decision No. 15 [1984], para. 21.)

[17] Statute, Article II, para. 2(ii).

series of events, particularly the occurrence of the event giving rise to the application, or the notification of this event. The Tribunal does not recognize any obligation of the Bank to remind an affected person of his or her right to apply to the Tribunal upon its notification of the decision.[18]

There are two other relevant situations, both of which have as a starting point the receipt of notice by the applicant. The first runs from the receipt of notice that the relief asked for or recommended at a pre-Tribunal stage will not be granted, when such remedy was foreseen as being available within the Bank Group and was sought by the applicant. The second applies when the aggrieved party receives notice that relief will be granted, but such relief is not in fact granted within thirty days after receipt of the notice.

The use of any procedure leading to alternative remedies (i.e., those not originating from the Tribunal) has in one way or another a suspensive effect on the time limit for submitting the application. This is an important point because the application has no suspensive effect on the administrative decision being challenged. Some confusion may arise, however, in respect of this interpretation of the tolling doctrine, given the Tribunal's reading of the rule when reviewing specific decisions of the Bank's Pension Benefits Administration Committee.[19] It is clearly stated for the latter type of case that the time limit is counted from the day on which the contested decision is communicated. It could be argued that this is an exception to the rule that the time limit runs from the day on which the event took place. Such an interpretation would be erroneous, however. The pension-case rule specifies that the starting point of the filing period in pension cases is limited to only one ruling, and this arrangement is natural for most pension cases, as the applicant is normally no longer in the service of the Bank.

There can be a different starting point, this being when the applicant and the President of the Bank have agreed to submit the application directly to the Tribunal. In such a case, the time limit is ninety days from the date on which the applicant is notified of the President's agreement to a direct submission. The question in this type of situation is whether the discussions between the applicant and the President may start after the expiration of the initial one hundred and twenty days commencing with the notification of the event giving rise to the dispute. It seems that in such a case the general time-limit rule may be threatened by an agreement, given that all time limits are in the public interest. The answer to the

[18] *Matta*, Decision No. 12 [1982], para. 52.
[19] Rules, Rule 24.

question should then be that if the applicant, before trying to exhaust all other remedies, applies directly to the President under the rule and within the general time limit, then whatever the President's answer may be, it will constitute the starting point of a separate procedure. Otherwise, the President could, upon receipt of the petition, delay the answer and thereby negate the agreement when it is too late for the aspiring applicant to file a regular application with the appropriate body. The petition to the President should not, after all, lead under this rule to a worse procedural treatment than that available under any other Bank internal administrative remedy procedure. At the same time, however, a revival of the time limit effected by agreement of the parties is not acceptable if the petition to the President takes place after the expiration of the general time limit. Such an outcome would be against all legal traditions for this type of procedure, since it would infringe on the public character of time limits.

III. *The Procedure*

It should be noted once again that the World Bank Administrative Tribunal's procedure has more or less the same characteristics as those of all other international administrative tribunals.

The pleas must specify the decisions whose rescission is requested, the obligations invoked and any specific performance requested, and the amounts of compensation and other relief claimed under the Statute of the Tribunal. In addition, the applicant may seek the ordering of any preliminary or provisional measures before he or she enters into normal proceedings or the Tribunal examines the case on the merits. These measures may, for example, be the production of additional documents or the hearing of witnesses. This means that in this part of the application, the applicant is given the opportunity to ask for the discovery of documents and facts which he or she may not already possess.

The explanatory statement sets out the facts and legal grounds on which the pleas are based, including the relevant contract clauses. The annexes, meanwhile, contain the texts of all documents referred to in the application.[20]

The application is filed with the Executive Secretary in one original and eight copies. The Executive Secretary has significant power to determine whether an application entirely fulfils the legal prerequisites for admissibility. When the application presents defects, the Executive Secretary is permitted to take action to have corrections made so as to avoid the risk

[20] See also Rules, Annexes I and II.

of the application's rejection for purely formal reasons. When defects do not affect the substance of the application, the Executive Secretary may ask the President to allow him or her to perform the necessary corrections. Otherwise, the Executive Secretary is allowed to call the applicant to have them made. The Executive Secretary may also return the application documents to the applicant and set a time limit within which the applicant must resubmit them. It is entirely within the discretion of the Executive Secretary to undertake any of these procedures, and there is no remedy offered to the applicant in those cases in which the Executive Secretary does not exercise this corrective function.[21]

From the moment that the Executive Secretary is satisfied that the formal requirements for admissibility have been fulfilled, he or she will proceed to secure the case's adversarial character by transmitting a copy of the application to the respondent. If the Executive Secretary believes that the application may be irreceivable or devoid of merit, however, he or she will introduce the file to the President of the Tribunal. The President makes a first, *prima facie*, examination of the application, though his power to stop the proceedings can be exercised only through the Tribunal in session.[22] This examination is what is called reservation of application. If it appears to him or her that the application is clearly irreceivable or devoid of all merit, he or she may ask the Executive Secretary not to follow the normal course of procedure, but to wait until the next session of the Tribunal. The Tribunal will then consider the case at its next session, outside the normal adversarial procedure, since it will decide only according to the elements brought to its attention by the application. It may, in keeping with the *prima facie* impression of the President, decide to dismiss the case summarily as being clearly irreceivable or devoid of all merit, or it may order normal proceedings to continue in the ordinary way.[23]

---

[21] Rules, Rule 7, para. 9.

[22] Rules, Rule 7, para. 11.

[23] A clear distinction can be drawn between correction of the application under both Rule 7, paragraph 9, and Annex I, Part II, of the Rules of the Tribunal, and summary dismissal of the application under Rule 7, paragraph 11. The Executive Secretary checks whether the formal (or standard) requirements stipulated in Rule 7 regarding the filing of the application have been met. Unmet formal requirements can include a failure of the applicant to number the annexes to his or her application, or to inscribe the phrase "Certified true copy" on the copies of the original annexes. In practice, whenever the Executive Secretary is not satisfied that the formal requirements have been met, he or she will return the application for corrections under Rule 7, paragraph 9, without the intervention of the President of the Tribunal. On the other hand, regardless of whether the formal requirements have been met, if the Executive Secretary believes upon examination that the application is clearly irreceivable because, for example, it has been filed too late, he or she may point this out to the President, who may then instruct the Executive Secretary to act under Rule 7, paragraph 11.

This power of the President and the Tribunal to preclude normal proceedings demonstrates the importance of the application being fully and well presented by the interested party, as at this stage the applicant risks seeing his or her application dismissed without having any chance to add further elements. On the other hand, the importance of the President's power becomes more clearly evident when one also considers the President's ability to request additional documents. It is in fact up to him or her either to introduce the case to the Tribunal for summary dismissal, or alternatively to give to the applicant a chance to submit additional documents[24] which could alter the first impression given by the application.[25]

The same procedure applies, *mutatis mutandis*, to the respondent's answer,[26] which is submitted to the Executive Secretary within sixty days of the respondent's receipt of the application. The answer is, like the application, composed of pleas, an explanatory statement and annexes. It is presented in one original and eight copies, of which one is transmitted to the applicant once the Executive Secretary is satisfied that all formal requirements under the Rules have been fulfilled. The Rules do not actually provide for the situation in which the Executive Secretary is not satisfied, but it can be concluded that he or she would simply not proceed to the transmission and that the application would remain unanswered. And yet, even if this function is to be exercised at the discretion of the Executive Secretary, the solution of non-transmission is unequal to the process offered to the applicant and contradicts the general principle of procedural law regarding the equality of litigants. Therefore, it should be accepted that the Executive Secretary may exercise *mutatis mutandis* the same powers vis-à-vis the respondent as he or she does with respect to the applicant.[27]

Opportunities for a reply[28] and a rejoinder[29] are given to the litigants. The reply of the applicant must be submitted to the Executive Secretary within forty-five days of the transmission of the respondent's answer to the applicant. The rejoinder of the respondent must be submitted to the Executive Secretary within thirty days of the transmission of the reply to the respondent. Both of these pleadings should be supported by any document to which the pleading refers. It is interesting to observe that among

---

[24] Rules, Rule 12.

[25] The production of additional statements or documents is usually requested under Rule 12 after the closure of the proceedings. Before this point, the parties are able to develop their arguments in their pleadings.

[26] Rules, Rule 9.

[27] Indeed, in practice, if the Executive Secretary is not satisfied that the formal requirements have been met for any pleading, he or she may return the pleading to the filing party for correction.

[28] Rules, Rule 10.

[29] Rules, Rule 11.

these documents are to be included the sources of law, so that these pleadings are obviously not covered by the old maxim *jura novit curia*, "the Court knows the law," since in principle the law is also to be proven.

During this phase in which pleadings are collected by the Tribunal, the President has another important power, albeit only in what he or she would consider exceptional cases. At his or her initiative, or at the initiative of one of the parties, he or she may call upon the parties to submit additional statements or documents of his or her choice. The President cannot, however, give them the opportunity to add new pleas, as this power to obtain further information is restricted in scope to the facts and legal grounds as well as to their supporting documents. These additional items are, like the pleadings, submitted in one original and eight copies to the Executive Secretary, who is responsible for their communication to the other party.

It is natural to suggest that the applicant's personnel file should be made available to the applicant at the earliest possible moment in the proceedings, as it very often contains information unknown to the applicant and thus could be useful to his or her argumentation. It should for such reason be concluded that the personnel file should be part of the annexes to the respondent's answer, or that the discretionary powers of the President should be used to request the respondent to provide it as an additional statement or document under Rule 12, paragraph 2.

It is interesting to observe that, unlike in a typical adversarial procedure up to this point, important deviations from the general rules are introduced in favor of the President's investigatory powers. He or she has an independent role in collecting information from the parties, witnesses or experts, and may act insofar as he or she thinks fit. The President may also ask one of the members of the Tribunal, or any other disinterested person, to take oral statements whose scope and usefulness are defined by the President. When the President is finally satisfied that the file of the case is sufficiently complete and mature for trial, he or she will ask the Executive Secretary to place the case on the list.[30] The need for the President to be satisfied that the case is mature for trial is another important element of the investigatory powers of the President.

When the case has been put on the list, no additional statements or documents may be filed with the Tribunal. It is the Executive Secretary's responsibility to inform the parties of the date of the case's placement on the list, as well as of the date of the opening of the session for which the case has been entered.

---

[30] Rules, Rule 14.

Oral Proceedings

Oral proceedings[31] are not a necessary part of the Tribunal process, as the Tribunal may decide not to hold them. The parties may for their part choose not to request them. But if either party does so, it is within the Tribunal's discretion to accept the request.[32]

Oral proceedings may include the presentation and examination of witnesses and experts, as well as oral argumentation and commentary on the evidence given, even when such evidence has already been given in writing. The procedure, despite its adversarial character, is in the hands of the Tribunal, which will decide conclusively if witnesses and experts should be examined, and will, through its President, direct and control the questioning undertaken by the parties. The investigatory element of the Tribunal's procedure reappears at this stage, as the Tribunal has the power to call as it sees fit for the production of any document or evidence, as well as for any measure of inquiry.[33] Indeed, the Tribunal may permit any person over whom its jurisdiction extends to furnish information by submitting written or oral observations.

Any party may ask for the adjournment of the oral proceedings. The decision then lies with the President or, if the Tribunal is in session, with the latter. The use of a lawyer is not required in any oral proceedings, as the applicant is allowed to present his or her case in person or through an official or retired official of the Bank Group. When a party chooses to be represented by a lawyer, however, the lawyer must be qualified with the Bar of any of the respondent's member states.

Each party must notify the Tribunal, in sufficient time before the opening of the oral proceedings, of the names and descriptions of the witnesses and experts, as well as of the points to which their evidence will refer. If the Tribunal decides that the proposed evidence is irrelevant, frivolous or otherwise lacking in probative value, it can exclude it altogether.[34] It may

---

[31] Rules, Rule 17.

[32] *Skandera,* Decision No. 2 [1981], Preamble ("[The Tribunal] has decided that oral proceedings as requested by Applicant pursuant to Rule 14(1) are unnecessary and shall not be held").

[33] See, e.g., *Fernandes,* Order [1989], para. 4 ("Because the Tribunal considers that any such information might prove to be relevant to the Tribunal's decision on the merits of this case, it concludes that the Respondent should be directed to respond to the interrogatory posed and produce any related documents as requested"); *Fabara-Núñez,* Order [1990], para. 5 ("The Tribunal orders that the Respondent shall within ten days of the receipt of this Order produce for examination by the Tribunal the IAD Investigative Panel Report referred to in the Respondent's answer and letter"). See also *Abdi,* Order [1991], paras. 2, 4; *Vollmer,* Order [1991], paras. 3–9; *de Jong,* Order [1992], paras. 1–2; *Rae (No. 2),* Order [1993], paras. 1–5; and *Courtney,* Order [1994], paras. 1, 3–4.

[34] *Buranavanichkit,* Decision No. 7 [1982], Preamble ("The Tribunal has decided that the hearing of witnesses in this case is unnecessary").

also direct that the evidence be given in writing instead, or limit the oral testimony where it considers the written documentation to be adequate.

Interventions

It is interesting to observe that the right to intervene is granted to various categories of parties.[35] Interventions are permitted in the first place to individuals who could themselves qualify as parties in the case before the Tribunal, if they allege that a right of their own might be affected by the judgment to be given by the Tribunal. A mere interest is insufficient, however, no matter how strong it might be. The representative of any institution to which the jurisdiction of the Tribunal applies – including the Chairman of the Bank's Pension Benefits Administration Committee – may also intervene at any stage if the administration might be affected by the judgment. Finally, the Tribunal may permit any person or entity with a substantial interest in the outcome of the case, not excluding the Staff Association of the respondent institution, to participate as an *amicus curiae*.[36] The Tribunal has in any case the power to transmit a copy of the application to any person who might have an interest in intervening.

Interventions may be made in favor of either party, or simply of the intervening party itself, and will follow the general rules of procedural law since no restrictions are otherwise provided. This is more obvious in cases of interventions by individuals, whereas institutional interventions will be rarer since in most such cases the interested institutions are already respondents. On the other hand, it is interesting to observe that the Staff Association may participate in the proceedings only as an *amicus curiae*.[37] This is to be expected, as it could not qualify for intervention given its difficulty in meeting the condition of having an affected right. Interventions by individuals, meanwhile, are made in the form of applications, and are transmitted to the parties in litigation by the Executive Secretary only if the Tribunal decides that they are admissible.

---

[35] Rules, Rules 21–23. Sometimes an intervention is due to the wish of the intervenor not to see his file disclosed due to its confidential nature. See, for example, *Jassal*, Decision No. 100 [1991], paras. 1, 66.

[36] Rules, Rule 25, para. 2. See also *Agodo*, Decision No. 76 [1989], para. 1; *Hammond*, Decision No. 86 [1989], para. 1.

[37] Rules, Rule 25, para. 2.

IV. *Grounds for Review*

Paradoxically, not much is stated in the Statutes of the World Bank Administrative Tribunal and similar administrative tribunals with respect to the grounds for review. Only non-observance of the contract of employment or of the terms of appointment can form the basis on which the Tribunal will appraise applications coming under its consideration. This statutory rule gives evidence of the kind of law that will be applied by the Tribunal, and this appears to be contract law. In this context, the litigation is not objective, in that it does not seek to unveil and restore rights established by an objective legality, but rather is subjective, in that the contract is the law of the parties. A question could be raised in this regard as to the relevance of pertinent rules and regulations in force at the time of the alleged non-observance, including the provisions of the Staff Retirement Plan. The answer would be supplied by the Statute itself, according to which all such rules and regulations are included in the terms "contract of employment" and "terms of appointment."

A further question is whether those sources of law are applicable objectively as rules of law, or simply as part of the contractual agreement, i.e., as just the law of the parties. It may be recalled here that the history of administrative law in continental European countries has known two phases. During the first phase, in the 19th century, the relationship between civil servants and the State was contractual. At the beginning of the 20th century, however, the theory of the statutory relationship prevailed throughout continental Europe. The debate between the two schools was interesting, as it marked the consolidation of the State as being the one and only source of power in a given country. According to the second theory, which still prevails in most continental countries, we witness a unilateral decision by the administration to appoint someone to public service, despite the contractual appearances of the relationship. The appointee, by declaring his or her willingness to accept that decision, voluntarily subjects himself or herself to the rules governing the civil service as they then exist and as they could eventually be amended at the free discretion of the State.

It was natural for the WBAT to be faced with such questions from its inception, and it indeed did so in its first judgment, the *de Merode* case.

In *de Merode*,[38] the Tribunal faced the dilemma of addressing whether the basis of the employment relationship is a contract or a status. The Tribunal knowledgeably reviewed the existing administrative legal theories

[38] *de Merode*, Decision No. 1 [1981].

mentioned above, and concluded that the basis of the employment relationship in the Bank Group is contractual, the result of an offer made by the Bank and an acceptance given by the recruit. The Tribunal had to reach such a conclusion because in its terms of reference it was clearly indicated that the object of its adjudication is the contract between the parties. On the other hand, under the same terms of reference, the pertinent rules and regulations in force at the time of the alleged non-observance, including the provisions of the Staff Retirement Plan, are to be considered as part of the contract. It is important to underline that these rules are considered to be part of the contract not in the form in which they existed at the time of the contractual stipulation, but rather as they were constituted at the time of the event which gave rise to the conflict. This can only mean that there has been an acceptance of the principle that the Bank Group can change its rules at will.

The Tribunal decided not to follow the traditional continental European tradition, which distinguishes between the part of the relationship which cannot change, and the other, which can be freely changed at the will of the administration as pertaining to the organization of the public service and the administration's duty to keep it functioning through appropriate, unilaterally established regulations. Despite the authoritarian profile of this old European doctrine, which was repudiated by the Tribunal, its reasoning is clear and useful, and it is a fundamental principle that the organizational rules of the public service cannot be the object of any bargaining with prospective recruits. This doctrine underlines the clause of Article II, paragraph 1, of the Statute that clearly results from citing, among other sources, the Staff Retirement Plan.

The Tribunal stated, nevertheless, that the Bank has the power to amend conditions of employment unilaterally, as is implied in the Bank's duty to pursue fully and efficiently the purposes and objectives for which it was created. The existence of objectives and rules implies also the power to amend them, and to apply changes immediately to employed personnel. This discretionary power cannot, on the other hand, be totally unlimited because of the risk of abuse. The criteria as to how this discretion should therefore be used were fixed by the Tribunal itself in the *de Merode* case, and consist of the following: changes must be reasonably related to the objective which they intend to achieve, and specifically to the proper functioning of the organization and the Bank's duty to ensure that it has a staff possessing "the highest standards of efficiency and of technical competence"; changes must be made in good faith and be properly motivated; they must not discriminate in an unjustifiable manner; they must seek to avoid excessive and unnecessary harm to the staff; and they must give evidence of the care with which the relevant reform was studied and of the conditions attached to the change.

The Tribunal distinguished between an employment contract's fundamental or essential elements and its non-fundamental or non-essential elements. This distinction has its roots in the Roman contract law's *essentialia* and *non essentialia negotii*. The first cannot be altered without the consent of the employee, whereas in the second case the opposite rule applies. The Tribunal might have believed in adopting this distinction that it had honored the theory of contracts, but it found itself in the difficult position of defining what is and what is not fundamental or essential in a contract of public-service employment. It is true that the rules of organization and of the functioning of services are necessarily fundamental, as they constitute the legal framework into which the staff member enters upon his or her employment. The Tribunal must work within this framework to develop its case law regarding the violation or non-violation of clauses falling, or not falling, under its jurisdiction.

The Statute and Rules of the Tribunal distinguish only between the required procedure on the one hand and the merits or substance of a case on the other. The distinction is of importance because if the Tribunal finds that the required procedure was not respected, it may ask the respondent institution to fulfill its obligation before the case is finally decided. This is not, however, a distinction that should be applied at this stage, as procedural questions go also to the merits of a case if the Tribunal proceeds to a final judgment.

One should therefore avoid following the pragmatic approach of the Anglo-Saxon tradition in categorizing the grounds for review, and instead simplify the approach by dividing such grounds under two simple headings: external and internal illegality.[39] External illegality comprises all questions of jurisdiction involving the acting authority and the relevant procedure, while internal illegality comprises substantive violations of law, errors of law and of fact, and *détournement de pouvoir* or the misuse of powers. This distinction corresponds to the above-mentioned one only if "procedure" is understood to include jurisdiction, as must in fact be the case, since a lack of jurisdiction is a relatively simple form of procedural irregularity. As for internal illegality, the Tribunal has elaborated upon all concepts that modern administrative law has developed, including the principles of proportionality,[40] *détournement de pouvoir*,[41] *détournement de procédure* or abuse of

---

[39] As they are indeed codified in French administrative law.
[40] *Gregorio*, op. cit., para. 47; *Georgiev*, Decision No. 96 [1990], paras. 32–33, 39–40.
[41] *Jassal*, op. cit., para. 31.

procedure,[42] irregular purpose,[43] reasonableness,[44] discrimination,[45] abuse of discretion and arbitrariness in general,[46] error of law,[47] error of fact,[48] etc.

V. *Judgment*

Whether or not oral proceedings are held, the World Bank Administrative Tribunal will reach its decision by a majority vote of the members pre-

[42] *Suntharalingam*, Decision No. 6 [1981], para. 35; *King*, Decision No. 131 [1993], paras. 62, 64; *Sjamsubahri*, Decision No. 145 [1995], paras. 16–17. In regard specifically to due process, see *Salle*, Decision No. 10 [1982], para. 50; *Gyamfi*, Decision No. 28 [1986], para. 47; *O'Humay*, Decision No. 140 [1994], paras. 43–45; *Thompson*, Decision No. 30 [1986], para. 28; *Rossini*, Decision No. 31 [1987], para. 32. In regard to the requirement that a statement of reasons be given for an action, see *Skandera*, op. cit, paras. 27–29; *Suntharalingam*, op. cit., paras. 34–37; *Fernandes*, Decision No. 90 [1990], para. 43. In regard to the right of defense, see *Suntharalingam*, op. cit, para. 38; *A. Berg*, Decision No. 73 [1983], paras. 37–41; *Gyamfi*, op. cit., paras. 42–44; *Rae*, Decision No. 74 [1988], para. 46; *Spier*, Decision No. 77 [1989], para. 19; *Kassab*, op. cit., paras. 55–56; *King*, op. cit., paras. 33–38, 49–53; *Snyder*, Decision No. 135 [1993], paras. 38–39. In regard to notice, see *de Raet*, Decision No. 85 [1989], paras. 60, 63, 66; *de Jong*, op. cit., paras. 41–45; *Wahie*, Decision No. 93 [1990], para. 38; *Pavesich*, Decision No. 94 [1990], para. 43. In regard to disciplinary warnings, see *Sjamsubahri*, op. cit., para. 13; *Samuel-Thambiah*, Decision No. 133 [1993], paras. 31–33. In regard to job classification, see *A. Berg*, op. cit. In regard to failures of the administration to act, see *Broemser*, Decision No. 27 [1985], para. 34; *Singh*, Decision No. 105 [1992], para. 54; *Sjamsubahri*, op. cit., paras. 10–11. In regard to a failure to provide information to an affected staff member, see *Buranavanichkit*, op. cit., para. 28.

[43] See, e.g., *Courtney*, op. cit., paras. 49–53.

[44] See, e.g., *Saberi*, Decision No. 5 [1982], para. 24; *Sebastian (No. 2)*, Decision No. 57 [1988], paras. 21–22; *Pinto*, Decision No. 56 [1988], paras. 35–36; *Hammond*, op. cit., paras. 27–28, 34, 37; *Lindsay*, Decision No. 92 [1990], para. 29.

[45] See, e.g., *Skandera*, op. cit., para. 26; *Salle*, op. cit., para. 57; *Gyamfi*, op. cit., paras. 37, 45; *van Gent (No. 9)*, Decision No. 34 [1985], para. 25; *Suntharalingam*, op. cit., paras. 28–29; *Matta*, op. cit., para. 45; *Mendaro*, Decision No. 26 [1985], paras. 19–22; *Agodo*, op. cit., para. 33; *de Raet*, op. cit., paras. 55, 74; *Gavidia*, Decision No. 66 [1988], para. 26; *Fabara-Núñez*, Decision No. 101 [1991], para. 47; *Mathew*, Decision No. 103 [1991], para. 32; *Snyder*, op. cit., paras. 28–31; *Addy*, op. cit., para. 50; *Chhabra*, Decision No. 139 [1994], paras. 51–53; *Planthara*, Decision No. 143 [1995], para. 36.

[46] *Einthoven*, Decision No. 23 [1985], paras. 43, 59; *Saberi*, op. cit., para. 24; *Gyamfi*, op. cit., paras. 31, 35, 37, 39; *Polak*, Decision No. 17 [1984], para. 43; *von Stauffenberg*, Decision No. 38 [1987], paras. 69, 112, 119; *de Vuyst*, Decision No. 39 [1987], paras. 23–24; *K. Berg*, op. cit., para. 29; *Sebastian (No. 2)*, op. cit., paras. 22, 24, 27–29, 35; *Apkarian*, Decision No. 58 [1988], paras. 35, 47; *Apergis*, Decision No. 83 [1989], para. 57; *Klempin*, Decision No. 88 [1990], paras. 21–22; *Fernandes*, op. cit., para. 40; *Lindsay*, op. cit., paras. 23, 25, 28–29; *Georgiev*, op. cit., paras. 41, 44; *Kassab*, op. cit., para. 54; *Jassal*, op. cit., paras. 30, 37, 55, 59, 61; *Vollmer*, Decision No. 112 [1992], para. 29; *Shaffer*, op. cit., paras. 30–31, 34–38; *de Jong (No. 2)*, Decision No. 127 [1993], paras. 39–41, 44–46; *King*, op. cit., paras. 67–68, 74; *Carew*, Decision No. 142 [1995], paras. 31–32; *Chhabra*, op. cit., paras. 54–56.

[47] *von Stauffenberg*, op. cit., para. 116; *Sebastian (No. 2)*, op. cit., paras. 21–22, 25–29; *Arellano*, Decision No. 98 [1990], para. 42.

[48] *K. Berg (No. 2)*, Decision No. 99 [1990], paras. 30–38, 40–41.

sent. In cases where there is an equality of votes, the President of the panel (or, in a plenary session, the President of the Tribunal) will cast the deciding vote. The judgment must state the reasons on which it is based.[49] No appeal is possible and judgments are final.[50] Judgments are also to be made public and published. In practical terms, finality means that pursuant to the generally accepted meaning of *res judicata*,[51] no further application may be filed with the Tribunal when it has the same object as the application already decided upon.

Can the Tribunal decide to reinstate a staff member? The WBAT Statute states at Article XII, paragraph 1, that "[i]f the Tribunal finds that the application is well-founded, it shall order the rescission of the decision contested or the specific performance of the obligation invoked." At the same time, however, if the Tribunal finds that the respondent institution "has reasonably determined that such rescission or specific performance would not be practicable or in the institution's interest," it shall order such institution to pay restitution in the amount that is reasonably necessary to compensate the applicant for the actual damages suffered.

The rescission of a decision does not by itself lead to a positive effect, but rather does so only indirectly and according to the circumstances of the case. If the applicant had his or her contract terminated by the Bank, for example, it has to be admitted that the rescission of that decision has the automatic, logical consequence of reviving the contract. If the contested act was a decision of non-promotion, however, the rescission of that decision does not automatically imply the promotion of the staff member, but only affirms his or her right to be re-evaluated. The Tribunal may, therefore, only add to its judgment a further clause asking the Bank to *"perform"* an evaluation in accordance with its own standards of good practice.

The matter of reinstatement has been raised in a small number of Tribunal judgments, wherein it was decided and ordered that the only appropriate remedy was the reinstatement of the staff member.[52]

---

[49] This requirement is laid down in the sense given by the International Court of Justice in *Application for Review of Judgment No. 158 of the UNAT*, ICJ Reports 1973, pp. 210–211, which was cited by the WBAT in *van Gent (No. 2)*, Decision No. 13 [1983], para. 28: "This statement must indicate in a general way the reasoning upon which the judgment is based; but it need not enter meticulously into every claim and contention on either side."

[50] See *van Gent (No. 2)*, op. cit., para. 21 ("No party to a dispute before the Tribunal may . . . bring his case back to the Tribunal for a second round of litigation, no matter how dissatisfied he may be with the pronouncement of the Tribunal or its considerations. The Tribunal's judgment is meant to be the last step along the path of settling disputes arising between the Bank and the members of its staff").

[51] Statute, Article XI.

[52] See, e.g., *Jassal*, op. cit.; *Fabara-Núñez*, op. cit.; *Brannigan*, Decision No. 165 [1997]; *Niedzviecki*, Decision No. 189 [1998].

Such is the normal practice of various international administrative tribunals. In the Rules of Procedure of the Administrative Tribunal of the Organization of American States (OASAT), it is stated in Chapter IX, Article 50, para. 7, that "[t]he Tribunal's judgment may include any form of redress it deems necessary and appropriate to properly settle the matter in dispute, including but not limited to reinstatement, affirmation of individual rights and responsibilities, and damages."

The Statute of the Administrative Tribunal of the African Development Bank is not so explicit. It does, however, permit any kind of redress through its Article XIII, which states that "[i]f the Tribunal concludes that an application contesting an administrative decision is well-founded, it shall order the rescission of such a decision, and may order any other measures, whether involving the payment of money or otherwise, required to correct the effects of that decision."

The WBAT organizes its deliberations into two phases. First, the Tribunal is bound to examine whether the procedure prescribed by the rules of the respondent institution has been observed. Whenever the Tribunal concludes that it has not, it then decides whether the case should be remanded to the respondent so that the respondent can make the necessary corrections. The President of the respondent institution has two working days from his or her notification of this decision to request a remand for such a purpose. When such a request is made, the Tribunal will proceed on that basis.[53] At the expiration of the two-day time limit, however, if there is no positive answer, the Tribunal is bound to proceed to the second phase and to decide the case on its merits.

It is strange to exclude procedural omissions or mistakes from the merits of a case. It seems, nevertheless, that the Statute is intended to simplify litigation as much as possible. It should be noted in this respect that the remand procedure has never been applied in practice. This remand procedure is also different from a remand of a case to the administration for the purposes of reconsideration and adaptation to the Tribunal's findings upon the quashing of an administrative decision. Remand in the latter case occurs only because it is impossible for the Tribunal to substitute its own judgment for that of the administration.[54]

The Tribunal will base its judgment on the facts as presented by the parties in their pleadings and on the application of the facts to the relevant law, and will order either the rescission of the decision contested,[55]

[53] Statute, Article XII, para. 2; Rules, Rule 20.
[54] See, e.g., *Rae*, op. cit., for an example of a remand in this sense.
[55] As for example in *King*, op. cit., para. 66.

or the specific performance of the obligation invoked. The reform of an administrative decision by the Tribunal is not one of the remedies offered by the Statute, and thus if such a need arises, the Tribunal has to order the administration to conform to the Tribunal's findings and to reform the decision itself. This has been stated by the Tribunal in *de Merode* and many subsequent judgments.[56]

Can a decision be declaratory? This question was raised before the Tribunal in one case, *Agodo*, but no precise answer was given.[57] In fact, the Tribunal found that under the circumstances, the applicant in that case had no *locus standi.* Nevertheless, both the phrasing of the judgment and the general principles of procedural law lead to the conclusion that such a possibility exists since a declaratory judgment is a lesser protection than rescission, specific performance or compensation.[58]

The Tribunal is further permitted to decide and fix the amount to be paid to the applicant for the injury sustained. This compensation should not be confused with specific performance,[59] for which the applicant might apply. This distinction between the remedies becomes especially obvious in cases of alleged intangible (i.e., moral) injury.[60] It has to be noted in such cases that the applicant's request is not one for compensation but rather one for specific performance,[61] notwithstanding any further request made for compensation. In any event, however, the Tribunal may decide to make a separate award of compensation as part of its inherent power to provide remedies.[62]

Compensation must be paid by the Bank upon the judgment of the Tribunal.[63] No enforcement procedures are foreseen, however. Thus, in a

---

[56] *de Merode*, op. cit., para. 86 (holding that "[i]t is not for the Tribunal to substitute its judgment for that of the Bank in choosing the average deduction system, rather than some other system, to replace the previous system").

[57] *Agodo*, op. cit., para. 32.

[58] *Id.* (stating that "[j]ust as specific performance, rescission and compensation may be issued by the Tribunal only when the Respondent has made a 'decision' adversely affecting a staff member, the same is true regarding the issuance of a declaratory judgment").

[59] Compensation very often accompanies rescission, as for example in *Lamson-Scribner*, Decision No. 32 [1987], para. 57, wherein it was stated that "[i]t is also appropriate to award the Applicant a sum of money to compensate him for the intangible injury caused by the Respondent's breach of these conditions of his employment." See also, e.g., *Singh*, op. cit., paras. 55–58; *King*, op. cit., para. 82.

[60] As for example in *Gyamfi*, op. cit.; *King*, op. cit.; *Samuel-Thambiah*, op. cit., para. 43; *Sjamsubahri*, op. cit., paras. 18–21.

[61] In some cases, the applicant has asked for compensation because specific performance has become impossible, as for example when he or she asks to be paid his or her salary for annual leave not originally allowed by the Bank. See, e.g., *Moses (No. 2)*, Decision No. 138 [1994], para. 28.

[62] *Lamson-Scribner*, op. cit., para. 60.

[63] This is required by the express rule contained in Article XII, para. 3, of the Statute. See also *A. Berg (No. 2)*, Decision No. 87 [1990], para. 16.

hypothetical case of non-compliance with the judgment of the Tribunal, the only recourse available to the applicant is to make a new application against the failure of the Bank to comply.

Although the judgment of the Tribunal is final, a request for revision of the judgment is possible under certain circumstances.[64] Such circumstances can be found in any administrative litigation procedure of this kind, and are characterized by the fact that one of the parties is at the same time the main holder of information. It is possible that at a later date a party will discover a fact which at the time of the judgment was unknown to both that party and the Tribunal, and which by its nature might have had a decisive influence on the Tribunal's judgment. The party is then given the right to request a revision of the judgment within six months of learning of the fact. This party is, however, bound to produce with his or her request all necessary information proving both the existence of the fact and that the fact was unknown to him or her. The originals of all supporting documents must accompany the request.

A question may then be posed as to what happens when the fact was known to the Tribunal but not to the party (or vice versa), or when the fact was known to both of them, but under the circumstances could not have been interpreted in a way that would have had an impact on the case. Under the Statute, such a fact cannot be invoked as the basis for a request for revision. The true meaning of the Statute, however, leads to the opposite conclusion, and in these hypothetical situations the request should be declared admissible.

VI. *Costs*

The World Bank Administrative Tribunal has facilitated the right of staff members to be represented by legal counsel by making reasonable awards of costs in numerous cases. A newly developed practice requires applicants to submit statements of costs with some degree of specificity, and in 1998, the Tribunal amended its Rules to allow applicants more time to submit statements of costs, so that they are now accepted up to seven days after a case is listed.[65]

The established, general principle on the issue of costs, however, is that in international administrative law "[e]ach party shall bear its own costs in presenting a case to the Tribunal."[66] Article XV of the Statute of the

---

[64] Statute, Article XIII.

[65] Rules, Rule 29.

[66] Statute of the Inter-American Development Bank Administrative Tribunal, Article V,

IMFAT offers for its part a complete regulation of the cost problem as follows:

> 1. The Tribunal may order that reasonable compensation be made by the applicant to the Fund for all or part of the cost of defending the case, if it finds that:
>   a. the application was manifestly without foundation either in fact or under existing law, unless the applicant demonstrates that the application was based on a good faith argument for an extension, modification, or reversal of existing law; or
>   b. the applicant intended to delay the resolution of the case or to harass the Fund or any of its officers or employees.
> 2. The amount awarded by the Tribunal shall be collected by way of deductions from payments owed by the Fund to the applicant or otherwise, as determined by the Managing Director, who may, in particular cases, waive the claim of the Fund against the applicant.

It is obvious that this regulation is not in the spirit of offering potential complainants a guarantee of having their expenses covered, should the complaint be admitted. To the contrary, it is intended to restrain them from creating costs for the Fund with frivolous or malicious complaints.

Article 50, paragraph 7, of the Rules of Procedure of the OASAT addresses the situation differently by introducing a more equitable solution to the problem:

> [W]hen the Tribunal deems it appropriate, it may order the losing party to pay the prevailing party an indemnity for attorney's fees and costs. The payment of additional sanctions may be ordered in cases where the Tribunal considers that the losing party has brought a clearly frivolous claim or defense, did not have solid grounds for litigating, has been totally defeated, has clearly acted with disregard or malice toward the rights and interests of the other party, or has unnecessarily prolonged the proceedings. The maximum amount that can be awarded for the total of attorneys' fees and costs shall ordinarily not exceed the equivalent of one month's remuneration . . . in a judgment involving up to ten complainants, and twice that amount in a judgment involving more than ten complainants.

Another example is that of the Statute of the Council of Europe Administrative Tribunal. Under its Article 11, if the Board considers an appeal to be an abuse of procedure, it may order the appellant to pay all or part of the

para. 3. Article V further provides that, as an exception, transportation expenses incurred in the presentation of an application by a staff member who is stationed in any of the Bank's Field Offices, and which the Tribunal deems to be reasonable, shall be borne by the Bank.

costs incurred. If, on the other hand, it has allowed the appeal, the Tribunal may award reasonable reimbursement of the appellant's properly vouched expenses, taking into account the nature and importance of the dispute.

The question of costs also has to do with the wish of international civil servants to be provided with institutional help in the preparation and presentation of their cases. In 1995, the U.N.'s aborted grievance system reform provided, as an aspect of the Organization's duty to support its staff members, that legal counsel services would be offered to U.N. personnel.

On the other hand, a Labor Relations Advisor has been introduced to the Inter-American Development Bank's staff. His or her intervention in the grievance system, either through the offering of advice to staff members who turn out to have no case at all, or through the provision of services in the administrative review process, is considered as being of the first importance.

VII. *Interim Relief*

The World Bank Administrative Tribunal is not granted authority by its Statute to order interim relief measures, and the same limitation applies to other international administrative tribunals.[67] This statutory *lacuna* has been redressed by the case law of the Tribunal, which decided as early as 1981 that "this Tribunal, as an international tribunal, possesses an inherent jurisdiction to indicate provisional measures designed to preserve *pendente lite* the rights which are the subject of dispute in the proceedings . . . ."[68] Since January 1, 2002, the Tribunal's amended Rules have provided for provisional relief to be granted where the execution of a decision "is shown to be highly likely to result in grave hardship to the applicant that cannot otherwise be redressed."[69]

VIII. *Conclusion*

In conclusion, the World Bank Administrative Tribunal, when compared with other similar institutions, does not present areas in which drastic improvement is needed. In fact, what should eventually be required is that

[67] For example, the Statute of the International Monetary Fund Administrative Tribunal, Article VI, para. 4, states that "the filing of an application shall not have the effect of suspending the implementation of the decision contested."

[68] *Suntharalingam*, Order [1981].

[69] Rules, Rule 13.

the Tribunal use its investigatory powers more extensively, and accept some of the principles already introduced by the Statutes of other administrative tribunals. Examples of such principles can be found in the Statutes of the IMFAT and the OASAT, particularly with respect to applications brought against administrative acts of a general character, for the imposition of costs in frivolous cases, etc. Otherwise, however, the fact that the transcript of Appeals Committee proceedings is formally taken and then submitted to the Tribunal already constitutes a major reform.

REMARKS

Sir Elihu Lauterpacht, QC
Session Chair

Résumé

Je tâcherai d'identifier les questions sur lesquelles il serait utile d'avoir l'avis des participants:

- la question de la nature de la relation entre le tribunal et l'organisation dont il dépend présente un intérêt certain; celle-ci peut nous mener à nous interroger sur la prolifération des tribunaux administratifs internationaux et même sur l'utilité de ces tribunaux dans l'absolu: serait-il désavantageux aux membres du personnel de laisser au système judiciaire du pays d'accueil des organisations internationales le soin de régler les relations de celles-ci avec leur personnel?
- les rapports du tribunal avec les instances inférieures: le tribunal est-il lié par les conclusions relatives aux faits et par les moyens de preuve présentés devant ces instances?
- le rythme de travail des tribunaux ainsi que la question des pouvoirs implicites ou inhérents des tribunaux internationaux
- le comportement inapproprié de certains conseils représentant les parties
- le processus qui aboutit aux jugements du tribunal ainsi que le rôle du secrétariat dans ce contexte
- la forme des jugements (faits et droit séparés ou mêlés)
- la méthode de calcul des indemnités et la détermination des frais et dépens
- la question de savoir si des arrangements appropriés existent afin que la direction de l'organisation prenne conscience de l'importance des jugements du tribunal, et modifie son comportement pour l'avenir en conséquence.

* * *

It must be reassuring for most of us here to know that we are by our mere presence identified as "persons of high moral character" and of "demonstrable competence" – though I am sure that most of us assume that anyway.

We now proceed to the discussion, which is largely in the hands of the participants whose names appear on the sheets and who will presumably have identified the topics that they want to cover already. But I think it is perhaps desirable that I should say a few words to identify some of the issues that occurred to me as being ones on which it would be useful to hear the views of participants.

This morning, we were reminded of the interest of the nature of the relationship between the tribunal and the institution which it serves. In that connection, we might also want to give consideration to the whole question of the proliferation of administrative tribunals. Do we really need so many? Of course, each of us belonging to a different tribunal would feel that the answer is yes. But objectively approached, the answer may not be so obvious.

Indeed, we may even have to ask ourselves a fundamental question as to whether we need administrative tribunals at all. The source of the need as presently conceived is the immunity of the organization from the local jurisdiction. Unless there is an internal body like the administrative tribunal, there is no place to which staff can have recourse to air their grievances. But supposing that the organizations did not have immunity in respect of employment matters and supposing that the staff were left to have recourse to the local host country's system of employment law, would that be a serious disadvantage to them? It is a question we may need to ask ourselves.

We ought also to consider the relationship of the tribunal to the lower instances, the question of whether the findings of fact or the evidence given before the Appeals Committee to any extent bind the tribunal itself.

We ought to ask ourselves about the speed at which tribunals operate. In the course of this afternoon, we have heard a couple of references to the most interesting question of the implied or inherent powers of international tribunals. It would be helpful to know whether participants can identify any other respects in which recourse has been had to such powers.

We have heard some talk about frivolous, vexatious and repetitive procedures on the part of litigants, but nothing about the behavior, or should I say the misbehavior, of some of the counsel who occassionally represent litigants.

We have not as yet heard much about the process by which the tribunal reaches its decision. We have been told about the distinction between a full tribunal and a panel, but it would be useful to bring out the most important role that the secretariat of the tribunals can play. We know that it varies from tribunal to tribunal. It may be that some tribunals may not wish to acknowledge the extent to which they are dependent upon their secretariat, but there is no doubt that the secretariats have an important role to play.

We have not heard about the form of judgments: the question of whether the form which some tribunals adopt of a judgment in two parts, the *qualité* and then the *considerations*, is necessarily the best form or whether it is simpler to have a single, unitary judgment in which the tribunal finds the facts and goes on to the law as it may deem appropriate.

We have heard about both remedies and damages, but we have not heard about the methods of calculating damages or the question of whether interest ought to be brought into it. We have heard reference to cost, but no identification of any common factors that are applicable to the determination of costs.

There is another aspect to the matter which is very important and that is the procedures, if any, that exist for making management aware of the significance of the decisions of tribunals. I recall that when I saw the President of the World Bank at the time that I left the World Bank Administrative Tribunal and he asked me if I had any bequest to offer the Bank, I suggested that there might be a procedure established by which the decisions of the Tribunal could be brought to the attention of management so that management would be more "careful" in their behavior in the future. "Oh yes," he said, "that is a good idea." I am not sure that it has been implemented.

These are the types of issues upon which we might touch this afternoon, to the extent that they fall within the framework of the speeches already prepared or of the willingness of other commentators to speak about them.

Having said that, let me now turn to the commentators.

COMMENTS

THE POINT OF VIEW OF TRIBUNAL MEMBERS

Mark Fernando*

Résumé

Je traiterai de deux questions: le caractère irrévocable des jugements et l'opportunité d'en admettre la révision. Ces deux questions doivent être considérées sous l'angle de l'absence d'appel concernant les jugements des tribunaux administratifs internationaux. Puisque le droit d'appel n'existe pas, il faudrait améliorer la procédure aboutissant au jugement. L'un des moyens de le faire serait d'élargir la recevabilité du recours en révision. Deux séries de cas tranchés par le Tribunal administratif de l'Organisation internationale du Travail (TAOIT) serviront à clarifier ce point.

Première situation: litiges relatifs à l'emploi

Dans la première série de cas, des jugements affectant gravement les droits d'une tierce personne (ayant été nommée au poste du requérant) ont été déclarés irrévocables et sans possibilité de recours à l'égard de la tierce personne sans que lui ait été donnée l'opportunité d'être entendue pour faire valoir ses droits. Ces affaires posent la question de savoir s'il serait opportun de notifier les tierces personnes de l'existence d'une procédure où elles seraient appelées à faire valoir leurs droits. Cette procédure de notification est admise par le Règlement du Tribunal qui prévoit non seulement qu'une tierce personne peut intervenir à une affaire pendante si certaines conditions sont réunies, mais aussi que le Tribunal peut notifier toute tierce personne qui serait intéressée à présenter des conclusions dans cette affaire.

Deuxième situation: plaintes relatives au harcèlement sexuel

Dans ces cas, il est arrivé (jugement *Mussnig*) qu'une allégation de harcèlement sexuel émise par une partie requérante soit admise par le Tribunal. Plus tard, un comité *ad hoc* nommé par l'Organisation concluait que le harcèlement allégué n'avait pas eu lieu. Quand l'Organisation saisit de nouveau le Tribunal, celui-ci (jugement *Mussnig (No. 2)*) refusa la révision pour absence de faits nouveaux. Le supérieur, accusé de harcèlement, introduisit un recours contre l'Organisation en réclamant une indemnisation: le Tribunal la lui accorda (jugement *Eben-Moussi*), concluant implicitement que le supérieur n'était pas coupable de harcèlement

* President, Asian Development Bank Administrative Tribunal; former Judge, International Labour Organization Administrative Tribunal.

sexuel. Cet exemple est troublant car pour les mêmes faits, deux jugements ont abouti à des conclusions contradictoires.

En conclusion, le recours en révision devrait être plus largement admis au TAOIT, notamment pour découverte de faits nouveaux, violation de la justice naturelle, violation grave de la règle de droit et aussi en cas de contrariété de jugements rendus par le même Tribunal relatifs à une même affaire.

* * *

Thank you, Mr. Chairman. I am sorry that you did not give us this litany of matters to be discussed at the beginning of the day, as I am not ready to address them without careful thought. I wish to deal with two questions: the finality of judgments and when revision of judgments should be allowed.

I believe that the approach to these two matters needs to be considered against the background of the absence of a right of appeal. Because a complainant has no right of appeal, I think that administrative tribunals should be more cautious before they declare a judgment to be final and beyond review. There have sporadically been demands for a right of appeal against judgments of tribunals: a demand reiterated today by Judge Ajibola who posed the question: "How can the judges be judged?"

As the number of tribunals increases and their workload expands, this demand will become more insistent. Yet giving a right of appeal will entail further delay and expense, and will elevate Judge Ajibola's question to a higher plane: "Who will judge the judges of the appellate body?" My contention is that so long as there is no right of appeal (and indeed, even if there is a right of appeal), there is a need to improve the process of adjudication which takes place before the delivery of any judgment which by Statute is declared final and beyond review.

Improving the practice of tribunals in regard to revision is an important part of improving that process of adjudication. It is my belief that a tribunal, faced with the choice of allowing or not allowing revision, should lean in favor of revision, looking at the matter broadly rather than narrowly. I wish to refer to two sets of cases decided by the ILO Administrative Tribunal which I believe fortify the view that the right to revision ought to be wider than many judgments say it is.

Situation 1: Disputed Appointments

In the first set of cases to which I will refer, the right of a complainant was upheld in such a way as to seriously affect the rights of a third party, another staff member who had not been given an opportunity of being heard. The question then arises whether, and to what extent, such a judgment should be declared "final and beyond review" at the instance of such an aggrieved third party.

The first of these cases is *More*, ILOAT Judgment No. 1390. Mr. More applied for a post as an internal candidate. An external candidate, Miss X, was appointed instead. Mr. More complained to the ILO Tribunal. In Judgment No. 1390, the appointment that had been offered to the external candidate was set aside, apparently without any notice to her. Had Miss X then applied for revision of that judgment, could she have been told that, under the Statute of the Tribunal, the judgment was final even though there was a mistake of law? Or because there was no new fact? Is it not clear that, in so far as Miss X was concerned, there was a serious breach of natural justice and the judgment was, therefore, voidable?

The need for such notice, and an opportunity of being heard, was recognized in a subsequent case, *Saunders (No. 15)*, ILOAT Judgment No. 1468. Here, faced with a very similar situation, the Tribunal did not immediately set aside the disputed appointment. Instead it notified the third party and invited the third party to make submissions. Only thereafter, in a subsequent judgment (*Saunders (No. 15)*, ILOAT Judgment No. 1527), was the appointment quashed.

That procedure of giving notice finds support in the Rules of the Tribunal. Article 13(1) of the Rules of the ILO Administrative Tribunal entitles anyone to whom the Tribunal is open to intervene on the grounds that the ruling which the Tribunal is to make may affect him. However, recognizing that such a person may not be aware of pending proceedings, Article 13(3) provides that "[t]he Tribunal . . . may instruct the Registrar to give notice of a complaint to any third party if it appears that such third party may want to make submissions." In the *More* case, if the external candidate Miss X had sought revision, she might well have argued not only that the Tribunal had the *discretion* to give notice but that, under the circumstances, the Tribunal was under a *duty* to give such notice. Therefore, apart from a denial of natural justice, a serious breach of the rules of the tribunal may give rise to a right to revision.

There are other cases where, faced with a similar situation, the Tribunal did not quash the disputed appointment but instead granted damages, thereby avoiding any adverse consequence to a third party and not impairing the finality of its judgments (*Broere-Moore (No. 5)*, ILOAT Judgment No. 1706; see also *Flores*, ILOAT Judgment No. 1497).

Situation 2: Complaints of Sexual Harassment

There is another series of cases – arising from allegations of sexual harassment – which illustrates the anomalies that can occasionally result from tribunal judgments. In Judgment No. 1376 (*Mussnig*), Miss Mussnig complained that she had been subjected to sexual harassment by her supervisor and that, consequently, there had been a refusal to renew her contract. When the complainant filed her case, the organization took technical objections but did not deal with the merits. The Tribunal overruled the objections, refused to send the case back to the Appeals Committee for a decision on the merits, and accepted the complainant's uncontradicted version.

The organization thereafter appointed an *ad hoc* grievance panel to investigate the allegations of harassment. Both parties were heard. The panel ruled that there had been no sexual harassment. The Director-General apologized to the supervisor who had been accused of sexual harassment and acknowledged that the organization had erred in failing to notify him of the proceedings.

The organization then applied for review of the judgment based on the panel's findings. In Judgment No. 1504 (*Mussnig (No. 2)*), the Tribunal held that this was not a new fact and that the judgment was final, and refused review. What if the official charged with harassment had himself requested review? Could he not have relied both on a substantial breach of natural justice as well as a serious non-compliance with the rules of the Tribunal relating to intervention? However, he did not ask for review, but instead asked the organization for compensation. When that was refused, the matter came up again before the Tribunal. In Judgment No. 1619 (*Eben-Moussi*), the Tribunal held that the organization's failure to adduce evidence in the previous case was in violation of the complainant's rights and ordered it to pay him compensation of 10,000 United States dollars. Impliedly, therefore, the Tribunal seemed to agree that he was not guilty of sexual harassment; if he had been, there would have been no basis for giving him substantial damages.

Let us apply the principle of finality to those two judgments. In Judgment No. 1376 between Miss Mussnig and the organization, it was held that the supervisor was guilty of sexual harassment in proceedings to which he was not a party. In Judgment No. 1619 between that supervisor and the organization, to which Miss Mussnig was not a party, it was held that there was no sexual harassment. What is the final answer arising from the Tribunal's judgments to the question whether sexual harassment did take place? In Judgment No. 1376, the answer is that there *was* harassment. In Judgment No. 1619, the answer seems to be that there was *no* harassment.

Conclusion

Clearly, the possibility of review exists in many circumstances. Since tribunals expect organizations to comply strictly with their rules, it follows that tribunals must themselves ensure even stricter compliance with their own rules of procedure. I would suggest, particularly in relation to the ILO Administrative Tribunal (which does not have an express rule permitting review but which has nevertheless held that it has an inherent power to grant such review), that there are other matters besides the discovery of new facts which might fall under the category of exceptional circumstances. These include a breach of natural justice, a serious violation of the rules, or even an inconsistency between two judgments of the same Tribunal which involve the same issue.

I feel therefore that tribunals must scrutinize the pleadings in every case at an early stage to ensure compliance with natural justice, as well as its own rules, thereby avoiding injustices which could impair the finality of their judgments and encourage applications for revision.

Robert A. Gorman*

Résumé

Je répondrai à la question de savoir quelle est la meilleure façon de gérer la relation entre le tribunal administratif et l'organisation dont il dépend.

Même si la fonction première du tribunal administratif est d'agir de la même manière qu'un tribunal, il n'en reste pas moins qu'il remplit aussi une fonction éducative, et ce, aussi bien vis-à-vis de la direction que du personnel de la Banque en leur communiquant les règles relatives à la bonne gestion et au traitement équitable des membres du personnel.

Trois voies pourraient aider le tribunal à mieux remplir cette fonction éducative vis-à-vis de l'administration.

La première consiste pour les tribunaux, bien que soumis à des limites établies par leurs statuts, à s'enhardir et à admettre les recours contre les actes réglementaires promulgués par les organisations.

La seconde voie serait d'encourager l'usage des *obiter dicta* dans les jugements des tribunaux administratifs: il est conseillé, quand l'opportunité se présente, d'aller au-delà du cas considéré et de donner à l'institution des conseils sur la manière d'améliorer ses règles de fonctionnement et de traiter son personnel plus équitablement.

Enfin, la troisième voie consiste à tenir des réunions entre les membres du tribunal, les représentants du personnel et les représentants de la direction de l'institution pour avoir l'opportunité de discuter du comportement de chacune de ces trois entités.

Les jugements du Tribunal administratif de la Banque mondiale sont lus par l'Administration de la Banque. Par conséquent, ils peuvent influencer son comportement futur.

* * *

I, too, was unaware of the fact that Judge Lauterpacht was going to impose a rather daunting list of suggested topics for our discussion. He appears to be very comfortable playing the role of an American law professor who educates by shock and surprise. Nonetheless, I will do my best to respond in a constructive way.

My remarks are largely born of the fact that I came to the World Bank Administrative Tribunal, and subsequently to the Asian Development Bank Administrative Tribunal, through a rather unusual route – not as a scholar or practitioner in the field of international law or in an international orga-

* President, World Bank Administrative Tribunal; Vice President, Asian Development Bank Administrative Tribunal.

nization, but rather as a student and professor of labor and employment law. In that capacity, I served as an arbitrator for many years resolving claims brought by unions on behalf of individual employees for alleged violations by the employer of the terms of collective bargaining agreements. In many respects, there has been a parallel between the types of claims that were presented to me as a labor arbitrator in the private sector in the United States, and those claims presented to us in this room as judges on administrative tribunals. My comments are inspired by the work I have undertaken on tribunals, as well as on my continuing service as a labor arbitrator.

I will address one of our Chairman's earlier questions, i.e., how best to articulate the relationship between the administrative tribunal and the institution. Most of the morning's conversation bears out the thesis that administrative tribunals function principally as courts. We interpret documents in a legalistic way and apply rules drawn from both civil and common law to curb abuses of administrative discretion.

However, I would like to identify another function that we serve. It is a function mentioned this morning by Ko-Yung Tung, General Counsel of the World Bank, and might be known as the educational function. He stated that the World Bank Administrative Tribunal has the function of providing guidance to the staff and the management of the Bank regarding good management practices and the just treatment of staff members. I do believe that the Tribunal serves a useful non-judicial function by seeking to communicate to the Bank, its staff members and its management guidelines for proper management practice and treatment of staff members.

That leads me to raise some questions. I will be both making comments and raising questions that we might be able to explore in the balance of the afternoon. How best can an administrative tribunal achieve this educational function, the function of informing and guiding management? There are three possible ways that come to my mind on the basis of the discussions that we have had so far today and the papers that have been presented.

First, might it not be appropriate to allow an administrative tribunal to pass judgment upon the general terms of a legislative regulation promulgated by the institution or, in most of our cases, the Bank? Apparently, the practice among our tribunals is to decide the validity of staff rules and similar instruments only in the context of a claim by a specific individual who asserts direct injury (typically economic injury) as the result of the application of a promulgated rule. Even though we are subject to the limitations provided by the Statutes that create us and give us our power, we should be more assertive in hearing cases that challenge the general substance of a legislative rule.

For example, suppose a Bank were to announce, through a staff rule, that it was going henceforth to require the mandatory retirement of all staff members at the age of 60, rather than at the prevailing age of 62. Our standard jurisprudence is such that we would require a staff member to go through the ages of 55, 56, 59 and 60 and be told to retire, contrary to the staff member's expectations, before the tribunal would be able to assert jurisdiction. It is not clear to me why tribunals should be denied the jurisdiction to pass judgments upon the validity of that reduction in the retirement age as a general matter of the lawmaker's authority.

Now I will take up the example presented this morning by Mr. Shihata. Suppose an institution were to adopt a general regulation stating that all financial delinquencies or misconduct on the part of a staff member would warrant an immediate termination of employment. It is not clear to me why a staff member has to engage in such misconduct in order to precipitate an adverse action against him in order to precipitate judicial review by the administrative tribunal. I gather from the remarks of Professor Flogaitis that it is unheard of for tribunals to assert such an authority. It would be interesting if we had the opportunity to explore why that should be so.

A *second* technique by which a tribunal can discharge its educational or interactive function with the management or administration of the Bank is to engage in what I might generously call the excessive use of *obiter dicta* in the judgments written by the administrative tribunals. My experience clearly shows that administrative tribunals feel required to do more than simply rule on the outcome of a case and state the respective rights and duties of the staff member and the Bank. Rather, we give reasons. In the course of giving reasons, we give guidance and to some extent, at least in my own experience, the guidance that we give sometimes goes beyond the precisely cabined issue that is presented to the administrative tribunal. As a technical legal matter, perhaps that is inappropriate for the tribunal to do. However, if you believe that the tribunal is to discharge more than a judicial role, but also to engage in an educational process, I would suggest to you that it is often appropriate, when the opportunity and context present themselves, to go beyond strictly the issue to be decided and give the institution some gentle advice as to how it might alter and improve its rules and treat staff members more fairly.

Finally, a *third* technique for communicating and educating between the administrative tribunal and the institution is to do what the World Bank Administrative Tribunal intends to do six months from now. We intend to precipitate a meeting involving the members of the Tribunal as well as representatives of the Staff Association and representatives of management of the Bank. We will have the opportunity to exchange views with one another on the respective performances of the three entities present.

Administrative tribunals write their decisions and send them out without any formal way of ascertaining whether, as the Chairman mentioned, they are even read by management, let alone have an impact on managerial action. I have no doubt that the decisions of the World Bank Administrative Tribunal are read by management, are taken seriously and affect what management does and how it acts. Nonetheless, it would be helpful to learn that directly. In turn, it might be helpful for management to hear from the Administrative Tribunal about how, for example, it might improve its presentations before the Administrative Tribunal, if that is possible.

I would have liked to present some comments about oral proceedings, which the World Bank Administrative Tribunal has embarked upon for the first time in 19 years only this past January. It was an intriguing and valuable experience. However, given the limitations on my time I will refrain from discussing this experience and raising questions with you, from other administrative tribunals, as to your experience with oral proceedings and their role in shaping your deliberations and decisions. Thank you very much.

Jean Massot*

Summary

Neither the proliferation of international administrative tribunals nor excessive uniformity among the existing ones is desirable. As to the latter, it is preferable that the rules of procedure of each tribunal take into account the specific characteristics of the organization within which the tribunal must function.

The two tribunals over which I preside, the European Space Agency Appeals Board (ESAAB) and the Organisation for Economic Co-operation and Development Administrative Tribunal (OECDAT), have certain similarities and differences.

Concerning composition, the ESAAB and the OECDAT each have six members, with cases decided by panels of three members. However, unlike the six members of the ESAAB who hear cases on a rotational basis, three of the members of the OECDAT are alternates, which means that they might not sit on a case for many years. The OECDAT's advantage is, however, that there is a jurisprudential continuity arising from the stability of its primary panel's composition. It may be noted that while in the OECDAT all of the members must have judicial experience, one of the three panel members in the ESAAB may be a person with practical experience in the highly technical work of the organization.

As to workload, both the ESAAB and the OECDAT hear a small number of cases per year, which indicates that the organizations know how to resolve disputes before they reach their tribunals. Nevertheless, there are occasionally in both tribunals applicants who do not accept unfavorable judgments and who consequently attempt to return to the tribunal. These repetitive cases are, however, dealt with in a relatively expedient manner. Requests for revision, rectification or interpretation of judgments, which are in reality appeals of the original unfavorable judgments, are addressed according to a streamlined procedure by the president after consultation with the two other members of the panel.

Concerning attorneys' fees, the respective Rules of the ESAAB and the OECDAT are relatively flexible. The practice is to grant such expenses on a flat-rate basis rather than on the basis of the actual expenses incurred. Moreover, even when a staff member loses his or her case, partial attorneys' fees are sometimes granted so long as the claim on the merits is not abusive and has a serious foundation.

Lastly, regarding the drafting of judgments, the practice of the ESAAB is to make the ruling known immediately, before the judgment is finalized, while in the OECDAT the practice now is to finalize the judgment before making the ruling known to the parties. As to the actual drafting of the judgments, in both tribunals I, as president, draft all judgments before circulating them to the other members of the panel. One could just as well imagine a rapporteur system for drafting judgments.

* * *

* Président, Commission de recours de l'Agence spatiale européenne; Président, Tribunal administratif de l'Organisation de coopération et de développement économiques.

Je vous remercie de m'avoir invité à participer à cette très intéressante réunion. J'ai le privilège d'être président de deux tribunaux administratifs: la Commission de recours de l'agence spatiale européenne et le Tribunal administratif de l'Organisation de coopération et de développement économiques (OCDE). Ces deux organisations ont leur siège à Paris. J'illustre donc ce qu'évoquait mon éminent collègue Gilbert Guillaume: la possibilité de remédier partiellement à la prolifération des tribunaux administratifs en leur permettant d'avoir des membres communs. J'en profite pour répondre à l'une des questions impromptues que vous nous avez posées, Monsieur le Président: bien que ma double appartenance en soit une illustration, je ne suis pas un partisan de cette prolifération. Je dirais simplement à ce sujet que j'ai eu l'honneur, il y a quelques années, d'être consulté par une importante organisation internationale qui relève actuellement d'un tribunal commun et qui entendait créer sa propre juridiction et que j'ai fortement déconseillé cette création d'un tribunal autonome. J'ai eu la satisfaction de voir que ce projet était resté sans suite. J'aimerais reprendre rapidement un certain nombre des points qui ont été très bien développés par nos rapporteurs et vous-même, Monsieur le Président, et qui se posent de façon tout à fait commune aux différents tribunaux.

Je retire de mon expérience d'environ vingt ans dans chacun de ces tribunaux – un peu plus de vingt ans pour la Commission de recours de l'Agence spatiale européenne et un peu moins de vingt ans pour la Commission puis le Tribunal de l'OCDE – l'impression que des systèmes relativement différents, quant aux règles de procédure notamment, peuvent avoir chacun leurs mérites. Aussi, si je ne suis pas favorable à la prolifération, je ne le suis pas non plus à l'uniformisation. Je crois qu'il est bon que les règles applicables à chaque tribunal tiennent compte des spécificités de l'organisation au sein de laquelle ce tribunal doit fonctionner.

La composition du tribunal

Je prendrai un premier exemple qui concerne la composition même du tribunal. En apparence, les deux tribunaux dont je suis le président ont la même composition de six membres mais, en réalité, la règle est fondamentalement différente. Dans le cas de l'Agence spatiale, les six membres se trouvent à égalité et siègent à tour de rôle, en principe en suivant un ordre aléatoire tel que l'ordre alphabétique. Au contraire, dans le cas de l'OCDE, il y a trois membres titulaires et trois membres suppléants. Ces derniers ne siègent qu'exceptionnellement, lorsqu'un membre titulaire a un empêchement. A titre personnel, je peux dire qu'être membre suppléant dans le cas de l'OCDE est un peu frustrant. Je l'ai été près de dix ans sans jamais être appelé à siéger. Cela n'a donc pas été une très lourde charge pour moi. Mais maintenant que j'ai l'honneur d'être titulaire, je vois l'avantage qu'il y a à siéger pratiquement toujours dans la même composition, quant à l'éventuelle continuité de la jurisprudence et notamment lorsqu'un cas doit être traité à plusieurs reprises. Ainsi, je crois que les deux systèmes ont leurs avantages et leurs inconvénients.

Toujours en ce qui concerne la composition, dans le cas de l'OCDE, la règle qui a été signalée comme la plus courante par Monsieur Ziadé est celle que tous les membres doivent avoir une expérience juridique et doivent être en principe qualifiés pour occuper des fonctions juridictionnelles dans leur Etat d'origine. Dans le cas de l'Agence spatiale, la règle est un peu différente. Dans les textes, mais aussi en pratique, cette exigence de qualification juridique n'est requise que pour deux des juges appelés à siéger. Le troisième peut être une personne qui a une expérience pratique du fonctionnement de l'Agence, soit parce qu'elle a appartenu au personnel de l'Agence, soit parce qu'elle a appartenu, dans son pays, à une administration en relation avec l'Agence. Je constate que pour un tribunal chargé de traiter essentiellement de personnels à qualification technique (ingénieurs ou techniciens), la présence d'un membre non-juriste, mais bon connaisseur de ce milieu professionnel, peut être tout à fait utile. Sur ce point encore, je crois qu'il faut tenir compte des spécificités de chaque organisation et que ce système a lui aussi ses mérites, au moins pour les organisations à caractère très technique comme l'Agence spatiale.

La charge du tribunal

En ce qui concerne la charge de ces deux tribunaux, elle est relativement comparable si l'on rapporte le nombre de recours à l'effectif du personnel. Pour l'Agence, 1700 personnels actifs et 600 personnels retraités relèvent de la Commission de recours; il y a en moyenne un peu moins de 3 affaires par an. Pour l'OCDE, qui compte 2300 actifs et 1250 retraités, il y a à peu près 6 affaires par an. Il y a un peu plus d'affaires dans le cas de l'OCDE, mais c'est relativement comparable. Ce nombre relativement limité de recours montre que, dans les deux cas, les organisations savent assez bien gérer le pré-contentieux et régler un certain nombre de problèmes sans qu'ils viennent devant le Tribunal ou la Commission de recours.

Je voudrais maintenant aborder trois des questions évoquées dans les rapports généraux.

Les recours répétitifs ou abusifs

Monsieur Ziadé nous a présenté une affaire portée devant la Commission de recours de l'OCDE, lorsque je n'étais que juge suppléant. De manière exceptionnelle, la Commission a prononcé une sanction. Il ne s'agissait pas d'une amende, puisque les textes ne le prévoient pas, mais du non-remboursement du cautionnement qui existait à l'époque. En pratique, nous connaissons, dans chacun de ces tribunaux, des requérants qui comprennent mal qu'une première décision leur soit défavorable et qui essaient ensuite de multiplier les recours, mais, au final, ce genre d'affaires se règle relativement facilement.

Certains recours se présentent comme des recours en rectification d'erreurs matérielles ou des recours en révision ou en interprétation. Ils n'en sont pas véritablement et sont des appels ou des contestations au fond de la décision rendue et jugée non satisfaisante. En ce cas, les règles permettent de répondre assez facilement et grâce à une procédure allégée, dès lors que le Président, après avoir éventuellement consulté deux autres membres, estime que le recours n'est pas véritablement un recours en rectification ou en révision mais, en réalité, une contestation au fond de la première décision rendue.

Les frais

En ce qui concerne les frais, je constate que, dans le cas des deux tribunaux, les règles sont relativement souples et que le tribunal peut traiter l'affaire de façon relativement libre. La pratique des conseils des requérants n'est pas toujours de formuler explicitement une demande, sans doute parce que, dans leur propre pays, les règles applicables aux demandes de remboursement de frais d'avocat ne sont pas les mêmes. En pratique, les tribunaux les traitent toujours. Il nous a été présenté un recours en rectification dans un cas où nous avions omis de répondre à une demande de remboursement de frais. Mais la pratique de ces deux tribunaux est d'accorder généralement une somme relativement forfaitaire, certainement inférieure aux honoraires réels perçus par les avocats. Nous tenons évidemment compte des mérites de la demande, du fait qu'elle est accueillie ou non, mais nous n'excluons pas le remboursement d'une partie des frais, même si la requête n'est pas accueillie, dès lors qu'elle n'est pas abusive et qu'elle a un fondement sérieux.

La rédaction et la publicité de la décision

J'aimerais, pour finir, parler de la rédaction et de la publicité de la décision. La pratique des deux tribunaux que je connais est un peu différente. Dans un cas (Commission de recours de l'Agence spatiale), la pratique est de faire connaître immédiatement le dispositif de la décision, quitte à différer, jusqu'à sa rédaction définitive et l'approbation, l'ensemble de la décision avec ses motifs. L'autre tribunal (Tribunal de l'OCDE) avait la même pratique mais s'est finalement rallié à la solution d'attendre la rédaction complète de la décision pour notifier à la fois les motifs et le dispositif.

J'aimerais avoir l'expérience de mes collègues quant aux pratiques de rédaction de ces jugements. Je constate, d'ailleurs avec une certaine vanité, que mes collègues me font très largement confiance au sein des tribunaux que je préside en me confiant la rédaction des projets. C'est un honneur auquel je suis sensible, mais c'est aussi une charge. On pourrait imaginer qu'un rapporteur soit désigné pour rédiger le projet de jugement. Cela ne se passe pas toujours ainsi dans les deux tribunaux que je préside. Il reste que la circulation des projets avec les autres membres du tribunal est très facile, grâce à l'aide très précieuse des greffes des deux tribunaux et que les réactions des collègues sont à la fois rapides et pertinentes, ce qui permet, la plupart du temps, d'avoir une décision rédigée dans un délai inférieur à un mois.

Je vous remercie encore une fois de votre invitation et de votre attention cet après-midi.

Stephen M. Schwebel*

Résumé

Il existe au Fonds monétaire international (FMI) une catégorie d'employés contractuels qui n'ont pas accès au Tribunal administratif car ils ne sont pas considérés comme des membres du personnel alors que l'accès au Tribunal est limité à ces derniers. Dans le cadre du rejet de l'appel de l'un de ces employés contractuels, le Tribunal a relevé ce fait avec inquiétude. Ces employés peuvent avoir recours à l'arbitrage, mais un tel recours n'embrasse pas la question du renouvellement de leurs contrats.

Le Tribunal administratif du Fonds monétaire international (TAFMI) n'est pas une instance d'appel des décisions du Comité des doléances. Le Tribunal est tout à fait libre d'apprécier à nouveau les faits et de tirer de nouvelles conséquences en droit. Le Tribunal se réfère, toutefois, aux procès-verbaux des audiences orales se déroulant devant le Comité.

Pendant de nombreuses années, la question de la prolifération des tribunaux administratifs internationaux ne se posait pas puisque de nombreuses organisations adhéraient à la compétence du Tribunal administratif des Nations Unies ou à celle du Tribunal administratif de l'Organisation internationale du Travail. Le processus de prolifération des tribunaux administratifs a été lancé par la Banque mondiale elle-même.

Au TAFMI, le travail du Secrétariat est très important. Celui-ci prépare pour chaque cas une analyse des précédents ainsi qu'un rapport relatif aux questions soulevées par l'espèce. Un projet regroupant certains éléments du jugement est également préparé par le Secrétariat, ce qui permet d'accélérer le rythme de travail du Tribunal.

Le Tribunal accorde des indemnités pécuniaires ainsi que des frais et des dépens qui peuvent être importants.

La direction du Fonds lit les jugements du Tribunal. Il lui arrive même de modifier son comportement de manière à éviter des recours devant le Tribunal.

Le Statut et le Règlement du TAFMI permettent l'intervention d'une tierce partie à l'instance. Cette intervention peut être favorisée par la circulation d'informations relatives au cas qui est faite à l'intérieur du Fonds par le Secrétariat du Tribunal.

Le Statut du TAFMI permet d'introduire un recours contre des actes réglementaires. L'Association du personnel peut également agir en tant qu'*amicus curiae.*

Une réunion a groupé le Président du Tribunal et son Secrétariat avec des membres de la direction du Fonds ainsi que des membres de l'Association du personnel. La direction du Fonds ainsi que l'Association leur ont assuré qu'elles avaient une perception positive du Tribunal.

* * *

* President, International Monetary Fund Administrative Tribunal; former President, International Court of Justice.

Thank you, Mr. Chairman.

First, I wish to advert to a remark of Professor Tomuschat this morning: the very real question he raised in respect of repeated term contracts. I might note that in the International Monetary Fund (IMF), there are staff who have permanent contracts and staff who have fixed-term contracts. Both categories have the right of recourse to the Administrative Tribunal. But there is a third category of contractual employees – a significant category in the practice of the Fund – who do not have access to the Administrative Tribunal because that access is restricted to "staff members" and their terms of appointment define them as not being "staff members."

Incidentally, as an illustration of *obiter dicta* to which Professor Gorman referred, the Tribunal, in rejecting an appeal of a contractual employee recently, remarked with concern on the fact that there is a category of employees at the Fund who lack the possibility of recourse to the Administrative Tribunal. They do have recourse to arbitration, but that recourse does not embrace consideration of renewal of their contracts.

On the question of whether the International Monetary Fund Administrative Tribunal is a court of appeal from the Grievance Committee, the answer by our precedents is clearly negative. The Tribunal regards itself as free to make findings of fact as well as conclusions of law *de novo*. However, the work of the Grievance Committee is very important for the workings of the Tribunal because the Committee prepares an extensive record of the hearings involving the claimant. The Tribunal takes them as obviating the need for holding oral proceedings itself, though it has recently decided to be more open to that possibility. None have, so far, been held.

On the issue of the proliferation of administrative tribunals, I would like to recall that, for many years, that was not the characteristic procedure. On the contrary, large numbers of organizations adhered to the jurisdiction of the United Nations Administrative Tribunal and even more to that of the ILO Administrative Tribunal, and continue to do so. Perhaps it was the World Bank itself that launched the course of proliferation, a phenomenon that has both advantages and disadvantages.

On the process of the IMF Tribunal's work, I might note that there is heavy reliance on the Registry staff or the Secretariat. For each case, it prepares an Issues and Precedents paper which analyzes the issues at bar in that case and surveys the precedents in other administrative tribunals. This is a very substantial piece of work (25, 50 or more pages) which is circulated among the panel disposing of the case before it meets. When it does meet, it is enabled to render a decision rather rapidly because a draft of elements of the decision has been prepared by the Secretariat with the key questions remaining to be filled in (namely, what is the decision, which way will the Tribunal go, etc.). Once the Tribunal has discussed the matter and made its decision, clearly on its own and without the participation of the Secretariat, then the President of the Tribunal (working with the Secretariat) is in a position to produce the judgment quite rapidly, normally the day after the deliberation. Thus, a case is concluded at that very session.

We have awarded monetary compensation where a judgment went in favor of the applicant in some measure and also awarded costs which were the subject of considerable conflict between the parties. These were not nominal costs; they were significant ones.

On the question of whether management reads the Tribunal's judgments. To do so is not a great burden because there have not been many judgments yet. I am told that they do. Indeed, the General Counsel has assured us that he has been able to persuade the direction of the Fund on more than one occasion not to pursue a certain course of action, cautioning that if that action were pursued, it would result in proceedings before the Administrative Tribunal which the administration would lose.

Third-party intervention is permitted, very definitely, under the Statute and Rules of the IMF Administrative Tribunal. Indeed, when a case is filed, a notice of the cause of action is prepared by the Secretariat staff and circulated throughout the Fund. The purpose of that is to enable a prospective third-party intervenor to intervene. I am unsure whether this has been wholly successful. Early on, the administration of the Fund began to object to any extended description of the cause of action, which it said was nothing more than a potpourri of unfounded allegations of some embarrassment to the administration. These notices have been attenuated, and it is not certain whether they fulfill their function.

Under the Statute of the IMF Administrative Tribunal, regulations as such can be challenged, not only when they impact upon a particular staff member as applied to that staff member. Moreover, *amicus* briefs are accepted: that provision looks particularly towards the possibililty of the Staff Association's serving as *amicus curiae.*

Finally, I might note that the Secretariat and the President of the Tribunal did meet a few months ago with senior officials of the Fund management and the President and other officers of the Staff Association to discuss with them the utility, or lack of utility, of the Tribunal. We were very graciously assured that, despite the fact of our only having had eight cases over the first six years, both management and the Staff Association regard the existence and performance of the Tribunal as positive. Thank you.

Hubert Thierry*

Summary

At the United Nations Administrative Tribunal (UNAT) over which I preside, the Secretariat does very good work, but its staff is limited to two professional-rank staff and two secretaries. It is therefore impossible for them to perform elaborate tasks.

The debate concerning the forthcoming amendments to the UNAT's Statute was initiated during the last session of the UN General Assembly and will be taken up again at its next session. I will summarize in this respect various proposals which were made, particularly by the French delegation.

It has been proposed that the Statute specify that the members of the UNAT must have legal qualifications. However, I agree with Judge Massot that the criteria should not be so restrictive as to exclude the participation of qualified persons who do not have direct legal training.

Another issue concerns the length of the members' terms. Currently, the members have renewable three-year terms. It has been proposed that the terms be for four or five years, so as to allow members to become accustomed to the work of the UNAT and its jurisprudence. A renewable four-year term would be the most practical.

The use of three-member panels to decide all cases is also being debated. Their use, which is mandated by the UNAT Statute, in effect allows judgments to be adopted by two members against one where there is a separate or dissenting opinion. The practice of issuing separate and dissenting opinions is inadvisable in international administrative tribunals. It is even more regrettable when important cases are decided by panels, as the participation of the Tribunal's other judges might have had an effect on the judgment. It has therefore been proposed that when a panel is unable to reach a consensus in a case, the case will be brought before the full Tribunal.

Other issues deserve reflection: Should we maintain the cap of two years' net salary on the amount of compensation that the Tribunal can award? Should the UN Secretary-General be able to choose to award compensation fixed by the Tribunal rather than accept the Tribunal's order to rescind a contested decision? Administrative law specialists would feel uncomfortable with the thought that a managerial decision could be considered null and void by a tribunal and nevertheless remain in force.

With respect to international administrative tribunals in general, it has been proposed by the General Assembly Joint Inspection Unit (JIU) that there be created an exhaustive, comparative table of the jurisprudence of the international

* Président, Tribunal administratif des Nations Unies; Professeur émérite, Université de Paris X.

administrative tribunals, particularly those within the UN family. This would be a good idea. Perhaps another good idea would be for the presidents or members of the different international administrative tribunals to meet together on a regular basis.

* * *

Vous avez eu raison, Monsieur le Président, d'attirer notre attention sur le rôle des greffes et sur la question de l'administration des tribunaux. Le Président Schwebel a traité, sous un certain angle, de cette question. Les greffes font du très bon travail et il convient de leur rendre hommage. On dit parfois greffe et parfois services administratifs. Celui qui joue le rôle de greffier au Tribunal administratif des Nations Unies n'en a pas le titre. Il a le titre de secrétaire exécutif. Mais je préfère l'appellation de greffier.

Sous le signe des économies qui sont imposées aux organes des Nations Unies, nous sommes au Tribunal administratif très mal lotis, non pas par la qualité des personnes, qui est très grande, mais par leur nombre. Notre secrétariat ne compte que deux personnes au rang professionnel, auxquels s'ajoutent deux secrétaires. Il nous est tout à fait impossible de leur demander des tâches aussi élaborées et aussi nécessaires que celles à laquelle vous avez fait allusion il y a un instant, Monsieur le Président.

Cela étant dit, j'aimerais appeler votre attention sur le débat relatif à la révision du statut du Tribunal administratif des Nations Unies. Ce débat a été amorcé lors de la dernière session de l'Assemblée Générale et sera repris lors de la prochaine session. Il a donné lieu à la formulation, tout particulièrement par la délégation française, de différentes suggestions qui sont pour l'essentiel les suivantes.

La qualification des membres du Tribunal

Tout d'abord, dans notre statut, il n'est pas question de la qualification des membres du Tribunal. Ceux-ci n'ont pas encore officiellement droit à l'appellation de juges. Mais il n'est rien dit sur les titres qu'ils doivent avoir. Il est demandé que l'on précise qu'il est nécessaire que les membres aient des qualifications de caractère juridique. Mais je partage ce que Jean Massot a dit tout à l'heure: il ne faut pas que les formules à ce sujet soient trop restrictives et nous avons eu, au sein du Tribunal administratif, le concours de personnes qui n'étaient pas de formation directement juridique, par exemple de l'ambassadeur Samar Sen. Celui-ci a été un Président très éminent de notre juridiction; il ne faudrait pas que des concours de cette qualité soient rendus impossibles par des formulations trop restrictives.

La durée du mandat des membres du Tribunal

Le mandat des membres du Tribunal administratif des Nations Unies est de trois ans. Un certain nombre de nos collègues – et je suis sûr que Monsieur Amerasinghe ne me démentira pas – considère que cette durée est trop courte. A peine le nouveau membre s'est-il habitué au Tribunal, à peine a-t-il acquis la connaissance et la pratique de nos affaires qu'il est appelé à remettre en cause son mandat! Très souvent, il est vrai, les membres sont réélus, mais il n'en reste pas moins que cette exigence de réélection est pesante. Il est proposé quatre ou cinq ans. Un mandat de quatre ans renouvelable serait à mon avis une bonne formule. Je le dis avec d'autant plus de liberté d'esprit que je me trouve dans la neuvième et dernière année de mon mandat.

Le système des panels

Le statut du Tribunal administratif prévoit que les jugements sont rendus par des panels de trois personnes. Il ne pourrait pas en être autrement au sens que si tout le Tribunal, qui est composé de sept membres, devait discuter de chaque affaire, nous n'y arriverions pas puisque nous traitons une soixantaine d'affaires dans l'année. Il n'en reste pas moins que le système des panels de trois membres n'est pas parfait. Je ferai deux remarques à ce sujet. D'une part, je crois qu'il n'est pas souhaitable que la pratique des tribunaux administratifs laisse place à des opinions individuelles et dissidentes. Si celles-ci sont justifiables au sein de la Cour internationale de Justice, elles ne le sont pas pour les tribunaux administratifs, et ce, d'autant plus que leur diffusion est limitée.

Je me suis efforcé, au cours des dernières années, de limiter autant que possible les opinions individuelles et dissidentes qui étaient assez nombreuses dans le passé. Mais le système des panels permet tout de même qu'un jugement soit adopté par deux membres contre un alors que le Tribunal est composé de sept membres. Dans des affaires importantes, il peut être regrettable que le jugement soit rendu par deux juges seulement. On peut imaginer qu'au sein du Tribunal, une majorité de juges n'aurait pas été, s'ils avaient été appelés à participer au jugement, de l'avis qui prévaut dans le jugement. Je pense pour ma part – et cela fait partie des propositions formulées dans le débat de l'Assemblée Générale – qu'en cas de désaccord, c'est-à-dire lorsqu'un panel n'arrive pas au consensus, l'affaire pourrait alors être portée devant le Tribunal dans son ensemble. Ces jugements en séance plénière seraient donc tout à fait exceptionnels mais possibles.

Quelques questions qui méritent également une réflexion

D'autres questions, dont certaines sont complexes et appellent des observations très développées pourraient être abordées. Je ne ferai que les mentionner. Le Tribunal administratif des Nations Unies prévoit que nous ne pouvons accorder des indemnités qu'au niveau de deux ans de salaire net des requérants, sauf exception dûment motivée par le Tribunal. Ces exceptions sont extrêmement rares. Doit-on ou non maintenir ce plafond? C'est une question qui mérite réflexion.

Le Statut de notre Tribunal nous donne un pouvoir d'annulation. Mais le Secrétaire général peut toujours préférer accorder une indemnité – étant entendu que c'est le tribunal qui fixe le montant de l'indemnité – plutôt que de tenir compte de la décision d'annulation. Il peut donc maintenir une décision considérée comme nulle par le Tribunal. Pour ceux qui, comme moi, ont enseigné le droit administratif au début de leur carrière, cette disposition est extrêmement choquante. L'idée qu'une décision considérée comme nulle par une juridiction puisse être néanmoins maintenue me heurte. Il se pose peut-être là un problème de rédaction mais également un problème de fond qui mérite en tout cas réflexion.

Je ferai pour finir deux observations. A propos des juridictions administratives, il existe un rapport établi par le corps commun d'inspection (CCI) de l'Assemblée Générale. Ce document propose, afin que les juridictions puissent tenir compte des décisions qui ont été prises par d'autres juridictions, que l'on établisse un tableau comparatif et exhaustif des différents tribunaux administratifs, tout au moins de ceux de la famille des Nations Unies. Cette suggestion me semble tout à fait heureuse.

Souvent, j'ai eu l'occasion de déplorer l'insuffisance des contacts entre nos différents tribunaux, notamment ceux de la famille des Nations Unies. Le colloque qui nous réunit aujourd'hui et qui est d'un grand intérêt permet de remédier à cette carence. Mais peut-être pourrait-on imaginer un processus permanent ou bien une structure permettant qu'une rencontre régulière soit organisée entre les Présidents ou certains membres des différentes juridictions administratives? C'est une suggestion que je me permets de formuler en vous remerciant de m'avoir accordé la parole.

THE POINT OF VIEW OF RESPONDENT INSTITUTIONS

Chris de Cooker*

Résumé

J'aimerais traiter de deux points:

Le premier concerne la méthode de sélection des juges. A mon avis, la procédure du choix des juges devrait aboutir à la création à l'Agence spatiale européenne d'une Commission de recours harmonieuse et équilibrée. A cette fin, la première chose à faire serait de sonder discrètement les juges en exercice quant à leur désir de prolonger leur mandat pour avoir une idée claire du nombre de postes à pourvoir. C'est alors que nous pourrions nous adresser aux Etats-membres pour les informer des postes disponibles, tout en essayant de préserver au sein de la Commission l'équilibre entre les Etats-membres quant à leur taille et à leur système juridique. En dernier recours, le Directeur-Général de l'Agence spatiale européenne pourrait, si le nombre de candidats proposés n'était pas suffisant, en proposer d'autres lui-même, après consultation de l'Association du personnel. En tout état de cause, le Règlement de la Commission de recours de l'Agence spatiale européenne permet à des non-juristes de faire partie de la Commission, ce qui est éminemment souhaitable dans une organisation scientifique comme la nôtre.

Le second point concerne la prolifération des tribunaux. Je suis convaincu de la nécessité d'une Commission de recours propre à l'Agence spatiale européenne. La Commission comprend la culture de l'Agence et s'exprime d'une manière claire et concise. Ses jugements sont acceptés par toutes les parties. Cette proximité que vise la Commission de recours est mieux servie par la procédure orale qui donne aux requérants (y compris à ceux qui perdent éventuellement leurs cas) une meilleure chance de s'exprimer.

En conclusion, je crois qu'une bonne procédure pré-contentieuse pour la résolution des conflits permettrait d'éviter nombre de procès et rendrait les procédures abusives extrêmement rares.

* * *

Thank you, Mr. Chairman. It is certainly not easy to take the floor after so many distinguished speakers who spoke before me, many of whom have addressed the points that I wanted to raise.

I have been invited to speak as a representative of a respondent institution. I would prefer to see my task as larger than that. My Director-General, whom I represent before the Tribunal, has many functions within the organization. One of these is to see to it that we have a proper system

* Head of Staff Regulations and Central Support Division, Personnel Department, European Space Agency; former Senior Lecturer, Law Faculty, Leiden University.

of justice in the organization. Therefore, his function goes beyond the concept of defending oneself in court.

I would like to raise one or two points that have not yet been addressed. The first one is the selection of judges. It is sometimes said and written that the selection and appointment of judges is political because the decision is taken by the Council. I should add a few footnotes here. As the Head of my organization and his staff see it, a procedure must be developed around the selection in order to allow for the creation of a harmonious and balanced Appeals Board.

The first step that has to be taken in this respect is to check who among the sitting judges are willing to serve for a further period. This sometimes requires a little bit of diplomacy. We can either approach a judge directly or through the delegation of the Member State. Under normal circumstances, we can quickly obtain an indication of the number of members who will stay on the Board and thereby an idea of the number of vacancies.

The Rules then provide that we should address ourselves to all of our Member States and inform them of the existence of the vacancies. A normal letter is sent out to all the delegations. Sometimes, we receive replies. It may seem surprising to you, but very often we receive no replies. It seems that people are not lining up to become members of the Appeals Board. We are, therefore, forced to undertake the delicate task of reminding certain delegations of the existence of these vacancies. We may remind some delegations less insistently than others. Here begins the process of building a balanced representation on the Appeals Board – our objective is to attract people from different Member States, from States of different sizes (big and small) and also the representation of different legal disciplines.

In the last instance, the Director-General may propose candidates after consulting with the Staff Association. This only happens if there are not enough candidates. In such a case, he will present only the number of candidates required to fill the positions. We have so far been able to avoid the embarrassing situation of holding a vote. We should avoid election campaigns, and we are modest enough to realize that an appointment to the Appeals Board is not like an appointment to the International Court of Justice.

As Mr. Massot has already indicated, our Rules also allow that non-lawyers sit on the Appeals Board. This has happened quite regularly. We are very satisfied with the different viewpoints, approaches and ideas that these people have brought to the decisions. Indeed, in a scientific and technical organization, projects come and go. Sometimes they are interrupted for budgetary or political reasons. The structures that go with that change rapidly as well. In order to assess the claims of certain claimants, a good insight into the functioning of the organization is required.

My next point is on the proliferation of tribunals. I am also convinced that the European Space Agency needs its own Appeals Board. The Agency is different from other institutions. We have been very lucky in that the Appeals Board understands our culture, is close to the people and is able to explain the judgments in clear and concise terms. The judgments are not very long. They are precise, to the point and acceptable to everyone.

For the Appeals Board, to be close to the people means that it needs to hold oral hearings. This is important to claimants even if they lose their cases. In our experience, individuals always have the chance to express themselves, even when they are represented by a lawyer. This is a very positive point.

Although it may not be appropriate to say this before so many distinguished judges, I do not like to go to court. This is not because I am afraid to go to court or afraid to lose a case. Statistics show that organizations win cases because the administrations in these organizations do not pursue cases that they might lose. The reason for which I do not like to go to the Appeals Board lies elsewhere. I think that many of you know that I am a strong believer in pre-litigation procedures. Neither we nor our organizations are perfect. It is never too late to explain situations and legislation or to hold discussions with or without the help of a third party. It is never too late to compromise. Even when written communications are being exchanged within the appeals process, it is still not too late. Pre-litigation only ends when the Chairman of the Appeals Board opens the hearing in a case. I have been present in several cases where the Chairman postponed the opening of a hearing by one hour in order to allow the parties to discuss one more time. Needless to say, the Chairman never opened that hearing.

As far as suggestions about vexatious and frivolous appeals are concerned, everyone finds them frustrating, irritating and a waste of time. I find that such appeals should be avoided by proper dialogue and proper pre-litigation. However, the existence of one such case every few years is the price to pay to have an open system. This is the last thing on which I would like to compromise. As you have probably understood, I view going to court as a lost possibility to settle a case. Thank you, Mr. Chairman.

Dominick Devlin*

Résumé

L'Organisation internationale du Travail (OIT) n'est pas seulement une organisation défenderesse puisque les services de son Tribunal sont ouverts à d'autres organisations: en effet, 37 organisations en font usage.

La question posée par le président de séance est déconcertante: "A-t-on vraiment besoin d'un tribunal administratif? Pourquoi ne pas saisir les juridictions locales?" Je soumettrai à ce propos deux considérations: l'une d'ordre philosophique, l'autre d'ordre pratique. La considération *philosophique* s'exprime en ce qu'une organisation internationale est supposée exécuter sa mission en totale indépendance, sans subir aucune influence de l'un ou l'autre des Etats en cause. C'est la raison pour laquelle les organisations intergouvernementales bénéficient d'une immunité. L'aspect le plus important de cette immunité commande que tous les litiges soient réglés de manière appropriée. La considération *pratique* est que nous avons des bureaux partout dans le monde, et que les différents tribunaux du monde n'offrent pas tous les mêmes garanties d'une bonne administration de la justice.

Les réflexions formulées durant cette session ont fait naître plusieurs questions. Je répondrai à deux d'entre elles: Que demandons-nous à notre Tribunal administratif? Qu'avons-nous obtenu de notre Tribunal administratif?

- Nous voulons que soit rendue la meilleure justice possible; une telle qualité de justice aidera certainement la direction de l'OIT à faire coordonner son comportement avec les solutions du Tribunal.
- Nous voulons un Tribunal efficace où le travail s'exécute rapidement. C'est dans ce but de célérité que nous préférons la procédure écrite et souhaitons être dispensés de la procédure orale. Se dispenser de la procédure orale nécessite d'avoir des comités internes d'appel de grande qualité qui serviront de lien entre le Tribunal et l'organisation concernée.
- Concernant les faits, notamment en matière d'investigation, il est important que les tribunaux n'aient pas à les établir mais qu'ils les admettent tels qu'ils leur sont présentés. A ce propos, mon interprétation des jugements *Mussnig* et *Eben-Moussi* est différente de celle du juge Fernando.
- L'idée d'une juridiction d'appel par rapport aux jugements des tribunaux administratifs ne nous paraît pas satisfaisante. Par contre, nous sommes en faveur de l'évaluation du rendement des juges et en faveur de la tenue de réunions entre les représentants des organisations et des associations du personnel en présence de membres du Tribunal.

* Legal Adviser, International Labour Office; former Senior Legal Officer, World Health Organization.

En bref, nous souhaiterions avoir le meilleur Tribunal composé des meilleurs juges.

Le Réglement du Tribunal administratif de l'OIT (TAOIT) est beaucoup moins développé que ceux des autres tribunaux: il ne contient pas de dispositions concernant les frais ou concernant la révision des jugements. Il est également silencieux sur la question relative aux opinions dissidentes, bien qu'elles soient admises en pratique par le Tribunal.

Le Statut du TAOIT prévoit la réintégration du requérant à son poste sans laisser à la direction elle-même le choix de lui payer une indemnité pour le préjudice subi.

Le TAOIT a jugé qu'il était possible d'attaquer les mesures de nature générale pourvu que ces mesures ne puissent pas entraîner des décisions individuelles. Ce jugement ne favorise pas la prévisibilité des solutions.

* * *

Thank you, Mr. Chairman. The ILO is another respondent organization. It could also be said to be a provider of services since it makes its Administrative Tribunal available to other organizations. At this moment, approximately 37 organizations avail themselves of the ILO Administrative Tribunal. The Administrative Tribunal of the International Labour Organization is also the oldest of the tribunals since it is the successor of the Tribunal of the League of Nations.

Before coming here, I had tried to put my thoughts into a logical order, but I am afraid that all the conversation and the interesting presentations have completely distracted me and pushed me onto other tracks. Our Chairman's statements were particularly disconcerting: to state before a legal adviser of an international organization, "Do you really need an administrative tribunal? Why not go before Swiss (or local) courts?" is like waving a red blanket before a bull. I will not answer the question in full since a lot has been written on it. Instead, I will submit two considerations: one philosophical and the other practical.

Firstly, the philosophical one. An intergovernmental organization is supposed to be at the service of the international community to perform its mission in full independence and without any kind of interference or the impression of influence from any particular State. It is for this reason that sovereign States have made intergovernmental organizations subjects of international law. Intergovernmental organizations do not have, of course, the same immunity as States. One very important aspect of the immunity of intergovernmental organizations is that all disputes have to be settled by an appropriate mode of settlement. Perhaps the case could be made for saying that organizations need not have immunity when they are acting on the local level of a State (for example, in the purchasing of goods). However, when they act in the international domain, why should disputes that belong to that international domain be submitted to a national court? It would, in particular, give a very bad impression to the other Member States.

The practical reason is that our headquarters are in Switzerland, and I believe that we can have every confidence in the Swiss courts. However, we are also located around the world in places where many people would not have confidence in the local courts. It would be impossible to state overtly: Swiss courts are trustworthy while others may not be.

The reflections at this session raised three questions in my mind: What do we want from our Administrative Tribunal? What do we actually have from our Administrative Tribunal? How should judges be appointed? I will not have time to address the last question. I can merge the first two questions by stating that we have what we want. Most legal advisers are satisfied with our Tribunal. I do not believe that what we want is very different from what the complainants want, though I stand to be corrected by Maître Sicault later.

We want the best possible justice, which will indeed strengthen our position. We cannot tell our administration, or indeed our Director-General, that what he or she proposes to do is unjust. However, we can easily say that if the matter goes before the Tribunal, we will lose the case. The Tribunal provides great support in this way.

We want an efficient Tribunal. This implies a Tribunal that works as quickly as possible. This is why we like written proceedings and we would prefer normally not to have oral proceedings. Taking into account what has been said here today, especially by Judge Schwebel, it is essential to have a high-quality internal Appeals Committee if oral proceedings are not held. Such a Committee could sift the facts and give the Tribunal a taste of how "normal" officials in the organization think. In other words, the link between the Tribunal and the organizations themselves could come through the internal Appeals Committee, if that Committee is reliable.

Another point concerns investigations. It is important that tribunals take the facts as they are presented. This is why I take a different view, with due respect to Justice Fernando, on the *Mussnig* decision (ILOAT, Judgment No. 1376), which I thought to be very logical. Whether or not sexual harassment actually took place in this case was not relevant in the light of the legal considerations. In my view, this judgment said that, where an organization receives a complaint of sexual harassment, it must investigate the accusation. The organization concerned in this case did not even invite a denial from the alleged perpetrator. The Tribunal, therefore, took the normal attitude: since the acts were not denied, it must act on the assumption that sexual harassment had occurred. Later, when the person who had been accused of sexual harassment came forward and said "You should have defended me, I did not commit harassment," the Tribunal was again correct in awarding compensation to that person for not having given him an opportunity to defend himself (*Eben-Moussi*, ILOAT Judgment No. 1619).

We have discussed matters with legal advisers of other organizations and have all agreed on the need for the best possible Tribunal made up of the best possible judges. We would expect certainty and predictability from our Tribunal. We are prepared to put up with wrong decisions from time to time in order to ensure greater speed. There is not great enthusiam – though some organizations would like it – to have an appeals jurisdiction above the Tribunal. Thus, in answer to Judge Ajibola's question as to who will judge the judges themselves, I would agree with Professor Gorman, who suggested that we draw up performance evaluations of the judges. We can also have meetings. One year ago, we had a very successful meeting with approximately half of our 37 other organizations. Our President, Michel Gentot, kindly agreed to attend as well. All of the legal advisers were very satisfied. We also had representatives of the Federation of International Civil Servants Associations.

I shall now address the questions raised by Mr. Ziadé. I have learned quite a lot on the general powers of the tribunals today. The ILO Administrative Tribunal is less regulated in many respects than many others as far as procedure is concerned: neither costs nor revision of judgments are covered. The Rules were laid down by the Tribunal and we are satisfied with the Rules. We want the Tribunal to stick to the law that it has to apply. But since the members of the Tribunal are all eminent judges, we also want them to be free as to the procedure that they will follow, provided that they set down what that procedure is. Again, it seems from what I have heard that the Statute of the ILO Tribunal is one of the rare ones that allows for reinstatement without stating that the executive head can decide to pay compensation instead. Incidentally, while nothing is said about dissenting opinions in the Rules, they are allowed by the Tribunal in practice.

Another issue that has been raised is a little bit worrying from the point of view of predictability. This is the question of whether or not a complainant can attack a measure of a general nature. (This possibility has been confused with the question of whether a Tribunal can strike down or nullify an act of the legislature by reference to a higher norm. It can of course always do so where the higher norm is one that has already been decided by the legislature.) The ILO Administrative Tribunal has decided that it is possible to attack measures of a general nature, provided that the measure concerned is not of a kind that would lead to individual decisions. Where, however, it could lead to individual decisions, it cannot be attacked. This position has a worrying consequence: whenever an individual decision is contested at a later time, the complainant is entitled to contest the legality of the old general measure to the extent that it is the basis of the individual decision attacked. This means that, twenty years later, we can suddenly find that a staff rule of ours is invalid, even though we have been acting on it for a very long time.

I think that I ought to stop there, Mr. Chairman, because I have exceeded my time. Thank you.

David Rivero*

Résumé

Les audiences relatives à l'instruction sont les audiences consacrées à l'interrogatoire et au contre-interrogatoire des témoins. Ces audiences sont-elles utiles? L'impression dominante, à la Banque mondiale, est que l'audition des témoins est nécessaire pour assurer une procédure équitable. Le personnel de la Banque souhaite que ces audiences aient lieu plus fréquemment au Tribunal administratif de la Banque mondiale (TABM). Si la tenue de telles audiences favorise la perception que la procédure est équitable, le TABM devrait y recourir plus fréquemment.

La répartition des frais et honoraires d'avocats encourus par l'institution est une question délicate où le souci de pénaliser les procédures abusives devrait aller de pair avec celui de ne pas dissuader les requérants de bonne foi.

Deux types d'indemnité pour la partie requérante sont concevables: la compensation pécuniaire et l'exécution en nature. Pour un grand nombre d'employés, la compensation pécuniaire n'est pas toujours adéquate et l'exécution en nature (à savoir le rétablissement du requérant dans ses fonctions) peut être plus appropriée. Cependant, au vu des problèmes que pourrait soulever l'exécution en nature, le Statut du TABM dispose que celle-ci devrait être laissée à la discrétion de l'institution défenderesse.

Les faits constatés par les comités d'appel devraient-ils lier les tribunaux administratifs? Je ne le crois pas car les règles de preuve et d'établissement des faits à ce stade ne sont pas très fiables à la Banque mondiale.

Enfin, je voudrais ajouter qu'un effort certain est fourni à la Banque mondiale pour assurer la communication des jugements du TABM à la direction: tout le monde devrait apprendre de nos erreurs.

* * *

Thank you, Mr. Chairman. This afternoon I would like to touch upon four areas that have been raised already: evidentiary hearings; the awarding of costs and attorney's fees; other types of remedies; and the binding nature of fact-finding at levels below the tribunal stage.

Like the American law professor, my goal is to raise issues and provoke some discussion following our comments today. Unlike the American law professor, I would like to supply answers to these issues, hopefully even the right ones.

* Chief Counsel, Administration, World Bank; former Associate, Cole & Corette, Washington, DC.

Evidentiary Hearings

The first issue that I would like to focus on today is: Do we need evidentiary hearings in tribunal proceedings? By evidentiary hearings, I mean hearings in which witnesses are called and subjected to examination and cross-examination. This raises the question of whether the written record is adequate to provide sufficient basis for an informed decision by the tribunal. It also raises the question of whether witness testimony helps to clarify the evidence on record or confuses it further. At the World Bank, there is a very strong feeling, among the staff at least, that the examination of witnesses is fundamental to due process. The staff also feel that they have the inherent right to call and examine witnesses and to cross-examine adversarial witnesses. They regularly point to the fact that, at some administrative tribunals, this is a routine aspect of their proceedings. They ask why that is not the case at the World Bank Administrative Tribunal or why it is not the case more frequently.

I feel that the staff's perception of the process is as important as the outcome of specific cases. If evidentiary hearings promote the perception, if not the fact, of full due process, then I would submit that they should be used as appropriate.

The Awarding of Costs and Attorney's Fees

The second issue that I would like to touch upon is the awarding of costs by tribunals. I am using the term "costs" in a restricted sense to refer to attorney's fees, in particular costs and attorney's fees that are assessed against applicants who do not prevail or who bring frivolous cases, however that might be defined. (A frivolous case is a very difficult concept to define in actual practice.)

Another related issue is what costs should be awarded. How do you assess the value of attorney's fees in a proceeding and the other costs associated with defending an action that has been brought? Nassib Ziadé raises a very fair point when he asks whether this action would have a chilling effect on applicants. Perhaps it is a matter of simple justice, to the organization in some cases, to have these awarded.

My own view is that this is a very difficult matter. I believe that if the controlling statute allows it, the responsible exercise of this power could have a very salutary effect, particularly in cases at least where frivolous actions are brought or repetitive consecutive actions arise from the same body of dispute.

Other Types of Remedy

I would like to move to my third point, namely the remedies awarded by international administrative tribunals. Is monetary compensation always adequate? In the Bank, we have the option between specific performance or monetary compensation. I wonder whether specific performance (in other words, reinstatement) should be the only just outcome in some cases. Should reinstatement ever be an option to the institution?

There is a widely held view among staff that compensation alone is not enough in some cases. I recognize at the same time that reinstatement can be very problematic in some cases. I would conclude that the Tribunal's Statute has found the appropriate balance by stating that it should be left to the respondent institution to determine in light of all these factors whether reinstatement is appropriate.

The Binding Nature of Fact-Finding Prior to the Tribunal Stage

The issue was raised whether the findings of appeals committees should be binding on administrative tribunals. I believe that we should be wary to adopt such a rule. The World Bank has not yet developed rules of evidence at the level below the Administrative Tribunal and the fact-finding there is not very reliable.

One final comment that I would like to raise is on the issue of whether management ever learns about the Tribunal's decisions. We are making a very strong effort – Mr. Shihata actually provided senior management with summaries of the Tribunal's decisions. In the legal administration unit, we are emphasizing outreach on lessons learned so that everyone learns from our mistakes. Thank you.

THE POINT OF VIEW OF COUNSEL FOR APPLICANTS

Giovanni Palmieri*

Summary

This Conference's organizers need to be commended for including staff representatives in its work.

Staff representatives must deal with both the administration and the board of directors of the organization. The board of directors is often inaccessible and immune from suit, but may be affected by class actions that succeed in rescinding the application of administrative decisions enacted by the board. The board is normally involved in the process of nominating tribunal members, which may raise questions as to a lack of impartiality on the part of board members. One way to promote impartiality is for staff associations to be involved in the nominating process, as is already done with respect to some international administrative tribunals.

Staff representatives view the legal and administrative competence of tribunal members as a prerequisite for maintaining impartiality. They prefer that former staff members as well as former government representatives before the organization be prohibited from membership of the tribunal. Staff representatives also prefer that tribunal members serve simultaneously on other tribunals, in that such experience helps the members to become specialists in international administrative law and promotes further consistency in the law.

Concerning international administrative tribunals in general, other ideas that merit approval include: (i) rendering judgments as expeditiously as reasonably possible, the more so since cases in which a tribunal provisionally suspends a contested administrative decision are extremely rare and limited; (ii) enabling applicants to submit pleadings in their own language, as is allowed by the European Space Agency Appeals Board (ESAAB); (iii) requiring those who represent applicants to be sufficiently qualified in international administrative law; (iv) awarding legal fees commensurate with market rates; (v) having organizations avoid unjustifiably accusing applicants of submitting abusive claims, as the International Labour Organization Administrative Tribunal (ILOAT) has found in 1988 in its *West (No. 10)* judgment that "[t]he existence of the right [to submit an internal appeal and to resort ultimately to the Tribunal] is in the interests of both sides since it serves to maintain harmony, general efficiency and good morale in the Organisation"; and (vi) creating a procedure for applicants to appeal international administrative tribunal judgments, as is the case in domestic administrative law.

* * *

* Président du Comité des représentants du personnel des organisations coordonnées; Chef de la Division Union Européenne, Conseil de l'Europe.

J'aimerais féliciter les organisateurs de ce colloque qui ont associé à la réflexion des juges et des représentants des administrations également les représentants du personnel.

Dans la plupart des cas, les représentants du personnel ne se trouvent pas en face d'un monolithe mais plutôt d'un système à deux têtes: d'un côté, le visage de l'Administration, de l'autre, celui de l'organe directeur de l'organisation. Ce dernier est souvent inaccessible et inattaquable. Mais le recours collectif, notamment le recours en matière de rémunérations et de pensions, peut casser les actes d'application des décisions administratives prises par les organes directeurs. Ces derniers peuvent donc être atteints par les foudres d'une sentence. Parfois, cela soulève des problèmes politiques très difficiles. Je me réfère par exemple au recours du Comité du personnel du Conseil de l'Europe No. 2 qui mettait en cause une dérogation *ad hoc* et *ad personam* au Statut du personnel. Cette dérogation était mise en œuvre par le Secrétaire général mais autorisée par le Comité des ministres. Il a fallu au Secrétaire général faire preuve de beaucoup de pédagogie pour expliquer aux diplomates qui représentent les ministres à Strasbourg que dans tous les Etats de droit, modèle que défend le Conseil de l'Europe, il y a des législateurs qui croient bien faire, des administrés qui s'estiment lésés et des juges qui sont susceptibles de donner raison tantôt aux uns, tantôt aux autres.

Je saisis cette occasion pour souligner l'opportunité d'améliorer la formation des diplomates en matière de fonction publique internationale. Je pense aux diplomates appelés à servir dans une organisation internationale pour représenter leurs pays et aux fonctionnaires nationaux appelés à siéger dans des organes internationaux.

L'importance du recours collectif au cours des dernières années a jeté une lumière nouvelle sur la procédure de nomination des membres des tribunaux. En effet, la circonstance que le choix des juges revient aux organes directeurs n'est pas sans soulever des problèmes de principe. Or le personnel est très attaché au principe de l'impartialité. Au Conseil de l'Europe, comme vous le savez, le président et le président suppléant du Tribunal administratif sont élus par la Cour européenne des droits de l'homme parmi les juristes qui exercent ou ont exercé des fonctions judiciaires nationales ou internationales. Pour les représentants du personnel, il s'agit d'un gage important d'impartialité.

Les consultations des représentants du personnel quant au choix des juges poursuivent un objectif analogue. On nous a dit que ce type de consultations existait à l'Agence spatiale. Au sein de l'OTAN, des négociations durent depuis plus d'un an entre les représentants du personnel et le Secrétaire général. Elles devraient permettre à court terme aux représentants du personnel de proposer des noms de personnes qualifiées et impartiales au conseil de l'Organisation qui resterait souverain pour les désigner, bien entendu.

La compétence juridique et/ou administrative des juges constitue l'un des présupposés de l'indépendance. Les représentants du personnel ont toujours admis que les anciens membres du personnel ne pouvaient en principe pas faire de bons juges. Pour des raisons de symétrie, ils sont très méfiants lorsqu'un diplomate qui a servi dans la représentation permanente auprès d'une organisation déterminée, jusqu'à la veille ou presque, devient juge d'un tribunal administratif. Or cela se produit parfois.

Le personnel voit d'un œil favorable la circonstance qu'une même personne soit juge de deux juridictions administratives à la fois. En effet, non seulement le rapprochement entre la jurisprudence des différents tribunaux peut contribuer à un plus grand degré de certitude du droit de la fonction publique internationale mais le personnel a tout intérêt à ce que les juges soient au départ, ou deviennent rapidement, des spécialistes du droit de la fonction publique internationale.

Par ailleurs, les juridictions administratives internationales, lorsqu'elles rendent leurs sentences, se devraient de respecter le plus possible le délai raisonnable, délai consacré par exemple par l'article 6 paragraphe 1 de la Convention européenne des droits de l'homme. Cette exigence est d'autant plus forte que les cas où le tribunal suspend les effets d'une décision administrative pouvant faire grief sont extrêmement rares et limités.

Pour ce qui est de l'emploi des langues, la disposition applicable à la Commission de recours de l'Agence spatiale européenne, citée dans le rapport introductif de Monsieur Ziadé, est particulièrement intéressante dans la mesure où un agent d'une nationalité donnée peut choisir, pour l'assister, un juriste de la même nationalité. Il s'agit malheureusement d'une disposition isolée en raison, je suppose, des coûts d'interprétation qu'elle implique pour l'organisation. Cependant, elle octroie au requérant un droit supplémentaire, droit dont la portée n'est pas négligeable.

En ce qui concerne la représentation des requérants, une pratique était assez répandue il y a quelques années. Elle permettait à un autre agent de la même organisation de représenter un collègue devant le tribunal. Cette pratique s'est quelque peu perdue. J'y vois un signe de la complexité accrue des affaires et du profil hautement professionnel et spécialisé que l'on demande aux conseils des requérants. Ces conseils se trouvent, en effet, confrontés aux conseillers juridiques des organisations et à des collaborateurs rompus à l'exégèse des textes de l'organisation et à l'analyse de la jurisprudence administrative internationale.

Ces considérations sur l'opportunité d'avoir recours à des juristes ou des avocats spécialisés m'amènent à souligner que certaines juridictions octroient des remboursements de frais de recours excessivement bas. C'est le cas par exemple de la Commission de recours de l'OTAN. Ce clivage entre les honoraires du marché et le remboursement que l'on peut espérer constitue un frein au bon fonctionnement de la justice administrative.

Nous avons beaucoup parlé aujourd'hui de l'abus de droit de recours. J'aimerais pour ma part en parler autrement. Certaines organisations ont parfois tendance à accuser à tort un requérant d'abus de droit de recours. Cela tient sans doute au fait que dans la culture de certaines organisations, le recours est vu comme une sorte de crime de lèse-majesté. En revanche, le Tribunal de l'Organisation internationale du Travail a affirmé, dans son jugement No. 885 du 30 juin 1988 relatif à l'affaire *West (No. 10)*, que "le droit de recours existe dans l'intérêt des deux parties, car il sert à maintenir l'harmonie, la bonne exécution du travail et un bon moral au sein de l'Organisation". Bref, le recours constitue une occasion pour enrichir le patrimoine juridique de l'organisation, pour répondre à des questions restées jusque-là sans réponse, pour dénoncer l'existence de lacunes juridiques (par exemple, la récente décision du Tribunal administratif du Conseil de l'Europe rendue sur recours No. 255/1999) ou pour indiquer au législateur la voie à suivre (par exemple, la décision du 28 février 1992 relative à l'affaire *Parsons* en matière d'égalité entre les hommes et les femmes de la Commission de recours du Conseil de l'Europe rendue sur le recours 167/1991).

J'aimerais souligner l'importance que nous accordons à la tendance pour la création d'instances d'appel. L'absence d'une procédure d'appel constitue à notre époque une situation qui contribue à isoler la fonction publique internationale de l'évolution propre au droit administratif et aux fonctions publiques des Etats de droit. La fonction publique internationale est liée au droit international public mais elle est déconnectée du droit administratif national. C'est un sujet sérieux sur lequel le législateur et les représentants du personnel seront amenés à se pencher dans un avenir proche. L'institution des procédures d'appel serait un bon garde-fou.

Une intervention d'un représentant du personnel semblerait louche si elle ne revêtait pas un aspect revendicatif. C'est pourquoi j'ai essayé de ne pas susciter votre perplexité et de donner à mon discours une petite touche revendicatrice!

Jean-Didier Sicault*

Summary

I will address the following three themes in my capacity as counsel for applicants before international administrative tribunals: (i) oral proceedings; (ii) revision of judgments; and (iii) the use of jurisprudence to guide potential applicants.

With respect to oral proceedings, which are generally favored by individual applicants and staff associations, a distinction should be made between the evidence-gathering and pleadings phases. The evidence-gathering phase, which is the more important of the two, has been highly developed in the Inter-American Development Bank Administrative Tribunal (IDBAT). There, evidence-gathering precedes pleadings by weeks or even months. Prior to hearing testimony at the oral evidence-gathering proceedings, the President of the Tribunal rules on the points on which evidence will be heard as well as on the admissibility of the different witnesses' testimonies. This can lead to a long evidentiary hearing, during which the Tribunal can also order the production of documents. Moreover, after the hearing both parties must submit memorials on the probative value of the testimonies heard. This procedure, though complex, is extremely useful and informative for the Tribunal.

Regarding revision of judgments, applicants who win their cases are very happy that judgments are final, while those who lose complain bitterly that they have no further avenue of appeal. Such losing applicants sometimes resort to the only legitimate means by which they can change the outcome of their cases, namely procedures allowing for the revision of judgments. While some tribunals allow for the revision of a judgment only upon the discovery of a new fact, the International Labour Organization Administrative Tribunal (ILOAT), starting with the *de Villegas (No. 4)* case, has also allowed for the revision of judgments on other grounds such as, notably, an omission by the Tribunal to pass judgment on a claim or to take account of essential facts, or, even more importantly, a material error which involves no exercise of judgment. These grounds for revision, and particularly that of material error, represent important safety valves for losing applicants.

Lastly, when potential applicants seek advice as to the possibility of success, their cases are examined not only in the light of the applicable sources of law but also with specific reference to the jurisprudence of the relevant tribunal. Such an approach cannot always guarantee predictable results, however, as the tribunal may in a given case: (i) accept new arguments dictated by new circumstances; (ii) rely on the jurisprudence of other tribunals; or (iii) change its existing law on a given point. Another problem is that different panels of judges from the same tribunal sometimes develop different case law with respect to the same issue. This

* Chargé du cours de droit de la fonction publique internationale aux Universités Paris I et Paris II; Avocat à la Cour d'appel de Paris.

latter problem can be remedied by submitting such divided panel opinions to the tribunal in plenary session for final determination.

* * *

J'ai le triste privilège d'être le dernier intervenant au titre des représentants des requérants. J'ai, en effet, été invité en qualité de représentant des requérants et mon propos sera donc fondé sur les préoccupations de ceux-ci. J'ai d'ailleurs modifié les sujets dont je voulais vous parler en fonction de vos remarques introductives, Monsieur le Président. Je ne vais certainement pas vous parler, malgré votre suggestion, du comportement inapproprié ou de l'inconduite des conseils, certainement par ignorance de la chose. J'aimerais traiter trois thèmes: la procédure orale – je partage assez sur ce sujet les propos de Monsieur Rivero –; le recours en révision à la lumière du caractère définitif des jugements, et ce, dans une optique légèrement différente de celle du Président Fernando; l'utilisation de la jurisprudence pour l'orientation des requérants potentiels.

La procédure orale

Je crois qu'on peut très bien se débrouiller sans procédure orale. Mais les requérants individuels ou les associations du personnel sont cependant plutôt en faveur de ces procédures. Je distinguerai dans la procédure orale, deux phases complètement distinctes et qui ont un objet tout à fait différent: la phase de l'instruction et la phase des plaidoiries. De mon point de vue, la phase de l'instruction est la plus importante dans la procédure orale. En cela, je rejoins tout à fait ce que mon parfois adversaire institutionnel, Monsieur Rivero, a dit. J'aimerais à cet égard donner en exemple les règles très particulières qui existent au Tribunal administratif de la Banque interaméricaine de développement.

Dans cette organisation, il y a presque toujours une instruction séparée de plusieurs semaines, voire de plusieurs mois, des plaidoiries. Avant que ne se tienne l'instruction, le Président du Tribunal demande aux conseils des deux parties d'indiquer les points sur lesquels devront porter les témoignages. Il statue sur la recevabilité de ces points comme sur l'admissibilité des témoignages de tel ou tel témoin. Cette question réglée, l'audience relative aux témoignages est souvent longue: pratiquement une journée. Elle consiste en interrogatoires et contre-interrogatoires menés très librement sous la direction du Président. Au cours de cette audience, le Tribunal peut ordonner à l'une ou à l'autre des parties ou aux deux d'entre elles de produire des documents. Un laps de temps est ensuite accordé pour permettre la production de ces documents. Ensuite, il y a obligation pour les deux parties de soumettre un mémoire sur la valeur probante des témoignages entendus. Cette procédure, qui semble assez complexe, est extrêmement utile. Elle donne un éclairage très différent de l'affaire. Quelquefois, elle la fait basculer pour le meilleur ou pour le pire, selon le camp dans lequel on se trouve. Je crois que le Tribunal est beaucoup mieux informé après une procédure de cet ordre. Je dois dire que si l'on me donnait à choisir entre abandonner l'instruction ou abandonner les plaidoiries, j'abandonnerais très volontiers les plaidoiries, car un mémoire définitif peut très bien résumer l'argumentation. En revanche, ce qu'apporte le témoignage oral est tout à fait important.

Le recours en révision à la lumière du caractère définitif des jugements

Les requérants sont très satisfaits que les jugements des tribunaux administratifs internationaux soient, sauf l'exception mentionnée de la procédure de réformation du Tribunal administratif de l'OIT, définitifs. Surtout quand ils gagnent! En revanche, ils se plaignent amèrement de l'absence d'un double degré de juridiction lorsqu'ils perdent. C'est dans la nature des choses. Voilà peut-être pourquoi les requérants prêtent tant d'attention aux voies de recours ouvertes devant le tribunal devant lequel ils ont perdu leur affaire. En particulier, ils prêtent beaucoup d'attention au recours en révision.

Monsieur Ziadé, dans son rapport écrit si rigoureux, si minutieux, a réservé le vocable de recours en révision aux seuls cas dans lesquels un fait nouveau peut justifier un tel recours. Du coup, la jurisprudence *de Villegas* du Tribunal administratif de l'OIT de 1981 qui a été confirmée par la suite n'apparaît pas dans le texte. Cela est tout à fait normal car elle admet d'autres cas d'ouverture du recours, notamment l'omission de statuer sur des conclusions mais aussi l'omission de tenir compte de faits essentiels et surtout une erreur matérielle qui n'implique pas un jugement de valeur. Certes, le Tribunal n'encourage pas – c'est le moins que l'on puisse dire – les requérants à exercer une pareille voie de recours. Toutefois, je dirais que les 517 roupies (100 francs français environ) qui ont été attribuées par ce Tribunal dans son jugement No. 1255 (*Bansal (No. 4) et Harpalani (No. 4)*) de 1993 en raison d'une erreur matérielle qu'il avait commise, luisent d'un éclat particulier aux yeux des plaideurs qui viennent de perdre une affaire. En effet, cette somme est un peu la flamme de l'espoir, espoir d'ailleurs souvent fallacieux, que le Tribunal, s'il reconnaît s'être trompé, modifiera le sort de leur cause.

Malgré ce qui a été dit ce matin sur les plaideurs malheureux qui ont eu la satisfaction d'être entendus par un tribunal, je crois qu'ils vivent très mal le caractère définitif des jugements lorsqu'ils perdent. Aussi l'admission de davantage de cas d'ouverture que les seuls faits nouveaux, en particulier l'erreur matérielle, pour le recours en révision me semble constituer une soupape de sécurité importante. C'est une soupape sur le plan de la justice comme sur le plan psychologique. Or, comme on le sait, la justice est difficilement dissociable du sentiment qu'ont les plaideurs qu'elle est effectivement rendue.

L'utilisation de la jurisprudence pour l'orientation des requérants potentiels

Je m'autorise quelques mots sur le sujet bien qu'il n'ait pas été traité explicitement par les rapports de Monsieur Ziadé et du Professeur Flogaitis. Je crois que le problème peut se poser dans les termes suivants: quand un requérant envisage de faire recours et demande une évaluation de ses chances de succès, son affaire est examinée à la lumière de l'ensemble des sources du droit applicable mais une attention particulière est prêtée à la jurisprudence du tribunal devant lequel l'affaire est susceptible d'être portée. C'est là que les difficultés commencent. On ne peut certes pas enfermer, comme l'a dit l'un des orateurs, un tribunal dans sa propre jurisprudence. D'ailleurs, pour être honnête, la joie est grande de voir accueillir par un tribunal des arguments nouveaux qu'appelle une situation nouvelle ou alors la suggestion d'importer une jurisprudence d'un autre tribunal. L'intérêt est également grand quand une évolution jurisprudentielle se dessine et qu'une position dans laquelle on croyait un tribunal enfermé, se débloque. Il va sans dire que, si l'intérêt peut être partagé par les parties dans une même affaire, la joie de l'une fait évidemment plus souvent le malheur de l'autre.

Mais les vrais problèmes surgissent quand un tribunal fait marche arrière dans sa jurisprudence. C'est un point qui a été évoqué ce matin. Pour la partie qui perd, la déception est présente, même si elle peut parfois s'accompagner de compréhension. Mais la tâche devient ingrate lorsqu'on se trouve en présence d'une divergence de jurisprudence en provenance de deux formations de jugement d'un même tribunal sans que la chronologie puisse donner des pistes sur quelle jurisprudence est la bonne. D'ingrate, la tâche devient très complexe, voire carrément impossible, lorsqu'une telle situation se produit dans le domaine procédural. Certes, il y a toujours la possibilité de suivre de manière concurrente les deux procédures entre lesquelles on hésite. Mais alors vous conviendrez du gâchis engendré par ce "sur-verrouillage" procédural. Il serait très souhaitable que les règles de procédure, pour subtiles qu'elles soient, soient toujours dénuées de toute ambiguïté. En outre, pour les questions de fond, l'utilisation du tribunal jugeant en session plénière pour trancher des questions sur lesquelles toutes les formations de jugement restreintes d'un tribunal ne sont peut-être pas d'accord, peut se révéler très utile. Encore faut-il que le message soit suffisamment clair, notamment en ce qui concerne la similarité des causes. Mais peut-être mon exposé tourne-t-il là à la plaidoirie. Aussi est-il temps que je me retire. Je ne le ferai pas cependant sans remercier chaudement les organisateurs de ce colloque. Merci, Monsieur le Président.

OPEN DISCUSSION

Sir Elihu Lauterpacht, QC, Session Chair
We now have the opportunity for unscheduled commentators.

Bola A. Ajibola, Judge, World Bank Administrative Tribunal
Thank you, Mr. Chairman. I would like to make a few points on some of the issues raised.

The first one which I intend to touch upon is on dissenting opinions. Mr. Chairman, the founding fathers of the World Bank Administrative Tribunal – happily four of them are still alive and well – decided in their wisdom twenty years ago not to foster the idea of dissenting opinions. I do not know why they made this decision; I was not present at the time. The culture of the court to which I was used was such that, from my first day, I was poised to write my first dissenting opinion. But with the Administrative Tribunal I quickly discovered that dissenting opinions were not encouraged.

This is a very serious matter that should be brought to the attention of all administrative tribunals. I would like to listen to more discussion about whether it is desirable to write dissenting opinions in administrative tribunals. Should judges be allowed to write dissenting opinions or not? However, this could become an expensive exercise, a kind of undesirable luxury that many of these administrative tribunals could ill afford. This issue deserves to be studied in greater detail.

Judge Massot touched on the fact that the Chairman was a perpetual *rapporteur* in his own court. I do not think that this is desirable. The World Bank Administrative Tribunal was built on the idea that judges should all share in the burden of drafting and writing judgments. Judge Massot should look into that and ask his colleagues to help him. He may be tired of reading what he has written all the time.

Nassib Ziadé touched on frivolous litigants. How should we handle frivolous, rude or impertinent litigants who keep writing terrible letters to the tribunal, with or without the support of their counsel? That has occurred many times in some of our cases and needs to be discussed. Within a common law jurisdiction, the matter is very simple: the litigant is declared in contempt of court. What can administrative tribunals do? The time has come for a discussion of this aspect.

I have noted another problem, which relates to the functioning of administrative tribunals. How far can we go in the exercise of our power with respect to the rules and regulations of the Tribunal on the one hand, and policies of management on the other hand? To what extent can we turn around their policies without doing their job for them and making ourselves the policy-makers? What does it mean to tell management that what it has written is wrong and against the rules of law, natural justice or human rights? Where do our powers stop? Perhaps we should be very careful not to let ourselves get drawn into situations where we are judges as well as putting ourselves in the position of management. We need to study this in greater detail and draw up some limitations.

Lastly, Mr. Chairman, I would like to comment on the proliferation of tribunals. Who is afraid of proliferation? I am not. Proliferation is a positive phenomenon. This would provide jobs for competent jurists who would otherwise be "redundant." They will still be present to help, using their wealth of experience. A more serious point must be made as well. If all the activities of these tribunals were handled by a single institution, the caseload would be daunting or overwhelming. On the other hand, if they were spread amongst a number of institutions, that would be a positive development. While it is true that proliferation may be costly, we must look at the institutions bearing the cost: the UN, the World Bank, the ILO, etc. They all have their problems; yet, they have managed to carry the burden. There is no problem.

However, an advantage to having a single Tribunal may be this: if we create a single institution of all the existing tribunals, it may be easier to design an appellate body over that single institution. Thank you for allowing me to speak.

Nicolas Valticos, Ancien Président suppléant du Tribunal administratif du Conseil de l'Europe

Je serai bref – c'est ce que disent toujours la plupart des gens qui s'apprêtent à parler longtemps! Je vous promets cependant d'être vraiment bref et de ne faire que deux observations. Je félicite tout d'abord les organisateurs de cette réunion qui est vraiment très utile. Elle dépasse de beaucoup la seule expérience de l'Organisation de la Banque mondiale. Il est intéressant de faire un tour d'horizon aussi large et qui pose une question qui, en effet, mérite une réflexion non seulement sur le passé mais aussi sur l'avenir. Où allons-nous? Nous sommes nombreux à célébrer ce vingtième anniversaire du Tribunal administratif de la Banque mondiale mais justement ne sommes-nous pas trop nombreux? En d'autres termes, le nombre des tribunaux administratifs n'est-il pas devenu excessif, en raison de la multiplicité des organisations internationales? L'excès en tout étant un défaut et, comme l'a dit Monsieur Ajibola, il n'est pas question d'envisager un seul tribunal administratif. Il y a un certain nombre de décennies, il existait deux grands tribunaux administratifs: celui des Nations Unies, d'un côté de l'Atlantique; celui de l'OIT, de l'autre côté. Aucun nouveau Pascal n'est venu dire: "vérité en deçà de l'Atlantique, erreur en delà".

Le nombre des organisations internationales a crû et il était normal que le nombre des tribunaux administratifs augmente également. Dans certains cas, il y a eu des regroupements comme celui de l'OIT et d'autres. Mais ne sommes-nous pas arrivés au point où, sans vouloir trop simplifier les matières, il faut jeter un nouveau coup d'œil sur les compétences des tribunaux administratifs? On ne peut pas imaginer deux ou trois Tribunaux mais on peut imaginer au moins un certain regroupement des juridictions internationales qui permettrait une certaine coordination, voire une réunification, des jurisprudences. Cela nécessiterait évidemment des juges disponibles un peu plus longtemps, comme c'est d'ailleurs déjà le cas dans plusieurs tribunaux administratifs, mais la question mérite en tout cas d'être examinée. Il faudrait que nous nous demandions si nous ne sommes pas arrivés à un stade où les administrations, en coopération avec les organisations du personnel, devraient revoir la distribution actuelle des compétences et examiner dans quelle mesure il serait possible, pour promouvoir une unité de jurisprudence et de vision, de regrouper certaines des juridictions qui ont des bases juridiques communes et des compétences proches. Ce sont sans doute des vœux de fin de congrès mais il faut toujours regarder vers l'avenir et se dégager de l'obsession du passé. Nous sommes toujours jeunes, Messieurs et, par conséquent, nous devons regarder l'avenir!

Ranjan (C.F.) Amerasinghe, Judge, United Nations Administrative Tribunal
There are two sides to this issue. One aspect is of relevance to the administrations of the organizations. We, as judges, can only speak to the extent that they are willing to listen. Management will always take the action it wishes in the end. In short, we cannot do a great deal as judges. There are three points I want to make in this connection.

I have a very grave problem with the renewal of appointments. We need to have, e.g., one seven-year term with no renewals. This clearly tells staff members that the judges are not expected to be administration-oriented if they wish to continue on the tribunals by being renewed. The important point is that it is the respondent before the tribunals that makes the appointments. There should be no renewals.

The second point concerns the qualification of judges. While I agree that there exists a problem, it is not so severe in the case of civil law lawyers. Civil law lawyers have an exposure to civil service law and have a basic knowledge of the principles involved. It is with the common law lawyers that the problem arises. I believe that lawyers are necessary. Judges decide according to law. Therefore, we need lawyers. I do not agree that administrators or others such as diplomats can be substituted for them. Judges are neither conciliators nor mediators. However, we need to distinguish between the various types of lawyers. Apart from civil law lawyers, I believe competent international jurists can handle the work. Should common law lawyers have experience in both administrative and labor law? Professor Gorman has proved to us that such qualifications can be effective within the framework of common law. In any case, I am not sure that the ICJ formula is always useful for administrative tribunals. The UN General Assembly is currently looking into qualifications for the United Nations Administrative Tribunal (UNAT). While international jurists may be qualified to do the job, eligibility for high judicial office, particularly in a common law jurisdiction, does not seem to be a relevant qualification. In fact, it is probably a disqualification.

The third point – It is essential that legal departments within organizations be aware of their staff members. This does not mean that they should "lean toward the staff," but they must concede that the staff has rights. The ILO does not really have a problem, because it is a labor organization and is very conscious of labor values. In the World Bank, we never encountered such problems because the founder of our Tribunal, Dr. Golsong, was very staff-conscious. Mr. Shihata continued that tradition and I am sure that Mr. Tung will carry it on.

I would now like to speak more specifically about the work of tribunals. There are four points here.

Civil law lawyers clearly have a problem with separate and dissenting opinions. I believe that having them should be seriously considered. Decisions alone are not of any value; the reasoning behind them adds a world of richness and thought, besides being necessary to judicial functions. Tribunals need to give serious consideration to the possibility that judges disagree with the reasoning behind a judgment and even decisions. There may be separate opinions or dissenting opinions. It is not as easy as simply saying: "We do not want separate opinions" or "We do not want dissenting opinions. It is a nuisance, there is a lot of money involved and they are disruptive." I do not think the authority of the operative decision is affected by separate or dissenting opinions, although unanimity in every respect could be useful.

Some speakers mentioned the possibility of creating panels. The UNAT has found an effective answer. One of the problems with the UNAT is that it must deal with a vast number of cases and it is sometimes very difficult to do so with a full tribunal. The UNAT operates in panels of three. However, referring to the full bench when there is dissent or when the issue is important is a possible option. But in any case only the members of the panel would actually vote on the matter and participate in the judgment or judgments.

I would also like to address a point raised by Bob Gorman. In civil law, it is impossible for a tribunal to take up a case before an administrative decision has been made. Thus, the tribunal does not question legislation as such, it questions the administrative decision, although impliedly it may find legislation bad when it decides that it is inapplicable because of flaws. We need to look into this situation very carefully: Should tribunals have the power to question legislation *per se*? We have now to wade through administrative decisions that come before the tribunal to reach it. The situation is a problem for a lawyer from the common law tradition, but it is more normal for civil lawyers. I agree that because we are dealing with an *international* system the problem needs further examination.

My final point concerns papers on issues and precedents. I do not know how the European tribunals work. In the CJEC, the Court of Justice of the European Communities, an *Avocat Général* does much of the work that would be accomplished by preparing Issues and Precedents papers. I would like to mention that Prosper Weil was responsible for introducing these papers into the World Bank Administrative Tribunal. I took on the responsibility of preparing those papers personally in the registry because they were so important. The presentation of issues and precedents could affect the decision of the tribunal. We are trying to introduce a system like this into the UNAT, but, as my colleague Mr. Thierry said, we do not have enough resources. If the Registrar is to do Issues and Precedents papers for 25 cases per session, there must be adequate staff to help and do the other work. Papers on issues and precedents were always found most useful in the WBAT.

David Ruzié, Juge, Tribunal administratif de la Banque des règlements internationaux
Je voudrais faire trois brèves remarques. Tout d'abord, en ce qui concerne les voies de recours internes, je pense que d'efficaces voies de recours internes permettraient de faciliter le travail des juridictions. Mais pour cela, il faudrait que deux conditions soient remplies. D'une part, il faudrait que les juridictions internes soient composées de gens compétents. Il se trouve, en effet, que la complexité des affaires ne permet plus à n'importe qui de comprendre des questions juridiques. Il suffit de lire la jurisprudence des tribunaux administratifs de l'OIT ou des Nations Unies pour voir à quel point, dans certaines organisations, les commissions de recours interne font mal leur travail, parce qu'elles n'ont pas compris les problèmes juridiques qui étaient posés. D'autre part, il faudrait que ces organismes, qui sont notamment importants pour l'établissement des faits, travaillent dans un délai raisonnable. Or il arrive fréquemment, notamment dans le système des Nations Unies, que les commissions paritaires de recours mettent trois ou quatre ans pour faire des recommandations. Ensuite, le Tribunal accorde généreusement 5000 dollars ou un mois de traitement pour ce délai. Je

pense que cela permettrait d'améliorer le rendement des tribunaux, à condition qu'ils soient aidés par des gens compétents et travaillant dans un délai raisonnable.

J'aimerais ensuite aborder le problème des voies de recours contre les décisions des juridictions administratives internationales. Comme l'ont dit avec beaucoup de modestie les juges du Tribunal administratif de l'OIT il y a quelques années, "les juges sont humains et faillibles" (jugement No. 570). Par conséquent, un double degré de juridiction, qui ne porterait que sur les questions de droit, est indispensable. Par exemple, dans le système des Nations Unies, à propos des travaux de la commission de la fonction publique internationale, même s'il est vrai qu'il n'y a jamais eu jusqu'à présent de divergences de jurisprudence, ce double degré pourrait s'appliquer. Par ailleurs, il y a une divergence de jurisprudence dans le système des Nations Unies à propos du droit applicable. Le Tribunal administratif de l'OIT, à mon avis à juste titre, admet qu'un requérant puisse invoquer un accord de siège, dans lequel il est fait mention des droits du personnel (jugements Nos. 379 et 741), alors que le Tribunal administratif des Nations Unies considère que l'accord de siège est un acte qui ne concerne pas directement l'agent, qui ne peut invoquer que le règlement du personnel (jugement No. 588). Pourtant, dans l'accord de siège en question, il était fait état des privilèges et immunités de caractère fiscal dont bénéficient les agents de l'organisation. De même, une voie de recours me paraît indispensable dans le système des organisations européennes coordonnées. En effet, il existe des règles communes, soit de fait parce que les organisations reprennent à leur compte les recommandations du comité de coordination sur les rémunérations (CCR), soit parce que, juridiquement, les règles sont uniques en matière de pensions. Or, il y a des cas précis dans lesquels il y a eu des divergences sinon de jurisprudence, du moins de pratique. Il faudrait donc revoir sérieusement la question.

Enfin, en attendant, dans la mesure où les jugements sont définitifs, il faut revoir le problème des recours en révision et notamment la notion de fait nouveau. Il y a quelques années, un jugement a été rendu par une juridiction administrative internationale sur la base d'une déclaration faite par l'organisation qui déclarait que les dispositions réglementaires avaient été adoptées ou qu'elles étaient pratiquement sur le point d'être adoptées. La juridiction a cru en toute bonne foi que les textes avaient été adoptés. Or ce n'était pas le cas. Trois ans après, ces dispositions n'avaient toujours pas été prises. Un recours en révision a été rejeté, car effectivement, au sens strict, on ne pouvait pas parler d'un fait nouveau (Commission de recours de l'Agence spatiale européenne, affaire No. 62). On peut donc se demander si justice a effectivement été rendue.

Nassib G. Ziadé, Secrétaire exécutif, Tribunal administratif de la Banque mondiale
Je voudrais développer un point de vue différent et répondre brièvement à une question soulevée par Maître Sicault. J'ai évité à dessein de discuter la décision *de Villegas (No. 4)* rendue en 1981 par le Tribunal administratif de l'OIT (Décision No. 442) car je suis en désaccord avec celle-ci. Mais c'était sans compter sur la perspicacité de Maître Sicault. Du moment que la question a été soulevée, le Président Gentot et les autres membres du Tribunal administratif de l'OIT me permettront d'exprimer ici quelques propos libres.

La décision *de Villegas (No. 4)* est une décision de principe, rédigée de manière tout à fait remarquable, mais dont les implications pratiques peuvent s'avérer dangereuses pour le bon fonctionnement d'un tribunal. La raison en est que les motifs de révision développés par la décision s'apparentent davantage à un appel qu'à une révision. Et cela est tout simplement contraire aux textes de la plupart des statuts des tribunaux administratifs internationaux. Ceux-ci disposent, en effet, que les jugements sont définitifs et ne peuvent faire l'objet de recours en appel. Je ne suis pas partisan d'une interprétation figée des textes pourvu que l'on n'entrave pas la bonne administration de la justice.

Je suis, en revanche, en parfait accord avec une décision beaucoup plus récente du Tribunal administratif de l'OIT (Décision No. 1824) rendue en 1999 dans l'affaire *Sethi (No 4)*. Il y est dit que "l'autorité d'un jugement définitif – celle de la chose jugée – ne peut pas être si facilement mise en cause. Il y a deux parties à chaque affaire et celle qui perd estime habituellement que le Tribunal a commis une erreur. Il faut cependant bien mettre fin au litige, et la stabilité de la procédure judiciaire nécessite que les jugements définitifs du type de celui dont le requérant demande la révision ne peuvent être révisés que pour un nombre de motifs limités et pour les plus graves raisons". Il me semble que cette décision récente (peut-on déjà parler d'un revirement de jurisprudence?) s'accorde davantage avec les jurisprudences des autres tribunaux administratifs internationaux et, en tout cas, avec la nécessité de préserver la stabilité des relations juridiques.

Spyridon Flogaitis, Professor of Law, University of Athens
Thank you, Mr. Chairman. I would like to raise three points.

The first is costs, and especially punitive costs. This is a very delicate matter because it has to do with the right of access to justice. As we all know, after the Second World War, our societies became very sensitive to the question of access to justice. If there are severe rules about costs, then the impression is created that the right of access to justice is restrained. As a result, even when the statute foresees punitive costs, it is very difficult for the tribunal to impose them. The tribunal must come to the conclusion that it was a frivolous case or one that was created to harass the respondent institution. Such claims are very difficult to establish.

Instead, tribunals must reinforce the pro-active methods concerning costs: how first to consult the person about the case; how to free the complainant from lawyers who, for reasons of their own, will put them into a frivolous case situation; etc. (The Inter-American Development Bank realized this and has introduced a Labor Relations Advisor who is paid by the institution and whose duty is to help staff members see better their cases and to give them some idea of their chances at winning.)

The question of reservation of application in the World Bank Administrative Tribunal. The Statute clearly states that this right exists, adding that judges can end frivolous cases at a very early stage by exercising it.

In the debate over oral versus written proceedings, I believe that oral proceedings are very important, even during the preparation of the case. I do not believe that anyone can be a good judge in isolation. Take the example of my small country, Greece. The advantage of the Council of State is that anyone can meet with a judge personally to learn of his chances before the case is tried and talk about his case. In most cases, people who find that they will probably lose will not proceed with a case.

Heretofore, all administrative tribunals have been held to an *ad hoc* or fragmented jurisdiction. I would plead for a general clause jurisdiction. It is not only staff who can have claims against an international organization. Much litigation is left out of the jurisdiction of international administrative tribunals. We need to start thinking about the introduction of the general clause.

CONCLUDING REMARKS

CONCLUDING REMARKS

Ibrahim F.I. Shihata*

Résumé

Je soulèverai trois points qui méritent une attention particulière.

Le *premier* est relatif à la composition du Tribunal administratif de la Banque mondiale. En 1983, au moment où le mandat de quatre membres du Tribunal touchait à son terme, la question fut posée de savoir s'il était plus opportun de les remplacer ou de les reconduire dans leur mandat. Le point de vue dominant au sein de l'institution était favorable au remplacement des membres au motif que celui-ci affermissait l'indépendance du Tribunal et assurait en outre une représentation plus grande des Etats-membres. Mon point de vue, qui a fini par prévaloir, était favorable au renouvellement du mandat des membres du Tribunal le plus longtemps possible. Cette position a permis au Tribunal d'asseoir sa jurisprudence sur plusieurs points et de renforcer son autorité malgré la complexité des situations qu'il a dû affronter.

Le *second* se rapporte au rôle éducatif du Tribunal. Je crois à cet égard que le Tribunal ferait mieux de se limiter au rôle qui lui est imparti, à savoir celui de juger les affaires qui lui sont soumises. Si, exceptionnellement, le Tribunal considérait qu'un comportement nuisible devait être réprimé, il pourrait le signaler à la direction de l'Organisation.

Le *troisième* point concerne la multiplication des mécanismes de recours au sein de chaque institution. Je crois que cette prolifération nuit aussi bien à l'institution qu'à son personnel. Il vaudrait mieux, en revanche, limiter les recours et s'assurer de leur efficacité et de leur caractère équitable. Ce faisant, l'équilibre serait atteint entre les impératifs du traitement équitable des membres du personnel et ceux du fonctionnement efficace de l'institution.

* * *

It is not easy, Mr. Chairman, to make concluding remarks after a day-long meeting. By definition, these remarks come at a time when people are more interested in seeing the meeting concluded than in hearing concluding remarks. If I limit myself to summing up the discussion, I am likely to be boring and, worse, to be unfair to the speakers. If I come up with new ideas at this late hour, I am likely to be unfair to everybody. Finally, if I simply thank everyone and bid you farewell, I will be adding nothing. I shall therefore take a middle course: I will make three points that

* Secretary-General, International Centre for Settlement of Investment Disputes (ICSID); former Senior Vice President and General Counsel, World Bank.

deserve further attention and emphasize positions that I have taken during my over fifteen years as General Counsel of the World Bank.

The *first* point relates to the composition of the Tribunal. When I started in 1983, three years after the Tribunal was established, the terms of four members of the Tribunal had reached an end and I had to address the question of whether they should be renewed or whether we should look for new appointees. Interestingly, almost everybody else in the Management Committee of the Bank at the time was in favor of choosing new members of the Tribunal. The expressed idea was that this would be better for the independence of the Tribunal, but also that this would give more chance to nationals of more member countries to be represented in the Tribunal. I personally felt that, in a complex institution like the World Bank, which has very complex procedures, rules, papers, and even its own jargon or language, the Tribunal would be very weak if the members were changed every three years. I took the position that, unless there was a good reason for a change, members of the Tribunal should be renewed. It was not easy, but that view prevailed at the end. Some of the members of the Tribunal today have been members since 1980. This has enabled the Tribunal to establish a doctrine on many issues and to take strong stands in spite of the complexities of the situations that it has had to address.

The *second* point relates to the so-called educational role of the Tribunal, a role which goes beyond deciding on the specific cases brought before it. I personally fear that this is not advisable as a general matter. Perhaps the Tribunal could express its feeling to management only when it sees that there is a general trend which is threatening and which should be stopped. Our experience with another mechanism suggests that a tribunal would do best if it limits its role to what is stated in its Statute.

The *third* and last point is more general and pertains to the need to balance considerations of fair treatment of the staff with considerations of efficiency and economy of the work of the institution. Here my concern is not with the proliferation of administrative tribunals, but with the continuing proliferation of grievance mechanisms within each institution. It is very time consuming and, in my view, it is not even protective of the staff to maintain such varied possibilities. I have seen cases where staff members pursued their grievances for seven to ten years, only to become mental cases. It is not in their interest to have an open-ended process. If we have limited ways that are fair and efficient in addressing the complaints, these, in my view, would be much better for the institutions, and especially the action-oriented ones, and for the staff themselves.

QUESTIONS CONCLUSIVES

Prosper Weil*

Summary

The first question that needs to be considered is whether international administrative tribunals have jurisdiction only over individual decisions or also over decisions of a general nature. This problem was solved a long time ago by French administrative law but remains controversial in international administrative law. The approach adopted by the World Bank Administrative Tribunal (WBAT), and possibly by other international administrative tribunals as well, with respect to the general scope of their review powers is that the validity of institutional decisions of a general nature may be judged only while the tribunal is reviewing an individual decision. Having said this, all international administrative tribunals have questioned the right under which they may review the validity of the institution's policy decisions. It is, moreover, difficult to identify the substantive law under which a tribunal may review such policy decisions, as the tribunal is not guided by an authoritative text as in constitutional law, but only by rather vague provisions. The tribunal must thus establish its guiding principles, but cannot be a super-General Assembly or a super-board of directors, and must know how far it may go. This is a problem with which the French Conseil d'Etat has had to deal throughout its long history.

Individual decisions are the primary focus of international administrative tribunals. The general standard of review with respect to individual decisions is that the tribunal will not interfere with the organization's exercise of discretion, absent abuse of discretion or improper motive. This is a standard similar to the one used in French administrative law, according to which the judge reviews merely the legality (*légalité*) of a decision and not its wisdom (*opportunité*). The difficulty for all administrative tribunals is to draw such lines.

Certain judgments of international administrative tribunals echo the approach of French administrative law, which applies different levels of scrutiny to different types of decisions. Other judgments use Anglo-American rather than French standards, but reach essentially the same results.

In the light of the inherent difficulty in determining whether a staff member's claim is justified, a question arises as to whether international administrative judges have the technical grounding needed to pass judgment on individual claims when they do not necessarily understand very well the inner workings of the institution. While cases are relatively easy when they involve only questions of legal interpretation, this is not usually the situation when questions of fact are involved. At the same time, it must be understood that this is the nature of the job and that

* Ancien Président du Tribunal administratif de la Banque mondiale; Professeur émérite, Université de Paris II.

tribunals have no choice but to live with such uncertainty. It is not even a question of having a higher judicial body to review tribunal judgments, because such a body would encounter the same difficulties as the lower one. The uncertainties presented by highly fact-intensive cases could perhaps be relieved by evidentiary hearings or more extensive proceedings.

* * *

Je crois que tout a été dit aujourd'hui et je n'ai pas grand-chose à ajouter. Je me bornerai donc à vous faire part de mes sentiments personnels liés aux longues années que j'ai passées au Tribunal administratif de la Banque mondiale, de mes doutes, de mes quelques problèmes de conscience – le mot est peut-être un peu solennel – et de mes états d'âme que je partage sans doute avec certains membres de ce Tribunal et d'autres tribunaux.

I. *Jusqu'où va la mission des tribunaux administratifs?*

La mission des tribunaux administratifs est fondamentalement de juger les litiges entre le personnel et l'Administration et de régler les questions personnelles d'avancement et de discipline. Mais ces tribunaux sont-ils également compétents pour juger de la validité juridique ou de l'opportunité des décisions politiques, des décisions de principe prises par l'organisation? C'est là une très vieille question qui s'est traduite par un choix précis auquel Bob Gorman a fait allusion tout à l'heure. Les tribunaux ont-ils pour mission simplement de juger des actes individuels ou bien ont-ils aussi compétence pour juger les actes généraux? C'est un problème que les juristes français familiers du droit administratif connaissent bien. Il est réglé en France et sur le continent européen depuis très longtemps mais il reste controversé pour les tribunaux administratifs internationaux. La solution qui a été adoptée par le Tribunal administratif de la Banque mondiale, et je pense par d'autres aussi, c'est de dire que seuls sont recevables les recours contre des actes individuels mais qu'à cette occasion il est possible au Tribunal de juger de la validité d'un acte général, ce qui nous renvoie exactement au problème de fond.

Le Tribunal administratif de la Banque mondiale a rencontré ce problème dès sa première affaire parce que – ce n'est un secret pour personne – il a été créé sur l'initiative de son General Counsel, M. Golsong, pour se prononcer sur les difficultés nées d'un changement complet de structure et de politique du personnel. Finalement, le problème a été résolu parce que la Banque n'a pas soulevé d'objection et que nous nous sommes prononcés d'emblée sur des décisions générales à l'occasion de recours individuels. Cela étant, il n'en reste pas moins que tous les membres de tribunaux administratifs internationaux se sont demandés de quel droit ils pouvaient se prononcer sur des choix de politique administrative ou de politique de gestion des organisations internationales. De quel droit pouvaient-ils se substituer aux organismes compétents désignés par les gouvernements sur l'introduction d'une nouvelle politique de rémunération, d'une nouvelle grille de salaires, d'une nouvelle politique en matière de pensions et des modalités (*grandfathering*) des mesures transitoires jusqu'à ce que l'on ait adopté des mesures nouvelles?

Lorsque le système Kafka a été introduit à grand bruit à la Banque et qu'il a été abandonné quelques années plus tard au profit d'un système complètement différent, de quel droit pouvions-nous nous prononcer? Nous ne connaissions pas grand-chose au fonctionnement administratif des organisations internationales et à leurs besoins. La question à se poser n'était au surplus pas simplement: "de quel droit?", mais également: "au regard de quel droit?". Dans un système interne, il y a une Constitution. En droit administratif international, en dehors de quelques dispositions souvent vagues, il n'existe pas de système de droit constitutionnel. C'est donc au Tribunal qu'il aurait appartenu de poser les principes fondamentaux. Le problème posé était ardu et nous n'avons jamais réussi à le résoudre de manière absolument parfaite. Le tribunal administratif ne peut pas être un super conseil d'administration, une super Assemblée Générale, mais il ne peut pas non plus avaliser n'importe quoi. Il lui faut savoir jusqu'où ne pas aller trop loin. C'est un problème auquel le Conseil d'Etat français s'est heurté tout au long de son histoire. Il a su y répondre. Les tribunaux administratifs internationaux ont-ils su y répondre? Ce n'est évidemment pas à l'un de ses anciens membres de le dire.

II. *Comment juger les décisions individuelles?*

S'agissant des décisions individuelles, qui sont le pain quotidien des tribunaux administratifs (nomination, promotion, refus de promotion, validation des stages . . .), jusqu'où pouvons-nous aller? Les formules adoptées par les tribunaux administratifs internationaux, dont le Tribunal administratif de la Banque mondiale, sont connues. Premièrement, le pouvoir discrétionnaire n'est pas un pouvoir arbitraire. Deuxièmement, le tribunal n'a pas à se substituer à l'organisation, sauf lorsqu'il y a abus de discrétion (*abuse of discretion*) ou motif impropre. Ce sont de merveilleuses formules qui correspondent un peu à celles du droit français: le juge administratif est juge de la légalité et non de l'opportunité. Le malheur est que personne n'a jamais pu déterminer où était la limite entre les deux. Et comme je l'ai dit un jour – le Président Gentot s'en souvient et m'a fait l'honneur de m'approuver – c'est finalement une définition circulaire. On sait en effet ce qu'est la légalité lorsque le tribunal a accepté de contrôler et l'on sait ce qu'est l'opportunité lorsque le tribunal a dit qu'il ne contrôlait pas. Nous nous sommes heurtés à ce problème, comme sans doute tous les tribunaux administratifs du monde, dans presque chaque affaire. De quel droit pouvons-nous décider qu'un agent a bien rempli ses fonctions ou a mal rempli ses fonctions s'il n'y a pas une contradiction précise entre une conduite donnée et un texte donné? Comment pouvons-nous décider quel est celui des cinq agents se situant au même niveau dans un service qui doit être licencié lorsqu'une compression du personnel a lieu? Comment pouvons-nous juger si l'organisation a bien fait ou mal fait de titulariser un agent après sa période de stage? De quel droit des juges venus d'horizons différents, qui n'ont pas nécessairement une grande expérience de la vie administrative et qui de toute façon ne connaissent pas les réalités internes de l'organisation, peuvent-ils dire cela? Tout à l'heure, je disais: "de quel droit, mais aussi par rapport à quelle norme?" Cette fois-ci, je dirai: "de quel droit et avec quelle capacité technique?" Je ne me suis, pour ma part, jamais senti réellement capable de déterminer si un agent dont j'étudiais le recours était à la hauteur des *job requirements* ou s'il ne l'était pas.

Mais d'un autre côté, si le tribunal ne fait pas cela, que fait-il? Il est là pour cela. On se trouve alors devant un problème classique. Une juridiction administrative, pour reprendre une formule naguère célèbre, c'est un pouvoir hiérarchique sous une forme juridictionnelle. Tout l'art et toute la science d'un juge administratif international, comme probablement d'un juge administratif interne, c'est de savoir tracer la limite entre le "pas assez" et le "trop". La question ne se pose pas en termes de voies de recours et n'est pas: qui jugera les juges? Il est évident que les juges supérieurs ne seront pas meilleurs que les juges inférieurs. Ils n'en sauront pas davantage et le problème sera exactement le même. C'est à la fois la grandeur et l'impossibilité de la mission de juger qui est, en réalité, le problème devant lequel nous nous trouvons.

Le juge administratif français, le Conseil d'Etat français, a su élaborer, après de longues années d'hésitation et de progrès, un schéma de contrôle. Il existe un contrôle minimal dans certains cas, un contrôle normal dans d'autres et un contrôle étendu dans d'autres cas encore. C'est une technique très élaborée et il n'est pas question que des tribunaux administratifs composés de juristes venus d'horizons différents doivent nécessairement l'adopter. Certains jugements du Tribunal administratif de la Banque mondiale, du Tribunal administratif de l'OIT ou d'autres tribunaux font écho à la problématique du droit administratif français. D'autres utilisent des notions différentes venues d'horizons anglais et américains. J'ai eu le plaisir de constater que, par-delà un vocabulaire et une technique différents, on arrive à des résultats très voisins. C'est pourquoi je ne regrette pas trop que le Tribunal administratif de la Banque mondiale ait rarement adopté la terminologie et les concepts du droit administratif français.

Dernier point, dernier doute: Pouvons-nous réellement juger? Comment nous assurer de la réalité de l'affaire? Je dois dire que chaque fois que j'ai été rapporteur, je me suis posé cette question: qui a raison? qui a tort? Lorsqu'il s'agit d'un problème de droit ou d'une interprétation juridique, cela est relativement facile. Mais dans la plupart des cas individuels, c'est plus difficile. Les questions se bousculent. Sommes-nous en présence de la victime d'une persécution, d'une vendetta de bureau ou d'un maniaque de procédures (l'agent lui-même ou son avocat)? Nous n'arrivons en fait que rarement à nous faire une véritable idée. Peut-être l'audition des intéressés ou une procédure plus longue aurait-elle permis de trancher ce problème. Pour ma part, lorsqu'en tant que rapporteur j'étais en présence de recours écrits par l'intéressé lui-même sur des centaines de pages, j'ai souvent été incapable de discerner s'il était une victime ou un maniaque.

Voilà les quelques questions que je me suis permis de vous soumettre. Ce sont des questions auxquelles je n'ai pas de réponse mais dont je souhaitais vous faire part, au-delà des débats purement juridiques mais passionnants que nous avons eus aujourd'hui.

Sir Elihu Lauterpacht, QC, Session Chair

Thank you, Professor Weil, for your brilliant closing remarks. We have been privileged to be present at a remarkably rich session packed with information and insight. I do not feel that a moment of it has been wasted.

Many people deserve thanks for this event. First, we have to thank Nassib Ziadé whose imagination, initiative and administrative zeal have brought us to this point in the day. Secondly, we must thank the speakers who have shared their experience and their insight. Thirdly, we must thank the interpreters who, behind dark glass, have listened to every word and converted it into a language understood by others. Fourthly, we must thank the World Bank for its support of Nassib's initiative. Finally, we must thank ourselves for having had an interest and commitment to the subject-matter sufficient to give us a sense of satisfaction at a day well spent. The last word rests with Professor Gorman, the President of the World Bank Administrative Tribunal.

Robert A. Gorman, President, World Bank Administrative Tribunal

It is remarkable to look around the room and see almost as many people who were here when we began this morning.

On behalf of the Administrative Tribunal of the World Bank, I would like to thank you for your presence here at what might be called something of a very high-level birthday party. We also want to thank you for your participation, either as formal speakers or as members of the audience. Speaking personally and on behalf of my colleagues on the Tribunal, I hope that the suggestions that were made by Presidents Valticos and Thierry, that this be viewed as the beginning of a series of continuing conversations, will indeed be implemented.

ANNEXES

THE DEVELOPMENT OF INTERNATIONAL EMPLOYMENT LAW: MY EXPERIENCE ON INTERNATIONAL ADMINISTRATIVE TRIBUNALS AT THE WORLD BANK AND THE ASIAN DEVELOPMENT BANK

Robert A. Gorman*

Résumé

Susana Mendaro fut recrutée par la Banque mondiale en 1977 pour travailler à Washington. Peu de temps après, elle prétendit être victime de discrimination et de harcèlement sexuels. Elle intenta un procès contre la Banque mondiale devant la Cour fédérale alléguant la violation d'une loi américaine prohibant la discrimination et le harcèlement sexuels sur les lieux de travail. Son action fut rejetée de manière sommaire sans que ne lui fut donnée l'opportunité de présenter une preuve du comportement injuste de la Banque.

Pour rejeter l'action, le tribunal fédéral de première instance et la Cour fédérale d'appel se basèrent sur la loi fédérale relative aux immunités des organisations internationales qui étend à celles-ci l'immunité dont jouissent les gouvernements étrangers. Il est à noter que les Etats-Unis ont étendu cette immunité à la Banque mondiale. La Cour d'appel jugea que l'immunité s'appliquait aux contrats de travail conclus par la Banque ainsi qu'à ses relations avec les membres du personnel. La Cour d'appel observa que la cohérence de l'organisation interne de la Banque viendrait à disparaître si les relations de travail de ses employés de nationalités diverses et dispersés géographiquement dans des lieux de travail divers devaient être soumises à de multiples lois internes. Tout en rejetant l'action de Mme Mendaro, la Cour d'appel nota toutefois que "la Banque Mondiale a récemment créé un Tribunal Administratif pour résoudre les revendications des employés basées sur les contrats de travail".

La question à laquelle il faudrait tout d'abord répondre est celle de savoir ce qu'est un tribunal administratif international. C'est tout simplement un tribunal arbitral international du travail auquel les employés des organisations internationales peuvent recourir concernant les différends qui surviennent sur le lieu de travail et dont les jugements sont obligatoires pour l'organisation en question.

Je parlerai principalement du Tribunal administratif de la Banque mondiale (TABM) dans lequel j'ai été désigné depuis sa création en 1980, et du Tribunal

---

* Kenneth W. Gemmill Professor of Law Emeritus, University of Pennsylvania; Professor of Law, Arizona State University College of Law. This article is based upon remarks delivered at the European Public Law Center, Athens, in June 2004, and at the University of Pennsylvania Law School, Philadelphia, in December 2002, which largely explains much of its informal and personal tone. A previous version of this article was published in 25 *Comparative Labor Law & Policy Journal* 423 (2004) and also in 16 *European Review of Public Law* 631 (2004). The editors of those journals have kindly given their consent to republish. The author wishes to thank Nassib G. Ziadé and Zakir Hafez of the Secretariat of the World Bank Administrative Tribunal for their assistance in the preparation of this article.

administratif de la Banque asiatique de développement (TABAsD) qui a été créé en 1991 et dans lequel j'ai été désigné depuis 1995. Je tâcherai de répondre aux questions suivantes: Que représente le TABM? Pourquoi a-t-il été créé? De qui est-il constitué, comment fonctionne-t-il, quels sont les litiges dont il connaît et quelles règles de droit applique-t-il?

Le jugement *Mendaro* avait mis en relief le fait que la Banque mondiale opérait aux Etats-Unis et ailleurs de par le monde dans une sorte de vide juridique auquel la création du TABM était venue remédier: dorénavant, la Banque pourrait être tenue responsable des décisions prises par ses cadres à l'endroit des membres du personnel. La création du Tribunal administratif répondait au vœu du Président de la Banque mondiale de l'époque, Robert McNamara, de soumettre les opérations intérieures de la Banque à la règle de droit et d'assurer le traitement équitable des membres du personnel.

Le TABM est composé de sept juges choisis de par le monde pour être représentatifs des divers systèmes juridiques ainsi que des différentes traditions sociales et culturelles. La langue officielle du TABM est l'anglais. Le Conseil des Gouverneurs, qui est la plus haute autorité de décision de la Banque et qui est constitué de représentants de tous les Etats-membres, a créé le TABM et en a précisé la compétence dans un document intitulé Statut du Tribunal administratif. Le Statut indique aussi les qualifications que doivent posséder les membres du Tribunal. Ceux-ci "doivent être des personnes jouissant de la plus haute considération morale et doivent réunir les conditions requises pour l'exercice de hautes fonctions judiciaires ou être des jurisconsultes possédant une compétence notoire dans des disciplines appropriées telles que les relations de travail, la fonction publique internationale et l'administration des organisations internationales". En pratique, les membres du Tribunal doivent être des personnes réputées, qu'ils soient juges, avocats ou professeurs de disciplines juridiques. Des qualifications similaires sont requises des membres du TABAsD.

Les Statuts du TABM et du TABAsD leur donnent pouvoir "pour connaître de toute requête par laquelle un membre du personnel du Groupe de la Banque invoque l'inobservation des dispositions de son contrat de travail ou des conditions de son emploi et pour statuer sur ladite requête". Les termes "contrat de travail" et "conditions d'emploi" sont définis par les Statuts pour "inclure toutes dispositions pertinentes des règlements en vigueur au moment de l'inobservation invoquée". Les règlements sont donc des textes contraignants sur lesquels les membres du personnel peuvent se fonder pour réclamer leurs droits. Le "contrat de travail" auquel les deux Tribunaux sont appelés à donner effet est, à la différence des conventions collectives, un contrat individuel conclu par la Banque et le membre du personnel.

Le Statut du TABM pose certaines conditions de recevabilité de la requête. L'une d'elles est l'épuisement préalable des recours internes dans le cadre de la Banque mondiale, à savoir la soumission préalable du cas par le membre du personnel au Comité d'appel. Ce Comité est composé de membres du personnel, désignés pour partie par la direction et pour autre partie par l'Association du personnel. Le Comité mène une procédure probatoire et contradictoire. Après l'audience, le Comité d'appel présente des recommandations à la direction de la Banque mondiale, lesquelles dans la majorité des cas mettent fin au litige et sont acceptées par celle-ci. Si le requérant n'obtient pas satisfaction, il peut saisir à ce moment le TABM. Tout retard à saisir le Comité d'appel sera toutefois considéré par le TABM comme équivalant à un non-épuisement des recours internes.

La Banque mondiale a récemment créé un bureau de médiation interne auquel le membre du personnel et la Banque peuvent recourir avant, ou même après la procédure devant le Comité d'appel. Ce bureau a connu un succès considérable puisqu'il résout presque 90 pour cent des cas qui lui sont déférés.

Une deuxième condition préalable de recevabilité posée par le Statut du TABM doit être vérifiée, à savoir que la requête soit présentée dans un délai de 120 jours courant à partir de la décision contestée. Au terme de quatre années passées devant les tribunaux fédéraux américains, la Cour d'appel du district de Colombie repoussa l'action de Susana Mendaro. Celle-ci saisit alors le TABM qui jugea que sa requête était soumise de manière très tardive. Le TABM saisit néanmoins cette occasion pour préciser sous forme d'*obiter dictum* que la Banque était, en vertu des principes généraux de droit et de ses propres déclarations de politique interne, dans l'obligation d'éviter la discrimination et le harcèlement de ses employés.

L'affaire *Mendaro* a eu le mérite de clarifier les deux sources distinctes des obligations de la Banque mondiale, à savoir les règlements internes de la Banque et les principes généraux de droit. Si la première source est citée dans le Statut du TABM, la deuxième a été consacrée avec force par le TABM dès son premier jugement en 1981. Le TABM identifie, formule et applique ces principes en cas de nécessité. Une question se pose à ce niveau: d'où le TABM s'inspire-t-il pour donner corps à ces principes et quelles sont ses sources de droit?

Nous savons que la Banque mondiale n'est soumise ni aux lois ni aux tribunaux internes d'aucun de ses Etats-membres. Nous savons aussi que le TABM est chargé par son Statut de déterminer si la Banque mondiale a méconnu le "contrat de travail" ou les "conditions d'emploi". En sus de la lettre d'emploi émise lorsqu'une personne rejoint les services de la Banque, de quoi sont formés ce contrat et ces conditions d'emploi? Les principales sources dont le Tribunal s'inspire sont les documents émis par la Banque mondiale qui posent des règles détaillées concernant les droits et les responsabilités des membres du personnel. Ces règles, auxquelles s'ajoutent des mémorandums et des circulaires moins formels mais toujours relatifs aux membres du personnel, doivent être ajoutées aux directives plus générales contenues dans un document appelé "Principes d'emploi des membres du personnel" dans lequel les droits de ceux-ci sont décrits de manière générale (par exemple, le traitement équitable dans le fond et dans la forme, la non-discrimination, le payement égal à travail égal).

Le TABM a même décidé, dans son premier jugement, qu'au-delà des sources écrites, les pratiques non écrites pouvaient faire partie des "conditions d'emploi" sur lesquels les membres du personnel peuvent compter.

Les Tribunaux doivent même aller au-delà des documents écrits et des pratiques non écrites de la Banque pour déterminer les droits des membres du personnel. En effet, les Tribunaux ont développé un corps de règles contractuelles qui sont une distillation des principes aussi bien des pays de droit civil que de ceux de la *common law* avec lesquels les juges du Tribunal sont familiers. Ces règles contractuelles serviront notamment à interpréter les ambiguïtés de langage et à résoudre les conflits de documents et de pratiques. Sont aussi au centre de la jurisprudence des Tribunaux les règles du droit administratif national par lesquelles les organes judiciaires contrôlent l'action de l'Administration. La plus importante de ces règles est sans doute celle qui sanctionne l'abus du pouvoir discrétionnaire.

Les Tribunaux invoquent parfois les principes du droit international public et la jurisprudence d'autres tribunaux administratifs internationaux mais seulement à titre indicatif, comme l'a énoncé le TABM dès son premier jugement. Les principes directeurs du Tribunal dérivent aussi de règles sociales fondamentales dont les employés sont en droit d'attendre l'application, tels le caractère équitable de la procédure, la non-discrimination et le juste traitement.

Toutes ces sources écrites et non écrites, internationales et nationales, constituent ce que le TABM a appelé le "droit interne" de l'institution.

Dans de rares occasions, il peut y avoir conflit entre les directives expresses de la Banque faisant partie du "contrat de travail", d'une part, et les principes généraux de droit communément admis, d'autre part. Ce conflit est illustré par l'affaire *Amora* tranchée par le TABAsD. Dans cette affaire, un conflit avait surgi entre les termes clairs du contrat de travail écrit et les principes généraux du droit du travail. Le TABAsD trancha en faveur de ces derniers se référant à un détournement de pouvoir, notion bien connue dans le droit administratif des pays de droit civil, qu'aurait commis la Banque asiatique.

D'autres règles substantielles ont été développées par les Tribunaux. L'une d'elles concerne l'interdiction de la discrimination entre individus ou envers la classe à laquelle ils appartiennent. Dans une affaire tranchée par le TABM, ce dernier a repoussé une allégation de discrimination basée sur des études statistiques générales montrant qu'à travail égal les femmes étaient moins bien payées que les hommes, au motif qu'en l'espèce la requérante n'avait pas prouvé avoir été elle-même victime de telles pratiques discriminatoires.

Une autre règle, des plus importantes, développée par tous les tribunaux administratifs internationaux est la possibilité pour un tribunal d'annuler les décisions prises par l'institution si celles-ci ont été entachées d'abus de pouvoir discrétionnaire. Même si certaines décisions de l'Administration relèvent de la compétence liée, beaucoup d'autres relèvent du pouvoir discrétionnaire. A l'occasion de ces dernières, la jurisprudence de nos deux Tribunaux a constamment affirmé que "le Tribunal n'interfère pas avec l'exercice du pouvoir discrétionnaire, à moins que la décision contestée ne soit entachée d'abus, étant arbitraire, discriminatoire, improprement motivée ou prise en violation d'une procédure juste et raisonnable".

La notion d'abus de pouvoir discrétionnaire s'applique non seulement aux décisions individuelles concernant un employé chargé d'effectuer des photocopies, tel que M. Amora, mais aussi à un vice-président de l'institution, tel le cas soumis au TABM. La notion s'applique en outre aux décisions réglementaires adoptées par le Conseil des Gouverneurs ou le Conseil des Administrateurs des deux Banques. En témoigne une affaire portée devant le TABAsD. En l'occurrence, un membre du personnel avait contesté une décision prise par le Conseil des Gouverneurs de la Banque asiatique qui avait décidé de baisser l'âge obligatoire de la retraite. La Banque argua que les décisions du Conseil des Gouverneurs n'étaient pas susceptibles de recours devant le TABAsD. Ce dernier rejeta cette argumentation au motif que le Conseil des Gouverneurs est soumis à la règle de droit et que son pouvoir discrétionnaire connaît des limites.

Un autre principe substantiel de la jurisprudence des deux Tribunaux est qu'il existe certaines conditions du contrat de travail qui sont tellement "fondamentales et essentielles" qu'il est interdit à la Banque de les modifier sans l'accord des membres du personnel. Ainsi, dans le premier jugement rendu par le TABM dans l'affaire *de Merode*, le TABM a décidé que la périodicité de l'augmentation des salaires accordée par la Banque mondiale à ses employés dans le passé en faisait une condition "fondamentale et essentielle" des contrats de travail qui était devenue un "droit acquis" aux membres du personnel que la Banque ne pouvait retirer sans leur consentement. La doctrine des "droits acquis" est aujourd'hui un principe fondamental du droit administratif international, ainsi que la distinction entre les conditions "essentielles" de l'emploi et celles qui ne le sont pas. Seules ces dernières peuvent être unilatéralement modifiées par l'Administration, sous réserve de certaines limitations telle que l'interdiction de toute rétroactivité.

La détermination du caractère essentiel ou non essentiel de l'une des conditions de l'emploi est un point très subtil qu'il revient au tribunal de trancher. La question du remboursement par la Banque mondiale et la Banque asiatique de l'impôt payé par certains des membres de leur personnel sur leur revenu allait donner l'occasion au TABM et au TABAsD d'en fournir la preuve.

Alors que la plupart des pays n'imposent pas le revenu de leurs nationaux travaillant dans les organisations internationales, les Etats-Unis et les Philippines le font. La Banque mondiale a, de tout temps, remboursé à ses employés américains le montant de leur impôt sur le revenu. Le TABM jugea dans l'affaire *de Merode*, rendue en 1981, que le principe du remboursement des taxes était "une condition fondamentale et essentielle de l'emploi", et que, par conséquent, la Banque mondiale ne pouvait mettre unilatéralement fin à cette pratique. Mais dans cette affaire, la Banque n'avait pas abandonné son programme de remboursement; elle avait uniquement introduit un changement mineur aux détails du calcul du montant remboursé. Le Tribunal en conclut que ces détails ne portaient pas sur des conditions fondamentales et essentielles, et que la Banque pouvait donc les ajuster sous réserve du respect du traitement équitable et de la régularité de la procédure.

Le même problème fut soumis quelques quinze ans plus tard au TABAsD par un ressortissant américain, M. Mesch, et un ressortissant philippin, M. Siy. Dans la première étape de l'affaire *Mesch et Siy*, le Tribunal soutint que le principe du salaire égal à travail égal était une condition essentielle et intangible de l'emploi au sein de la Banque asiatique. Le Tribunal consacra ce principe, même en l'absence d'une pratique antérieure en ce sens et sans qu'aucune déclaration de la Banque asiatique n'ait confirmé l'existence d'un tel programme de remboursement. Le Tribunal conclut que les membres du personnel concernés devaient avoir droit à une compensation appropriée pour les deux années précédentes, même s'il ne soutint pas expressément que le principe du remboursement des taxes était fondamental et intangible.

Le Conseil des Administrateurs de la Banque asiatique répliqua promptement en adoptant une résolution décidant que la Banque ne remboursera plus à l'avenir les taxes payées par les membres de son personnel.

Les employés concernés (*Mesch et Siy*) saisirent à nouveau le TABAsD soutenant que le remboursement des taxes était une condition fondamentale et essentielle de l'emploi que la Banque asiatique était tenue de respecter pour le passé et pour l'avenir et que, par conséquent, la résolution du Conseil des Administrateurs n'était pas valide. La majorité des juges du Tribunal décida, qu'en l'absence de toute pratique antérieure et de toute déclaration de la Banque asiatique en faveur du remboursement des taxes, cette question ne constituait pas une condition essentielle et fondamentale du contrat de travail. Malgré une forte opinion dissidente, la majorité conclut, qu'en dépit de l'existence du principe fondamental du salaire égal à travail égal, l'exigence d'égalité pouvait être satisfaite par des compensations équivalentes octroyées par la Banque à ses employés avant que ne leur soit imposé l'impôt national sur le revenu sur lequel la Banque n'a aucun contrôle.

D'autres règles substantielles importantes ont été énoncées par les deux Tribunaux dans des procès relatifs aux sanctions disciplinaires imposées aux membres du personnel pour mauvaise conduite. Les Tribunaux ont posé l'exigence d'une procédure équitable et ont souligné l'importance de la "proportionnalité" de la sanction.

Bien que la doctrine de la proportionnalité ait été parfaitement comprise par tous les juges du TABM, qu'ils proviennent des pays de droit civil ou de ceux de la *common law*, certaines spécificités culturelles se sont fait jour concernant la sévérité des sanctions disciplinaires, et ce, bien que les règlements internes de la Banque mondiale relatifs au personnel contiennent des dispositions précises quant à la prise en compte, au moment de l'imposition d'une sanction disciplinaire, de "l'importance de l'affaire", des "circonstances atténuantes", de "la situation du membre du personnel" et de "la fréquence de la conduite en cause".

Deux affaires jugées par le TABM en 1995 permettront de s'en rendre compte. Dans ces affaires, deux membres du personnel avaient, chacun de son côté, falsifié le compte de leurs heures supplémentaires. Ils avaient, ce faisant, reçu un paiement injustifié de l'ordre de quelques centaines de dollars. Ces deux personnes avaient été licenciées par la direction sans avoir reconnu les faits qui leur étaient reprochés. Le Comité d'appel soutint dans chacun des deux cas la terminaison du contrat.

Si je devais juger l'affaire par moi-même en tant qu'arbitre unique, j'aurais confirmé la décision de la direction. En l'occurrence, je pris la décision de me rallier à mes collègues an sein du TABM. Le Tribunal estima donc que le comportement fautif des deux employés ne justifiait pas la terminaison du contrat. Il souligna l'absence de fautes antérieures malgré la longue période d'emploi, la modicité des sommes en cause, et la modeste position qu'occupaient ces deux employés et décida de leur accorder une compensation pécuniaire. Ces deux jugements du Tribunal firent l'objet d'une critique de la part du Conseiller juridique principal de la Banque mondiale quelques années plus tard au motif que le TABM n'avait pas en l'espèce tenu compte de l'un des buts que s'était fixée la Banque mondiale, à savoir l'éradication de la corruption.

En dépit de ces divergences quant à la mise en application du principe de proportionnalité, une convergence des valeurs et des conclusions a prévalu. Un exemple de la convergence des valeurs chez les différents juges du Tribunal peut être trouvé dans l'exigence d'une procédure équitable au moment de la terminaison d'un contrat pour raisons disciplinaires. C'est ainsi qu'il y eut dans le second jugement du Tribunal, en 1981, unanimité pour poser les exigences d'une procédure équitable. Celles-ci ont été précisées au fil des jugements comme suit: la notification au membre du personnel de toute faute alléguée à son encontre, l'opportunité de se défendre, l'existence d'une enquête équitable, de certaines mesures de confrontation avec les accusateurs, et une prompte délivrance des résultats de l'enquête.

Avant de conclure, j'aimerais passer en revue certains aspects relatifs à la composition du Tribunal et à la procédure suivie. Tout d'abord, il est à noter que chaque affaire est assignée à l'un des juges qui est chargé de l'analyser en détail et de préparer un projet de jugement. Durant les sessions du Tribunal, une discussion collective de chaque projet a lieu en vue d'assurer la continuité de notre jurisprudence et d'aboutir à un jugement acceptable pour tous les juges. Malgré la diversité culturelle des juges du Tribunal, une convergence des valeurs et des conclusions a toujours prévalu.

Un autre aspect du processus de décision du Tribunal ne laisse pas d'intriguer. Le TABM a rendu, en 24 ans, plus de 300 jugements, tous pris à l'unanimité, et ce, que les jugements aient été rendus, comme l'autorise le Statut du TABM, en assemblée plénière de sept juges ou dans le cadre de panels de trois juges au moins. Contrairement au Statut du TABAsD et de celui d'autres tribunaux administratifs internationaux, le Statut du TABM ne prévoyait pas, à l'origine, la possibilité d'émettre des opinions dissidentes. Bien que ses membres, eux, fussent convaincus que de telles opinions étaient inhérentes à toute bonne procédure judiciaire, aucune opinion dissidente n'a jamais été émise. La raison peut être attribuée à la convergence des valeurs et à la continuité de la jurisprudence déjà relevées, mais aussi au sentiment que les jugements obtenus à l'unanimité s'imposent avec plus de force et de clarté. Le récent amendement du Statut du TABM adopté par le Conseil des Gouverneurs et permettant aux membres du TABM de manière expresse d'émettre des opinions dissidentes m'a semblé inutile tant cette possibilité me paraissait inhérente à notre fonction juridictionnelle.

Par contre, deux opinions dissidentes ont été émises au TABAsD. Dans la première affaire, le Tribunal avait soutenu la décision de la Banque asiatique de fixer l'âge de la retraite obligatoire à 60 ans. Dans la seconde affaire déjà mentionnée, le TABAsD avait soutenu la politique de la Banque asiatique tendant à ne pas rembourser aux employés originaires des Etats-Unis et des Philippines leurs taxes payées, alors qu'un jugement antérieur avait paru considérer cette compensation comme obligatoire et intangible.

La caractéristique la plus controversée de nos deux Tribunaux administratifs est de ne pas procéder à l'audition et à l'interrogatoire des parties et des témoins. Dans la totalité des cas soumis au TABAsD et dans presque tous les cas portés devant le TABM, la résolution des questions contentieuses, factuelles aussi bien que juridiques, a eu lieu exclusivement sur la base des plaidoiries écrites. Nous considérons que les deux phases de plaidoiries écrites pour chaque partie, soutenues par des dizaines de documents annexés, constituent une base adéquate pour rendre un jugement. Cette tendance est renforcée par la pratique des membres du personnel de la Banque de garder une trace écrite (par courrier électronique ou mémorandum) de toutes les conversations et des réunions. Le fait aussi que le Comité d'appel tient des audiences relatives à la preuve des faits litigieux aide le Tribunal à se faire une idée nette de ceux-ci. De plus, beaucoup d'affaires ne soulèvent que des problèmes de compétence ou des questions strictement juridiques. La plupart des autres tribunaux administratifs internationaux s'abstiennent de manière similaire de tenir des audiences orales, et cette pratique me semble défendable. Il reste que cet aspect frustre les requérants qui pensent souvent qu'une comparution personnelle demeure au cœur d'une procédure équitable.

Il n'en demeure pas moins qu'il y a certaines affaires dans lesquelles il serait utile d'auditionner des témoins, d'avoir l'opportunité de les interroger ou de demander des éclaircissements aux avocats des parties. De fait, les deux Tribunaux sont autorisés par leurs Statuts respectifs à prévoir des audiences. Seul le TABM a eu recours à cette faculté. Dans ce cas, les audiences se sont avérées plus utiles au niveau de la collecte des preuves auprès des témoins et de l'audition des conseils des parties qu'au niveau de l'évaluation de la crédibilité des parties.

* * *

Susana Mendaro, a citizen of Argentina, was hired by the World Bank in 1977, and took up work as a researcher in Washington, D.C. She became part of a workforce of some 6000, overwhelmingly based in Washington but recruited internationally so as to reflect the wide range of member nations, then 140 in number. Soon after her appointment, Ms. Mendaro fell victim – so she believed – to a pattern of gender discrimination and harassment by her supervisors and fellow workers: fewer assignments than her male counterparts, obstruction in her work, unwanted verbal and physical advances, denial of a promotion, disinclination to investigate her grievances when she raised them, and ultimately unwarranted termination of employment in 1979. She commenced a lawsuit in federal court against the World Bank for violation of the U.S. statute that forbids workplace discrimination and harassment based on gender – known as Title VII of the 1964 Civil Rights Act[1] – but her case was summarily dismissed, without her being given an opportunity to present any proof of the Bank's wrongdoing. Why?

The trial court and the court of appeals[2] invoked a federal statute known as the International Organizations Immunities Act (IOIA), which provides that "international organizations, wherever located, shall enjoy the same immunity from suit and every form of judicial process as is enjoyed by foreign governments."[3] By action of the President and the Congress of the United States, this immunity has been extended to the World Bank.[4] Although the Bank has waived its immunity to lawsuits by vendors, suppliers and others outside of the Bank, the court of appeals held that the immunity from suit fully applies to the Bank's employment contracts and its relations with its own staff members, like Ms. Mendaro. The court found that the Bank's organizational purposes would be obstructed if its employees, of widely varying nationalities and at geographically dispersed work stations, were to have their employment relations governed by varying domestic laws.[5] That was true even in Washington, D.C., the Bank's headquarters.

The World Bank, in other words, had no duty under U.S. law, or any other national law, to refrain from gender discrimination and harassment of its staff members – or racial, religious, ethnic, age or disability discrimination, for that matter. In dismissing Ms. Mendaro's lawsuit under Title VII, however, the U.S. court of appeals stated – so as apparently to mitigate her hurt – "The World Bank has . . . recently established an administrative tribunal to resolve employees' claims based on employment contract

[1] 42 U.S.C. §§ 2000e et seq.
[2] *Mendaro v. World Bank*, 717 F.2d 610 (D.C. Cir. 1983).
[3] 22 U.S.C. § 288a(b) (2000).
[4] 22 U.S.C. §§ 286h and 284g (2000) – as well as the relevant Executive Orders, which grant IOIA protection to World Bank organizations. *See* Exec. Order 9751, 11 Fed. Reg. 7713 (1946); and Exec. Order 11966, 42 Fed. Reg. 4331 (1977).
[5] *Mendaro v. World Bank*, 717 F.2d 610 (D.C. Cir. 1983).

disputes."[6] But, so that her hopes not be raised unduly, the court pointed out that "the tribunal was not created until after the events giving rise to Mendaro's claim against the Bank" and "is not explicitly authorized to resolve claims based on sexual harassment and discrimination."[7]

Ms. Mendaro in fact then filed an application, the equivalent of a complaint, with the World Bank Administrative Tribunal – and more will be said about that application and its outcome later in this talk. More important for the moment is the question: "What is an international administrative tribunal?" The simplest answer is that it is an international employment arbitration court, to which employees of an international organization may take their claims or grievances that arise within the workplace, for a final determination that is binding on the organization. The League of Nations in 1927 established *its* tribunal, whose structure was taken over by the International Labour Organization in 1946;[8] the United Nations Administrative Tribunal was created in 1949;[9] the World Bank Administrative Tribunal was founded in 1980; and its related institution, the International Monetary Fund (a much smaller employer) created a separate tribunal in 1994. There are a myriad of other international organizations which have their own separate administrative tribunals; and some 50 organizations subscribe to the ILO Tribunal, which disposes of dozens of cases each year concerning the rights of staff members of those many organizations.[10]

My talk today will focus upon the World Bank Administrative Tribunal, on which I have served since its founding in 1980 (close to a longevity record in the world of administrative tribunals). I shall also make reference to the Asian Development Bank Administrative Tribunal. Headquartered in Manila, as is the Asian Development Bank (ADB) itself, the Tribunal was founded in 1991. I was appointed to it in 1995, and I have in August 2004 retired from that Tribunal after serving a term as its President.

What, then, is the World Bank Administrative Tribunal? Why did it come into existence, who sits on it, how does it operate, what kinds of cases does it decide, and what rules of law does it apply?

The *Mendaro* decision makes clear that the World Bank operates, within the U.S. and elsewhere around the globe, in something of a legal vacuum, within what is literally a lawless environment, in which it is free to treat

---

[6] *Id.*, at p. 616, footnote 41.

[7] *Id.*

[8] C.F. Amerasinghe, *The Law of the International Civil Service*, 49–53 (Vol. I, 2d ed. 1994).

[9] *Id.*

[10] *See* ILO Administrative Tribunal at www.ilo.org/public/english/tribunal

its employees without fear of statutory or contractual liability, or even of liability in tort. The Bank's creation of an administrative tribunal, having the purpose of resolving employment disputes, represents a determination by the Bank that it should be held legally accountable for the decisions made by supervisors and officials in managing the Bank's workforce.

Why would the Bank relinquish such a legally unfettered discretion? I remember being called, in 1980, into the office of then World Bank President Robert McNamara, who told me that the Bank was *voluntarily* creating the Administrative Tribunal in order to bring the rule of law to the Bank's internal operations, to regulate the behavior of management so as to assure fair treatment of staff members, and as a result to enhance the morale of the staff and to make the Bank a desirable and efficient place to work.

The Tribunal, then and now, had seven judges, chosen from around the world – from different legal systems and different social and cultural traditions. In 1980, the Tribunal judges were from England, France, Uruguay, Egypt, Nigeria, India and the U.S. (Today, the judges are from Australia, France, Chile, South Africa, Nigeria, the Philippines and the U.S.) Happily for me, the official language of the Tribunal is English, so that the parties' pleadings, the Tribunal's deliberations, and the text of our decisions, are all in English. Originally all male, the Tribunal presently, and for the past six years, has had two women judges.

The highest decision-making body within the management of the Bank is the Board of Governors, a large body with representatives from each of the Bank's 184 member nations. (A smaller body, the Executive Directors, meets more frequently to oversee the operations of the Bank.) The Board of Governors created the Tribunal and established its jurisdiction in a document called the Statute of the Administrative Tribunal, which also sets forth the lofty qualifications of the Tribunal members: They "shall be persons of high moral character and must possess the qualifications required for appointment to high judicial office or be jurisconsults of recognized competence in relevant fields such as employment relations, international civil service and international organization administration."[11] In short, they should be reputable judges, lawyers and legal academics. Through the years, my colleagues – for their full-time jobs – have been judges on the International Court of Justice at the Hague, world-renowned advocates before (or members of) international courts and arbitration panels, members of national supreme courts, and deans and scholars from university law schools. The scholars of international administrative law have offered historical and theoretical insights, the judges and other government officials

[11] Article IV(1), Statute of the World Bank Administrative Tribunal.

have brought a sense of reality and practical experience to the shaping of our governing rules, and I – until very recently, the only specialist in labor and employment law – have been turned to now and then for my familiarity with those fields. This same range of national and professional qualifications has characterized as well the membership of the Asian Development Bank Administrative Tribunal, which was purposefully created in the image of the World Bank Administrative Tribunal in 1991.

The Statutes of the two Tribunals tersely empower those bodies to "hear and pass judgment upon any application by which an individual member of the staff of the Bank Group alleges non-observance of the contract of employment or terms of appointment of such staff member."[12] The phrases "contract of employment" and "terms of appointment" are defined by the Statute to "include all pertinent regulations and rules in force at the time of alleged non-observance."[13] The World Bank has promulgated and disseminated staff rules, and they are contained in looseleafs several inches thick. Those simple phrases in the Statute have the effect of making these materials binding instruments upon which staff members can rely in their assertion of a wide range of rights, relating to such matters as salaries and other forms of compensation (particularly in very recent years at the World Bank, pension rights, as a large number of so-called consultants have been given regular appointments), their transfer and promotion, and the termination of their employment on account of redundancy, retirement and discipline.

The "contract of employment" that the two Tribunals are called upon to enforce is an individual contract, between the Bank and the individual employee or staff member. Unlike the employment contract in many European nations, and in a modest proportion of workplaces in the U.S., there is no collective agreement that gives rights to the workforce as a whole, and no labor union or other collective organization that bargains formally on behalf of the employees as a group. The governing rules for the staff members of the World Bank and the Asian Development Bank are thus very much of the Banks' own unilateral making and are not a product of collective negotiation with an employee representative. (It should be mentioned, however, that there is a Staff Association at the World Bank and a Staff Council at the ADB. These voluntary membership organizations have not been formally designated by a majority of the staff members but they purport to voice the concerns and views of the staff, and they are consulted by Bank management on a regular basis, particularly when significant changes in personnel policy are being contemplated.)[14]

---

[12] Article II(1), Statute of the World Bank Administrative Tribunal.

[13] *Id.*

[14] Principle 10.1, Principles of Staff Employment of the World Bank; World Bank Staff Rule 10.1 (Staff Consultations).

The Statute of the World Bank Administrative Tribunal sets forth certain jurisdictional prerequisites that have resulted in a quite substantial proportion of the cases before us being dismissed. One is that there must first be an exhaustion of internal remedies within the Bank,[15] most significantly the staff member's presentation of his or her case to a body called the Appeals Committee. That Committee is composed of fellow staff members, typically non-lawyers, some appointed by management and some appointed by the Staff Association. They conduct a full evidentiary and adversary proceeding, at which the aggrieved staff member has the right to be represented and at which there is the familiar form of examination, cross-examination and so forth.

After the hearing, the Appeals Committee makes a recommendation to the Bank's management (in particular, the Vice President for Human Resources) regarding the disposition of the employee's grievance, and in the great preponderance of cases those recommendations are accepted by the management in whole or in part, and the dispute is resolved. Basically, the proceeding before the Appeals Committee is a form of advisory arbitration – binding on neither the staff member nor the Bank. If the staff member remains dissatisfied after action upon an Appeals Committee recommendation, he or she may file an application with the Tribunal. Failure to proceed in a timely manner to the Appeals Committee will be fatal to an application to the Tribunal, on the ground of failure to exhaust internal remedies.[16] The Bank has fairly recently created an internal mediation office, to which the staff member and the Bank may together have recourse before (or even after) an Appeals Committee proceeding. The mediation office has had considerable success – a settlement rate of nearly 90 percent – in resolving disputes and avoiding the more formal and time-consuming proceedings before the Tribunal.

A second and related jurisdictional requirement in the Statute of the Tribunal is that the applicant coming to the Tribunal must have filed his or her application within 120 days of the decision that is challenged.[17] Typically, that decision is made (after an Appeals Committee proceeding and recommendation) by the Vice President for Human Resources, who confirms in whole or in part the decision of a supervisor concerning a staff member's job performance or job security. Only if the challenge to the Vice President's decision has been promptly brought does the Tribunal have the power to determine whether or not the staff member's rights under the employment contract have been violated.

---

[15] Article II(2)(i), Statute of the World Bank Administrative Tribunal.
[16] *See Malekpour*, WBAT Decision No. 320 [2004], para. 20.
[17] Article II(2)(ii), Statute of the World Bank Administrative Tribunal.

You may recall Susana Mendaro, who took her gender discrimination and harassment case against the World Bank to the courts of the District of Columbia, where the Bank has its headquarters. At the time she brought her lawsuit, she was informed by the Bank's management that, although her claim arose in 1979 – a year before the Tribunal was created – the Tribunal would have the authority to hear claims arising during that year. Ms. Mendaro chose to ignore the Bank's urging and invested some four years at the trial and appeals levels in the U.S. federal court. After her case was, as we know, dismissed by the District of Columbia Circuit Court of Appeals, Ms. Mendaro filed her application with the Tribunal.[18] We felt constrained to rule that her application was filed too late, more than three years beyond the period stipulated in the Tribunal's Statute.

But, as courts and arbitrators often do, the Tribunal believed it important to clarify in a forceful dictum what had until then been uncertain: that the Bank was obligated, by "general principles of law" and by the Bank's own internal policy statements, to avoid discriminatory and harassing treatment of staff members, that gender discrimination was an example of such proscribed conduct, and that the Tribunal had the authority to strike down and fashion appropriate remedies for any such conduct.[19]

Notice the two distinct sources of the Bank's obligations to which the Tribunal referred: the Bank's own internal policy statements, and "general principles of law." The former are expressly stated by the Statute of the Tribunal to be a part of the staff member's "contract of employment" which are thus directly enforceable by the Tribunal. But the Statute is silent with respect to the Tribunal's power to enforce "general principles of law." Yet the Tribunal declared – and actually had done so in its very first judgment in 1981 – that the actions of Bank managers and supervisors, and of all persons and bodies making decisions on behalf of the Bank, are restrained by legal principles going beyond the self-promulgated rules and regulations of the Bank.[20]

These general principles – which the Tribunal identifies, formulates and applies as is needed and appropriate on a case-by-case basis – are used much as a domestic court uses general principles of national law in reviewing the actions of government officials. As a sub-part of the body of international administrative law, they deal with the judicial review of decisions made by an international organization affecting the workplace rights of its

[18] *Mendaro,* WBAT Decision No. 26 [1985].

[19] *Id.,* at paras. 20–22.

[20] *de Merode,* WBAT Decision No. 1 [1981]. The Tribunal at para. 25 observed: "Another source of the rights and duties of the staff of the Bank consists of certain *general principles of law*, the applicability of which has in fact been acknowledged by the Bank in its written and oral pleadings." (Emphasis added.)

employees. As we shall see momentarily, the World Bank and ADB Administrative Tribunals have asserted the power to review not only the decisions of lower-level supervisors who appraise the workplace performance, salary increases and promotion opportunities of those who work with and for them, but even the decisions of the very highest policy-making organs of the institutions, the Boards of Governors and Directors. (One may wonder whether this is what President McNamara had in mind when he so eloquently endorsed the creation of the Administrative Tribunal in 1980.)

Where does the Tribunal look in shaping those principles? What are its sources of law? We know that the Bank is not subject to any nation's domestic law and courts, so that literally it operates within a lawless environment. We know, on the other hand, that the Tribunal is charged by its Statute with determining whether the Bank has violated a staff member's "contract of employment" or "terms of appointment." What constitutes that contract and those terms – apart from the letter of appointment that is typically issued when an individual becomes a member of the staff? Perhaps the principal source of the rules that the Tribunal applies are, as already mentioned, the Bank's own documents that set forth detailed regulations governing the rights and responsibilities of the staff on a host of workplace issues. These staff rules, along with less formal and often very detailed memoranda and announcements, are framed by the more general mandates set forth in a document titled Principles of Staff Employment which paint the rights of staff members in very broad strokes: for example, fair treatment in substance and in procedure, non-discrimination, and equal pay for comparable work.[21] Beyond those written sources, the World Bank Administrative Tribunal in its very first decision concluded that even unwritten practices – habitual ways in which employees are treated and compensated – can become a part of the "conditions of appointment" upon which staff members may rely.[22]

The Tribunals must, however, go even beyond the Bank's own written documents and unwritten practices in determining the rights of staff members. It is necessary, for example, to give meaning to ambiguous language in Bank documents, and to determine priorities among conflicting documents and practices. How do the Tribunals decide these matters? We have developed a body of contract rules that are a distillation of national law principles from legal systems with which the Tribunal judges are familiar, both civil law and common law.[23] Also central to our jurisprudence are rules of national administrative law by which judicial bodies control the

---

[21] *See* Principles 2 and 6, Principles of Staff Employment of the World Bank.
[22] *de Merode*, WBAT Decision No. 1 [1981], para. 23.
[23] *See Justin*, WBAT Decision No. 15 [1984], paras. 27, 32 and 36.

actions of government agencies; perhaps the most important of those rules is that the decision-maker has considerable discretion in taking decisions but that it may not abuse that discretion, or act arbitrarily or unreasonably, or utilize unfair procedures. More will be said, momentarily, concerning "abuse of discretion."

The Tribunals have also occasionally invoked principles of public international law and the jurisprudence of other international administrative tribunals.[24] For the most part, these are not controlling upon the Tribunals. In fact, the World Bank Administrative Tribunal – also in its very first judgment in 1981, when it was in effect introducing itself upon the international jurisprudential scene – pointed out that, in light of the World Bank's own particular history, operations and mission, the Tribunal intended to fashion its own jurisprudence, perhaps with helpful resort to the decisions of other international administrative tribunals, but only as persuasive and not as in any way binding.[25] The Tribunals have indeed sometimes cited in our own judgments the judgments of other Tribunals, and have had them cited to us in the pleadings filed by conscientious attorneys. Our governing principles also derive from core social norms that we believe employees can reasonably expect in the workplace – due process, fair treatment, non-discrimination and the like – which, as noted, often overlap with the norms established in the Banks' own internal documents.

All of these sources – written and unwritten, international and national – contribute to what the World Bank Administrative Tribunal has called an "internal law" of the institution.

On rare occasions, there may be a conflict between the express directives of the Bank, clearly stated to be a part of the staff member's "contract of employment" – which the Tribunals presumably must enforce – and more general commonly accepted principles of law. When that conflict cannot readily be resolved, the latter principles will commonly prevail. A particularly striking example is a case decided by the Asian Development Bank Tribunal in 1997, known as the *Amora* case.[26] Mr. Amora, a Filipino, worked over the course of some 15 consecutive years at what must be described as a fairly low-level job in the ADB's printing office; his job involved printing and copying Bank documents. His initial appointment was for one year, and it described Mr. Amora as an "independent contractor," and as such, the contract continued, "[He] shall not be entitled to any compensation, allowances, benefits or rights from or against the

[24] *See de Merode*, WBAT Decision No. 1 [1981], para. 108; *Rendall-Speranza*, WBAT Decision No. 197 [1998], para. 44.

[25] *de Merode*, WBAT Decision No. 1 [1981], para. 28.

[26] *Amora*, Decision No. 24 [1997], III ADBAT Reports 1.

Bank other than expressly provided therein." He was not included in the ADB's pension plan. Mr. Amora's appointment was extended, and eventually after a series of one-year and other very short-term renewals and extensions, he had worked 15 years, all in the ADB printing office. Eventually, he was given a regular staff appointment with a pension, doing the same work, but very soon after that, he was subjected to the Bank's recently revised retirement policy, and he was forced to retire with a very small pension. Mr. Amora's request to be accorded pension rights for the full 15 years of his service as a so-called "independent contractor" was denied by the Bank, and his case ultimately reached the Tribunal.

On the one hand were the clear and explicit terms of his written contract. On the other, was the fact that – applying generally prevailing legal principles concerning the line between employees and independent contractors – it could hardly be said that in truth Mr. Amora was anything other than an employee, with regular, essentially unchanging, full-time job responsibilities using the Bank's equipment and working subject to the directives of Bank supervisors.

The Tribunal concluded that no matter what legal relationship the Bank sought to create simply by using the term "independent contractor," Mr. Amora was an employee of the ADB who was entitled to pension benefits for his full term of service. The Tribunal, hinting that the Bank was purposely using a legal framework that would allow it to avoid its proper responsibilities for workers' benefits, referred to a *détournement de pouvoir*, a concept that is familiar in continental administrative law.[27] This concept has shaped a number of the decisions of the two Tribunals on which I have sat, and it is largely attributable to the influence within those Tribunals of our judges who have been distinguished scholars in nations such as France, Egypt and Uruguay.

I would like to touch briefly upon other substantive rules that have been developed by the Tribunals. One is that employment decisions based on invidious discrimination, either toward the individual or the class to which he or she belongs, are unlawful and will be overturned. Both the World Bank and the Asian Development Bank have stated that principle as part of their employment policies, and both Tribunals quickly took the opportunity (the World Bank Tribunal in Ms. Mendaro's case) to state that they had the jurisdiction to hear discrimination and harassment claims, and to remedy any such wrongdoing.[28] In a most interesting case, a high level staff member at the World Bank rested her claim of discrimination on no

---

[27] *Id.*, at pp. 10–11.

[28] *Rendall-Speranza*, WBAT Decision No. 197 [1998]; *Alexander*, Decision No. 40 [1998], IV ADBAT Reports 41.

more than a series of general statistical studies by the Bank itself that showed that overall women employed by the Bank were less well paid than men doing comparable work (although the gap had been closing through the years). The Tribunal concluded that such general statistics were insufficient to prove that the Applicant was a victim of gender discrimination in pay, particularly when the record showed that she had been initially hired at a suitable job level and salary, and that she had been fairly evaluated and promoted through the years with attendant suitable salary increases.[29]

Among the most important substantive principles in the jurisprudence of all international administrative tribunals is that a tribunal has the inherent power to overturn decisions made by the institution, through its officials and its supervisors, across a wide field of subject matters, if those have been tainted by an "abuse of discretion." Although certain Bank decisions are not matters of discretion – for example, those that are explicitly mandated by staff rules – a host of decisions are, where the criteria for action are spelled out only in broad terms or are not spelled out at all. Examples are whether a probationary staff member should be confirmed in an appointment because he or she has performed satisfactorily;[30] whether a staff member's performance justifies a 2% or a 4% salary increase;[31] whether the content of a job has been so changed as to justify declaring the staff member redundant and subject to termination;[32] whether the normal retirement age should be reduced from 65 to 60;[33] and so forth. These are properly characterized as decisions within the discretion of the institution. But, as already suggested above, that discretion is not unlimited. As the two tribunals, indeed all international administrative tribunals, have repeatedly stated, "the Tribunal will not interfere with the exercise of such discretion unless the decision constitutes an abuse of discretion, being arbitrary, discriminatory, improperly motivated or carried out in violation of a fair and reasonable procedure."[34]

This "abuse of discretion" standard applies not only to individual decisions about a staff member's job performance but even to policy decisions made at as high a level of authority as the Board of Governors or Board of Directors of the Banks.[35] With respect to individual staff members, for

---

[29] *Nunberg,* WBAT Decision No. 245 [2001]; *see also Sebastian (No. 2),* WBAT Decision No. 57 [1988].

[30] *See Suntharalingam,* WBAT Decision No. 6 [1981].

[31] *See Desthuis-Francis,* WBAT Decision No. 315 [2004]; *Marshall,* Decision No. 226 [2000].

[32] *See Brannigan,* WBAT Decision No. 165 [1997].

[33] *See Samuel,* Decision No. 15 [1996], II ADBAT Reports 51.

[34] *E.g., Peprah (No. 2),* WBAT Decision No. 310 [2004], para. 27.

[35] *See Mesch & Siy (No. 4),* Decision No. 35 [1997], III ADBAT Reports 71.

example, the protections afforded by the Tribunals are available not only to an individual employed to make copies in the Bank's printing shop, as was Mr. Amora, but even to a Vice President of the institution. Remarkably, the World Bank Administrative Tribunal reviewed a claim by a Vice President of the Bank that his transfer to a non-supervisory post – which was based upon decisions by *his* supervisor (a Managing Director of the Bank) and even by the President of the Bank – was an abuse of discretion. Ultimately, we rejected that claim as factually unfounded.[36] It is, of course, often a matter of fine judgment and delicate line-drawing to differentiate an arbitrary management decision from one that is merely unsound or unwise. But that kind of differentiation must be made – and that is why it is good to have three or five or seven heads available rather than one to address these often difficult questions.

Even more noteworthy was a judgment of the Asian Development Bank Administrative Tribunal, which challenged the decision of the Board of Governors to reduce the prevailing mandatory retirement age of staff members from 65 to 60.[37] The Applicant asserted that such a change was an abuse of discretion, while the Bank argued that it was altogether beyond the power of the administrative tribunal to review a decision of the Board of Directors, the Bank's highest decision-making authority. The Tribunal rejected the latter position. It held that even the Board is subject to the rule of law and to limits upon its discretion. Nonetheless, the Tribunal upheld the change in the mandatory retirement age; it was viewed as within the Board's discretion, as not unreasonable or arbitrary, and as consistent with prevailing Bank procedures and other more general principles of procedural law.[38]

I should mention that in the United States, an employer's decisions are almost totally beyond the reach of judicial or arbitral bodies, absent its violation of a statute or a governmental regulation or a precise public policy.[39] Abuses of discretion in employment relations must simply be tolerated. Even unionized employers operating under collective bargaining agreements typically have only specifically designated limitations upon managerial freedoms and nothing like the more general form of review that is given to decisions made by international organizations in *their* employment relations. The closer analogy in the U.S. is to judicial review of the decisions

[36] *Conthe*, WBAT Decision No. 271 [2002].

[37] *Samuel*, Decision No. 15 [1996], II ADBAT Reports 51.

[38] *See id.*

[39] *E.g., Wisehart v. Meganck*, 66 Pac.3d 124 (Colo. App. 2002); *Mackenzie v. Miller Brewing Co.*, 623 N.W.2d 739 (Wis. 2001). *See* Richard A. Epstein, In Defense of the Contract At Will, 51 U. Chi. L. Rev. 947 (1984).

of administrative agencies exercising their discretionary powers given to them by federal or state statutes.[40]

Another substantive principle of the two Tribunals' jurisprudence also would, I suspect, be absolutely startling to U.S. employer representatives, especially those who do not deal with unions and collective bargaining agreements. The Tribunals have held that there are certain conditions of employment that are so "fundamental and essential" that the Bank is forbidden to change them to the detriment of the staff members. In the very first case decided by the World Bank Administrative Tribunal, the *de Merode* case, the Applicants claimed that the Bank was obligated periodically to increase the salaries of staff members to accord with cost-of-living percentage increases in the Washington, D.C. area. Although the Tribunal did not go quite so far, it did hold that the frequency and regularity with which the Bank had in the past given salary increases to its staff, giving consideration *in part* to the Washington cost of living – along with recurrent Bank pronouncements referring to those increases – made such regular salary increases mandatory, despite the absence of any actual promise to that effect by the Bank. Such recurrent salary increases were held to be "fundamental and essential" terms of employment, resulting in "acquired rights" of staff members that could be withdrawn by the employer only with their consent.[41]

The so-called doctrine of "acquired rights" is central to the law of international administrative tribunals.[42] Coupled with that doctrine is a dividing line between so-called *essential* conditions of employment and *non-essential* ones. The latter conditions may unilaterally be changed by management, subject to certain understandable limitations, for example that the change cannot be implemented retroactively so as unfairly to defeat the expectations of the staff. Whether a term of employment is essential or not, unchangeable or not, is again a matter of subtle judgment for the Tribunal.

Perhaps the most noteworthy cases in which I participated on both Tribunals required making such a judgment. Coincidentally, both of the cases involved separate decisions by the World Bank and by the ADB about the same employment term – the reimbursement of taxes paid by certain staff members on their Bank income. Most nations that have their citizens working at international organizations do not impose a tax upon their income there, as a matter of informal comity. However, the United

---

[40] *See Chevron, U.S.A., Inc. v. Natural Resources Defense Council, Inc.*, 467 U.S. 837 (1984).

[41] *de Merode*, WBAT Decision No. 1 [1981], para. 112.

[42] *See* C.F. Amerasinghe, *The Law of the International Civil Service*, 402–40 (Vol. I, 2d ed. 1994). The World Bank Administrative Tribunal, however, has disassociated itself from the concept of "acquired rights." *See de Merode*, WBAT Decision No. 1 [1981], para. 44.

States and the Philippines are among the very few nations that do collect income taxes from their nationals working at the World Bank and the Asian Development Bank. This results in a net income for a U.S. citizen or a Filipino citizen that is less, often significantly less, than another nation's citizen who is doing precisely the same sort of work. At the World Bank, the Bank has through the years reimbursed United States citizens in an amount equal to their income taxes, so as to equalize their gross salaries with those of their fellow staff members from other countries. In the *de Merode* case, decided in 1981, the World Bank Administrative Tribunal held that the principle of tax reimbursement was a "fundamental and essential condition of employment," so that the Bank could not unilaterally end its long practice of reimbursing for taxes even if it wanted to. Were the Bank to wish to amend the program adversely, or to terminate it, the consent of staff members would have to be secured. (The Tribunal did not elaborate on just how the Bank would do that.) But in *de Merode* the Bank had not abandoned its tax-reimbursement program; it merely made a minor change in the details of calculating the reimbursement amount. The Tribunal concluded that such details were not "fundamental and essential" terms, but non-essential terms, which the Bank was free to adjust, subject to various limits to guarantee due process and fair treatment.[43]

Some 15 years later, the identical issue was presented to the ADB Tribunal in a case bearing the name of the two applicants Mesch and Siy, respectively nationals of the U.S. and the Philippines. Their case made its way to the Tribunal in several stages. In its initial decision, before I became a member, the Tribunal held that the Bank's own articulated principle of equal pay for comparable work was an unchangeable essential condition of employment.[44] The Tribunal applied that principle and concluded, even in the absence (in contrast to *de Merode*) of any previous program of tax reimbursement and in the absence of any ADB statements confirming such a program in any way, that tax reimbursement was *a* condition of employment. The Tribunal therefore ordered appropriate compensation to the U.S. and Filipino staff for the two past years that were in dispute. But there was no precise holding that tax reimbursement was fundamental and unchangeable. The ADB Board of Directors promptly threw down the gauntlet – to the staff and to the Tribunal – and adopted a resolution to the effect that "the Bank shall not reimburse the taxes paid by any . . . staff member of the Bank for the taxes paid by them on their salaries and emoluments paid by the Bank, effective upon the date of this Resolution."

When Messrs. Mesch and Siy returned to the Tribunal, they not sur-

[43] *de Merode*, WBAT Decision No. 1 [1981], paras. 49–89.
[44] *Mesch & Siy*, Decision No. 2 [1994], I ADBAT Reports 21.

prisingly argued that tax reimbursement – designed to achieve equal pay for equal work – was a fundamental and essential term, that the Bank was legally obligated not only to pay it for the past but to continue it in the future, and that the Board of Directors' resolution was therefore invalid. The three Tribunal judges who constituted the majority (myself included) distinguished the *de Merode* decision at the World Bank and held, particularly because of the absence of any past practice or confirming statements by the ADB with respect to tax reimbursement, that such reimbursement was a non-fundamental and non-essential condition of employment subject to complete withdrawal by the ADB Board of Directors.[45] Over a forceful dissent, we concluded that although there was indeed a fundamental principle of equal pay for equal work, the equality requirement could be satisfied by equal Bank compensation *before* the imposition of national income taxes, which was a circumstance over which the Bank had no control.

Another set of important substantive rules announced by both Tribunals have been in cases involving discipline imposed upon a staff member for engaging in misconduct. On such matters, the Banks have adopted detailed staff rules and they provide for internal investigations before serious discipline can be imposed. The Tribunals have added various due-process requirements, and have also made clear the importance of "proportionality" in the imposition of discipline. The doctrine of proportionality – that there be some reasonable "fit" between the wrongdoing and the severity of the punishment – is one that was perfectly well understood by Tribunal members schooled in the common law as well as Tribunal members with a civil law background. It is also a value that is embodied in the World Bank's own staff rules, which provide that the Bank when imposing discipline is to take into account "the seriousness of the matter," "extenuating circumstances," "the situation of the staff member," and "the frequency of conduct for which disciplinary measures may be imposed."[46]

Although the judges all agree upon the importance of the principle of proportional discipline, the *application* of that principle to particular circumstances has provided what I view as perhaps the only example of a significant disparity of attitudes based upon our differing cultural and societal backgrounds. In a pair of cases decided by the WBAT in 1995,[47] two staff members had each separately engaged in a conscious, repetitive and furtively executed plan to falsify their records for overtime work. Through an accumulation of improper claims for modest amounts, they were able, on between 15 and 20 occasions, each to steal several hundreds of dollars

---

[45] *Mesch & Siy (No. 4)*, Decision No. 35 [1997], III ADBAT Reports 71.
[46] Paragraph 3, World Bank Staff Rule 8.01 (Disciplinary Proceedings).
[47] *Carew*, WBAT Decision No. 142 [1995]; *Planthara*, WBAT Decision No. 143 [1995].

from the Bank. When confronted by management with the irregularities, the staff members persisted in fabricating their explanations, and they were discharged. They told the same story before the Appeals Committee – to fellow staff members – who in each case recommended that the termination should be sustained. If I were deciding the cases myself, as I have often done in the U.S. as an arbitrator under a collective bargaining agreement, I almost certainly would also have sustained the discharges.

Yet my colleagues were inclined to find that the wrongdoing – about which we had no doubt – was not so grave as to warrant termination. We stressed the staff members' long periods of employment, 14 years and 24 years, without previous incidents, as well as the modest amounts of money involved and the fact that the staff members did not occupy high managerial positions. Because, at the time, the Tribunal had no authority under its Statute to order reinstatement, it ordered the Bank to compensate the staff members – in one case, by paying six months of salary,[48] and in the other case, one and one-half years of salary.[49] I deferred to my colleagues' assessment, based on their own cultural norms, on the issue of "proportionality," because I thought it inappropriate to push for the application of stricter sanctions that I believe squared more with U.S. values. In an unusual public statement a few years after the decisions, the Bank's General Counsel criticized the Tribunal for having failed, in shaping our jurisprudence on the issue of discipline, to be mindful of the special values and goals of the Bank as an international institution – one of which is to eradicate governmental and corporate corruption in the use of funds on Bank-sponsored projects throughout the world.[50]

Despite these somewhat differing views about how to apply the principle of "proportionality," what has been perhaps most noteworthy in our decisions about the discipline of staff members for misconduct has been the congruence of values and of conclusions that have consistently prevailed over those differences. This community of values among all members of the Tribunals, regardless of our immersion in varying legal, social and cultural systems, has been one of the more startling lessons of my periods of service. We may sometimes use different terminology, and even different languages, to express our views, but the congruence in our substantive legal outlook has been quite extraordinary.

An example is the "due process of law" that must attach to the Bank's procedures in deciding that an individual's employment should be terminated for wrongdoing. There was immediate agreement – in only the

---

[48] *Carew*, WBAT Decision No. 142 [1995].
[49] *Planthara*, WBAT Decision No. 143 [1995].
[50] *See supra* at p. 63.

Tribunal's second judgment, filed in 1981 – that it was appropriate for the Tribunal to fashion "due process" requirements as an inherent element of workplace relations.[51] And never in subsequent cases has there been any ultimate disagreement as to the more precise components of due process in discipline cases – such elements as notice to the staff member of alleged malfeasance, an opportunity to respond, a fair investigation, some measure of confrontation with accusers, prompt delivery of any investigatory report on which discipline will be based, and so forth.[52] The Bank's own published rules set forth many of these elements of due process, but the Tribunal has not been shy about supplying a good number that are unwritten. There is thus a common answer to the question "what is fair treatment?" that transcends cultural differences.

Before I conclude my remarks, I would like to mention some aspects of the Tribunal's composition and procedures that I think raise some interesting issues.

First, as just noted, we are obviously quite diverse in terms of our nationalities, our legal systems, and the professional, political and social backgrounds from which we come. The most fascinating aspect of my Tribunal experience has been the way in which all of these varying viewpoints are articulated, discussed and accommodated within the text of our judgments. Each case to be decided in each of our sessions is assigned to one or another judge for especially close review of the record and for the drafting of a proposed Tribunal judgment. Our sessions are principally devoted to a group discussion of each draft, with a view toward assuring conformity with our jurisprudence, some consistency in style, and a final judgment to which we can all sign our name. Without fail, even though we may use different legal terminology and somewhat different analytical approaches, there has been a congruence of values and of conclusions that have consistently prevailed over those differences.

That leads to a second intriguing aspect of the Tribunal's decision-making. The World Bank Tribunal has rendered more than 300 decisions over the course of 24 years. Every one of them has been unanimous. There have been no dissenting opinions filed, and indeed there have been no separate opinions of any kind filed. Although there are 7 judges on the World Bank Tribunal, and 5 on the ADB Tribunal, our respective Statutes give us the authority to render Tribunal judgments in panels of at least three judges.[53] For the first 17 years of its existence, the World Bank

[51] *Skandera*, WBAT Decision No. 2 [1981].

[52] *See, e.g., C*, WBAT Decision No. 272 [2002].

[53] *See* Article V(2), Statute of the World Bank Administrative Tribunal; Article V(4), Statute of the Administrative Tribunal of the Asian Development Bank (as amended on 22 December 1994, effective 1 January 1995).

Tribunal sat in plenary, i.e., all 7 judges, in every one of our roughly 160 cases as of that time, whether the case involved the annual performance evaluation of a secretary or the salary increases of the entire 6000-person workforce. We simply believed that seven heads were better than three. In 1997, however, in response to a mounting backlog of cases, the Tribunal decided that it would be more efficient to handle certain cases in three- or four-judge panels, and we have done so since. Plenary sessions are reserved for the cases of more general import and cases that raise issues of a more complex and innovative nature.

As originally written, the Statute of the World Bank Tribunal made no reference to the possibility of separate or dissenting opinions, while the ADB Tribunal Statute expressly did so,[54] as is true with many other administrative tribunals. Although the WBAT members had no doubt that the filing of dissenting opinions was an inherent element of the judicial process, there has been an absolutely remarkable process of "coming together" around the decision ultimately reached, as well as the reasons given. In part, that is a product, as noted above, of the congruence in our jurisprudential values – even if some of us may start from a more philosophical perspective and others from a more pragmatic perspective. In part, also, dating back to the earliest days of the Tribunal, all of us have given great weight to the belief that our judgments have greater force and clarity, and that the Tribunal will have greater credibility, if we speak with one voice rather than several. The World Bank Staff Association began, a few years ago, to express its concern about the absence of dissents, suggesting that it derived from the suppression of disagreement, and presumably of voices on the Tribunal that were more sympathetic to the staff. Although not at all an accurate perception, the Staff Association succeeded in so convincing Bank management, and the Board of Governors recently revised our Statute so as expressly to allow for the filing of dissenting opinions[55] – an authorization that, as I say, was altogether unnecessary because already implied.

There have been two lengthy dissenting opinions filed at the Asian Development Bank Administrative Tribunal. In one case,[56] the Tribunal upheld (4 to 1) the Bank's decision to make 60 the mandatory retirement age, but my dissenting colleague strongly believed that this was a violation of staff rules and ADB practices which, to her, indicated that staff members were entitled to work until the age of 65. In the second case,[57]

[54] Article IX, Statute of the Administrative Tribunal of the Asian Development Bank (as amended on 22 December 1994, effective 1 January 1995).

[55] Article XI(2), Statute of the World Bank Administrative Tribunal, 1980 (as amended in 2001).

[56] *Samuel*, Decision No. 15 [1996], II ADBAT Reports 51.

[57] *Mesch & Siy (No. 4)*, Decision No. 35 [1997], III ADBAT Reports 71.

closer in vote (3 to 2) and also in my judgment closer on the merits, the Tribunal – as already mentioned – sustained the Bank's announcement of a policy not to pay tax-reimbursement benefits to staff from the U.S. and from the Philippines, in the face of an earlier Tribunal judgment that appeared to make such payments mandatory and unalterable. That latter case was surely the most vexing that I have had to decide as a member of either Tribunal and, although I understood how a Tribunal colleague, in fact two, could reasonably reach a result different from my own, I ultimately believed them to be wrong.

Finally, I want to mention what is perhaps the most controversial feature of the procedures by which the Tribunals operate – the almost uniform failure to hold evidentiary hearings. It is of course commonplace, in the U.S. and other legal systems with which we are familiar, to hold a hearing for the purpose of allowing the fact-finder – whether jury, court or arbitrator – to hear witnesses, through direct and cross examination, so as to make credibility assessments, resolve factual contradictions, and ultimately determine "what happened" when that is central to deciding a case. In almost all of the cases at the World Bank Administrative Tribunal, and in literally all of the cases at the ADB Administrative Tribunal, the disputed issues – factual as well as legal – have been resolved without seeing live witnesses, and on the pleadings alone.

We have found that the two rounds of pleadings for each party, the staff member applicant and the Bank as respondent, supplemented by the typically dozens of annexed documents, provide an adequate basis for decision-making. We are helped in this respect by the fact that the Banks' staff members, particularly those in supervisory positions, tend to write memoranda and today emails in great profusion and detail, contemporaneously documenting conversations, meetings, and the like. We are also helped by the fact that there is in most cases an evidentiary hearing by the Appeals Committee less than a year before the case is decided by us. Moreover, many of our cases raise only jurisdictional or strictly legal questions raising no pertinent evidentiary issues. In many cases, there is no dispute about the facts; and in other cases, factual disputes can be readily resolved by a careful perusal of the documents attached to the written pleadings. This accords with my own experience as a labor arbitrator who has heard many discipline cases in which credibility is in issue; I have come almost uniformly to ignore my unreliable sense of who "looks" to be telling the truth, and rather to rely upon inferences from external circumstances when determining whom to believe.

I am admittedly somewhat uncomfortable about the fact that most of our applicants may believe that they are being denied their "day in court," and that many observers may reasonably view an in-person hearing as a core element of due process of law. But for all of the reasons just recited, and because of the additional fact that it would be inefficient for tribunals meeting typically only once in six months to hold hearings in all cases, I can defend our practice of deciding cases on the pleadings alone. Indeed most other international administrative tribunals have the same reluctance to hold evidentiary hearings, although one or two do hold hearings in every case.

Of course, there are certain cases in which it would be very useful to see the witnesses, or to have an opportunity to question them or to question the attorneys for the parties. The two Tribunals are in fact authorized in their respective Statutes to hold hearings,[58] and although the ADB Tribunal has yet to do so, the World Bank Administrative Tribunal has held hearings in a handful of cases, and those have proved to be helpful in addressing very significant issues – less by helping us to assess credibility than by allowing us to elicit more evidence from witnesses and to hear arguments of counsel at greater length.[59]

In conclusion, I must say that my service on the Tribunals has been perhaps the most stimulating and rewarding professional experience of my life. The opportunity to work with, and intellectually engage with, esteemed lawyers, jurists and academicians from all corners of the globe in the very practical task of helping to resolve employment disputes has been unique and joyful. Particularly satisfying has been my appreciation that the knottiest of legal problems can be resolved, and an entire body of jurisprudence can be developed, by persons of good will who share the objectives of achieving for staff and managers alike a regime of law and fair treatment. I have been assured by representatives of the Bank management and of the staff that the Administrative Tribunal has achieved the objectives, communicated to me by President McNamara in 1980, of creating within the Bank a positive environment in which a highly qualified workforce can be attracted and retained.

---

[58] *See* Article IX, Statute of the World Bank Administrative Tribunal; Article VIII, Statute of the Administrative Tribunal of the Asian Development Bank (as amended on 22 December 1994, effective 1 January 1995).

[59] *See Prescott*, WBAT Decision No. 253 [2001]; *Nunberg*, WBAT Decision No. 245 [2001]; *Marshall*, WBAT Decision No. 226 [2000]; *de Merode*, WBAT Decision No. 1 [1981].

THE INTERNATIONAL MONETARY FUND ADMINISTRATIVE TRIBUNAL: A FEW OBSERVATIONS

Celia Goldman*

Résumé

En 2006, le Tribunal administratif du Fonds monétaire international ("Tribunal" ou "TAFMI") fête ses douze ans d'existence. Cet article nous donnera l'occasion de mettre en lumière certaines de ses caractéristiques essentielles.

I. *La composition du Tribunal*

Depuis sa création et jusqu'à ce jour, le TAFMI a eu l'avantage de bénéficier des services du même groupe de juges hautement qualifiés. Le Statut du Tribunal prévoit que ceux-ci doivent posséder les qualifications requises pour être nommés à de hautes fonctions judiciaires ou bien être des jurisconsultes d'une compétence reconnue.

Le Tribunal se compose d'un Président et de deux juges associés qui peuvent être remplacés par des juges suppléants lorsque les juges associés sont empêchés de participer à une session du Tribunal. Dans le but de se doter d'une jurisprudence mesurée et raisonnée, le Tribunal, quoique non requis par son Statut, a tranché à ce jour toutes les affaires qui lui ont été soumises à l'unanimité de ses membres.

II. *Les intervenants, les* amici curiae *et la pluralité de requérants*

Le TAFMI connaît des requêtes dirigées aussi bien contre des actes réglementaires que contre des actes individuels.

L'intervention de tiers à l'instance est permise. Le Statut prévoit l'intervention de personnes relevant de la compétence *ratione personae* du Tribunal dont les droits pourraient être affectés par le jugement à venir. Deux affaires sont venues illustrer cette règle.

---

* Registrar, International Monetary Fund Administrative Tribunal. B.A., University of Pennsylvania; J.D., Yale Law School. Any views expressed herein are those of the author and do not necessarily represent the views of the members of the IMF Administrative Tribunal. I am grateful to Mr. Nassib G. Ziadé, Executive Secretary of the World Bank Administrative Tribunal, for inviting these observations on the occasion of the publication of the proceedings of the WBAT's 20th Anniversary Conference.

Dans le premier cas, *M. "P" (No. 2)* (Jugement du TAFMI No. 2001–2), le requérant, un retraité du Fonds, contestait devant le Tribunal une décision du Comité d'administration du Plan de retraite du personnel ayant ordonné de déposer dans un compte séparé une portion de sa pension de retraite dans l'attente de la résolution d'un différend survenant en application d'une disposition du Plan permettant à un conjoint ou ex-conjoint de solliciter du Comité de donner effet à un jugement d'un tribunal national condamnant un retraité à payer une pension alimentaire. L'ex-épouse, Dame "Q", ayant eu connaissance de la requête, avait présenté une demande en intervention devant le Tribunal. Le requérant ainsi que la partie défenderesse contestaient le droit de l'ex-épouse à l'intervention. Le Tribunal observa que l'intervention devait être soumise aux mêmes conditions de recevabilité que l'action elle-même. En l'espèce, Dame "Q", ayant qualité pour agir d'après le Statut du Tribunal, avait donc qualité pour intervenir dans la procédure en cours.

Il est à noter que les Règles de procédure du TAFMI comportaient dès l'origine, dans un but de transparence, une disposition invitant le Greffier à faire circuler au sein du Fonds une note résumant les points soulevés par toute requête présentée au Tribunal. De plus, un amendement à ces Règles de procédure, adopté en 2004, permet désormais au Tribunal de solliciter l'intervention de toute personne vérifiant les critères statutaires.

Le deuxième cas, *Dame "G", requérante et M. "H", intervenant* (Jugement du TAFMI No. 2002–3), posait la question de savoir si l'intervention devait être permise lorsque la requête était dirigée contre une "décision réglementaire" de l'institution. Le demandeur à l'intervention, appartenant à la même catégorie d'employés que la requérante, devait-il être considéré comme étant fondé à intervenir à l'instance? En l'espèce, le Fonds prétendait que les droits de M. "H" ne seraient qu'indirectement affectés par le jugement du Tribunal et concluait au rejet de l'intervention. Le Tribunal admit néanmoins l'intervention sur la base de trois arguments: d'abord, que les droits de l'intervenant seraient affectés par le jugement du Tribunal; ensuite, qu'il n'était pas réaliste d'attendre que M. "H" intente une action de son propre chef si les prétentions de Dame "G" devaient être rejetées; enfin, que l'identité des demandes de la requérante et celles de l'intervenant militait en faveur de l'admission de l'intervention, non de son rejet.

L'Association du personnel n'a pas qualité pour intenter une action devant le Tribunal. Elle peut, par contre, lui faire parvenir son point de vue en tant qu'*amicus curiae*. Dans le seul cas de ce genre soumis au Tribunal, *Dame "J"* (Jugement du TAFMI No. 2003–1), le Tribunal, contre l'avis de l'institution défenderesse, admit l'Association du personnel à être entendue en tant qu'*amicus curiae*. Le Tribunal distingua le rôle de l'*amicus curiae* de celui de l'intervenant. Alors que le second est expressément invité à participer aux débats comme partie à l'instance, le premier est seulement autorisé à communiquer son avis au Tribunal. En l'espèce, l'avis de l'Association du personnel relatif au standard du contrôle devant être exercé par le Tribunal quant aux décisions du Comité d'administration du Plan de retraite du personnel concernant les demandes de retraite pour incapacité fut qualifié de judicieux et de constructif par le Tribunal. En bref, et quoique la décision contestée n'ait pas été réglementaire, elle affectait tout de même l'ensemble du personnel ainsi que le développement de la jurisprudence du TAFMI en la matière.

Enfin, le Tribunal a été saisi pour la première fois en 2005 de multiples requêtes entièrement identiques tendant également pour la première fois à annuler une décision réglementaire émanant du Conseil des Administrateurs du Fonds. Le Fonds a été invité par le Tribunal à présenter une réponse unique aux sept requêtes identiques.

III. *Les frais et dépens*

Une jurisprudence importante du TAFMI a été élaborée autour de la disposition de son Statut lui prescrivant de faire supporter au Fonds tout ou partie des frais et dépens du requérant lorsque la requête est partiellement ou totalement fondée. Une interprétation extensive de cette disposition a prévalu, qui a abouti à des décisions du Tribunal considérant que le requérant pouvait avoir également droit au remboursement de ses frais de représentation relatifs à la procédure de revue administrative préalable à la requête devant le Tribunal (*Dame "C"* (Ordonnance No. 1997–1) et *M. "F"* (Jugement No. 2005–1)). De plus, lorsque la requête s'est avérée partiellement fondée, le Tribunal a appliqué le principe de proportionnalité en vue du partage des frais et dépens entre les plaideurs (*Dame "C"* (Ordonnance No. 1997–1 et Ordonnance No. 1998–1) et *M. "F"* (Ordonnance No. 2005–1)).

Conclusion

Au regard de l'ensemble des sujets évoqués ci-haut, on peut conclure que le TAFMI a suivi une approche mesurée et flexible dans l'interprétation de ses pouvoirs statutaires.

* * *

At the time of the 20th Anniversary Conference of the World Bank Administrative Tribunal ("WBAT") in May 2000, the International Monetary Fund Administrative Tribunal ("IMFAT" or "Tribunal"), established in 1994, had been in existence for only six years.[1] The IMFAT now has doubled in age and, as of June 2006, has rendered twenty-four Judgments and nine Orders.[2] It faces a growing caseload, with the majority of its cases having been filed over the last four years, and a corresponding expansion of its jurisprudence. This paper offers observations on the IMFAT's development from the perspective of 2006, highlighting a few key features of its twelve-year history.

---

[1] For a review of the jurisprudence of the International Monetary Fund Administrative Tribunal for the years 1994–1999, *see* Goldman, "The International Monetary Fund Administrative Tribunal: Its First Six Years," in *International Monetary Fund Administrative Tribunal Reports*, Vol. I 1994–1999, pp. 1–33 (2000).

[2] The IMFAT's Judgments and Orders, along with its Statute and Rules of Procedure, may be accessed electronically at www.imf.org/external/imfat. Additional Volumes of *International Monetary Fund Administrative Tribunal Reports* are forthcoming.

Composition of the Tribunal

The IMF Administrative Tribunal, perhaps uniquely among international administrative tribunals, has had the benefit of the continuous service of the same group of highly qualified and diverse Judges from its inception.[3] By Statute, all must satisfy the requirement that they possess the qualifications required for appointment to high judicial office or be jurisconsults of recognized competence.[4] For purposes of deciding upon an Application, the Tribunal, by Statute, functions as a three-member body, comprised of a President and two Associate Judges.[5] When an Associate Judge is unable to participate in a session of the Tribunal, an Alternate Judge is called upon to serve in his place. The occasional participation of the Alternate Judges has enriched the points of view available to the Tribunal's decision-making. Also contributing to the articulation of a measured and carefully reasoned jurisprudence is the fact that while its Statute requires only that decisions be taken by a majority of the members participating,[6] the IMFAT, in each case decided to date, has acted with unanimity.

Intervenors, Amici Curiae, *and Multiple Applicants*

The typical case considered by the IMF Administrative Tribunal is that of a single Applicant contesting an "administrative act" of the Fund by which he alleges he has been "adversely affected."[7] Such "administrative acts" may, as provided by the IMFAT's Statute, include both "individual" and "regulatory" decisions of the Fund,[8] and it has not been uncommon

[3] Members of the Tribunal are eligible for reappointment. Statute, Article VII, Section 2.

[4] Statute, Article VII, Section 1(c). The composition of the IMFAT ably fulfills this mandate and reflects major legal systems of the world: Judge Stephen M. Schwebel (United States), President (Former President, International Court of Justice); Associate Judge Nisuke Ando (Japan) (Director, Kyoto Human Rights Research Institute; Professor Emeritus, Kyoto University); Associate Judge Michel Gentot (France) (Former President of the Judicial Chamber, Conseil d'Etat, France; former Director, Institute of Political Studies, Paris; President, International Labour Organization Administrative Tribunal); Alternate Judge Georges Abi-Saab (Egypt) (Emeritus Professor of International Law, Graduate Institute of International Studies, Geneva; Member of the Appellate Body, World Trade Organization); and Alternate Judge Agustín Gordillo (Argentina) (Emeritus Professor, University of Buenos Aires; Current President, Organization of American States Administrative Tribunal; Judge, International Labour Organization Administrative Tribunal).

[5] Statute, Article VII, Section 4. The Tribunal has functioned as a five-member body for the purposes of adopting, and later revising, its Rules of Procedure.

[6] Statute, Article XIII, Section 1.

[7] Statute, Article II, Section 1.

[8] Statute, Article II, Section 2(a). A "regulatory" decision is defined as "any rule concerning the terms and conditions of staff employment, including the General Administrative Orders and the Staff Retirement Plan, but excluding any resolutions adopted by the Board of Governors of the Fund." Statute, Article II, Section 2(b).

for an individual Applicant to raise a challenge to a Fund policy in the context of a complaint about the application of that policy in his individual case. In recent years, however, the IMFAT also has confronted questions relating to access to the Tribunal by Intervenors, *Amici Curiae* and multiple Applicants.

Intervention in the IMFAT is expressly authorized by its Statute, which directs the Tribunal to provide in its Rules of Procedure a mechanism for intervention by "... persons to whom the Tribunal is open under Section 1 of Article II [i.e. persons within the Tribunal's jurisdiction *ratione personae*], whose rights may be affected by the judgment."[9] In two cases in which Judgments have been rendered to date, individuals applied for and were granted the opportunity to intervene. In both instances, the Tribunal granted the application for intervention over the objections of the Applicant, Respondent or both.

In the first of these cases, *Mr. "P" (No. 2), Applicant v. International Monetary Fund, Respondent*, IMFAT Judgment No. 2001–2 (November 20, 2001), a retiree of the Fund had filed an Application with the Tribunal contesting a decision of the Administration Committee of the Staff Retirement Plan ("SRP" or "Plan") to escrow a portion of his pension benefits pending resolution of a dispute arising under a Plan provision that permits a spouse or former spouse to request that a court order for support be given effect under the SRP. The ex-spouse, Ms. "Q," who had independent knowledge of the retiree's having contested the decision in the Administrative Tribunal, filed an application to intervene. Both the Applicant and the Respondent objected to the application for intervention. The basis for the Fund's objection was that the ex-spouse allegedly did not fulfill both of the statutory criteria for intervention. In the Fund's view, while Ms. "Q" had rights that might be affected by the Judgment, she was not a person to whom the Tribunal was open under Article II, Section 1, of the Statute. The Fund suggested that she be invited to offer her views as an *Amicus Curiae*.[10]

The Tribunal observed that the question of Ms. "Q"'s right to be heard as an Intervenor was identical to the question of whether she could herself have filed an Application with the Tribunal contesting the decision of the SRP Administration Committee.[11] The Tribunal concluded, for purposes

[9] Statute, Article X, Section 2(b).

[10] *Mr. "P" (No. 2)*, para. 48.

[11] Accordingly, the application to intervene "... raise[d] the important issue of whether the amendment of Section 11.3 of the SRP, granting rights to spouses and former spouses of SRP participants to request the Fund to give effect to domestic relations orders, provide[d] a parallel right of review of such decisions of the Administration Committee in the Administrative Tribunal, in the case in which the decision of the Committee is adverse to the former spouse but not to the SRP participant [footnote omitted]." *Mr. "P" (No. 2)*, para. 51.

of Article II, Section 1(b),[12] of the Statute, that Ms. "Q" was ". . . a beneficiary under a Fund benefit plan, for purposes of challenging the legality of the Administration Committee's Decision on her Request to give effect to the [support] order." Her application for intervention accordingly was granted.[13]

While the ex-spouse Intervenor in the case of *Mr. "P" (No. 2)* possessed independent knowledge of the proceedings ongoing in the Administrative Tribunal, leading her to file her application to intervene, the Tribunal has recognized that not all persons within the Tribunal's jurisdiction *ratione personae* who have rights that may be affected by a Judgment in a pending case will necessarily have such knowledge, particularly in cases that affect non-staff members. Accordingly, the Tribunal, in adopting amendments to its Rules of Procedure in 2004, revised the Intervention Rule to provide, in the absence of an application for intervention, that the Tribunal may invite the participation as an Intervenor of any person who meets the statutory criteria.[14]

Notably, the IMFAT's Rules of Procedure have included from their inception a provision, unusual among the rules of international administrative tribunals, designed to alert potential Intervenors who are members of the staff of the Fund to pending Applications and to promote the overall transparency of the Tribunal's operations. This Rule, in its present formulation, requires the Registrar, upon the transmittal of an Application to the Fund, to ". . . circulate within the Fund a notice summarizing the issues raised in the application, without disclosing the name of the Applicant, in order to inform the Fund community of proceedings pending before the Tribunal."[15]

---

[12] Article II, Section 1(b), provides:

> 1. The Tribunal shall be competent to pass judgment upon any application:
>
> . . .
>
> b. by an enrollee in, or beneficiary under, any retirement or other benefit plan maintained by the Fund as employer challenging the legality of an administrative act concerning or arising under any such plan which adversely affects the applicant.

[13] *Mr. "P" (No. 2)*, para. 65. The Tribunal drew upon its earlier Judgment in *Estate of Mr. "D", Applicant v. International Monetary Fund, Respondent (Admissibility of the Application)*, IMFAT Judgment No. 2001–1 (March 30, 2001) in respect of the reach of its jurisdiction *ratione personae* with regard to non-staff members challenging decisions under the Fund's benefit plans. *Mr. "P" (No. 2)*, paras. 57–65.

[14] Rule XIV, para. 4, provides:

> In the absence of an application for intervention, the Tribunal may invite the participation as an intervenor of any person to whom the Tribunal is open under Article II, Section 1 of the Statute and who has a right that may be affected by the judgment to be given by the Tribunal. The views of the Applicant and the Fund may be sought, in a manner consistent with Paragraph 3 of this Rule, on the question of whether an individual should be invited to intervene. If the intervention is admitted, the intervenor shall thereafter participate in the proceedings as a party, and the schedule of pleadings shall be modified to accommodate his participation.

[15] Rule IV(f).

It was as a result of the circulation of such a Staff Notice that an application for intervention was filed in the case of *Ms. "G", Applicant and Mr. "H", Intervenor v. International Monetary Fund, Respondent*, IMFAT Judgment No. 2002–3 (December 18, 2002). Ms. "G" had challenged the Fund's eligibility criteria for expatriate benefits, which she maintained discriminated impermissibly among categories of Fund staff. She also challenged the Fund's refusal to grant an exception in her individual case. Mr. "H" shared the same visa status as Ms. "G" and hence also was ineligible for expatriate benefits under the Fund's policy. Upon notification to the staff of the filing of Ms. "G"'s Application, Mr. "H" sought to be admitted as an Intervenor.

The Applicant Ms. "G" opposed Mr. "H"'s effort to intervene on the ground that the intervention would create additional burdens for her as a litigant. The Tribunal rejected such a basis for denying the application for intervention.[16] Perhaps of greater interest was the position taken by the Respondent. While the Fund concluded that "on balance" it would not, in the particular circumstances of the case, oppose the intervention of Mr. "H", it urged the Tribunal to hold that it had discretion to deny an application for intervention by persons in the position of Mr. "H", who, in the Respondent's view, would be only "indirectly" affected by the Tribunal's Judgment.[17] Accordingly, unlike the case of *Mr. "P" (No. 2)*, the case of *Ms. "G"* required the IMFAT to analyze its Intervention Rule in the context of a challenge to a "regulatory" decision of the Fund.

The Tribunal rejected the Fund's contention that, because even without his intervention Mr. "H" would be in the class of persons who would benefit if Ms. "G" succeeded in her claim,[18] his interest in the case was only "indirect" and that the Tribunal had discretion to deny his application to intervene on that basis. "Indeed," observed the Tribunal, "that the prospective intervenor would be affected by such an outcome supported the conclusion that he should be admitted as an intervenor and thereby granted the opportunity to attempt to persuade the Tribunal of his views on the matter."[19] The Tribunal further noted, given Ms. "G"'s challenge to a "regulatory" decision, that it "may not be realistic" to expect, as the Fund had suggested, that Mr. "H" would be able to pursue an application

---

[16] *Ms. "G"*, paras. 27, 35.

[17] *Id.*, paras. 28–30.

[18] The Tribunal referenced Article XIV, Section 3, of the Statute, which provides:

> If the Tribunal concludes that an application challenging the legality of a regulatory decision is well-founded, it shall annul such decision. Any individual decision adversely affecting a staff member taken before or after the annulment and on the basis of such regulatory decision shall be null and void.

[19] *Ms. "G"*, para. 32.

of his own in the event that Ms. "G" was not successful in hers.[20] Finally, the Tribunal rejected the contention that the Tribunal has discretion to deny an application for intervention on the basis that it is "merely duplicative" of the claims of the Applicant. Such a view, concluded the Tribunal, ". . . runs counter to the purposes of intervention. An identity between the claims of an applicant and of an intervenor is ordinarily the touchstone for a decision to admit an intervention."[21]

The IMFAT's Rule requiring notification to the staff of a newly filed Application serves not only to alert potential Intervenors to pending cases but has the additional benefit of providing notice to the Staff Association of the Fund, which otherwise would not have knowledge of pending Applications. While the Staff Association does not have standing to serve as an Applicant before the IMFAT,[22] the provision of the Tribunal's Rules of Procedure providing for *Amici Curiae* looks particularly to a role for the Staff Association in communicating views to the Tribunal.[23] In one case to date, *Ms. "J", Applicant v. International Monetary Fund, Respondent*, IMFAT Judgment No. 2003-1 (September 30, 2003), the Staff Association Committee ("SAC") requested the opportunity to file an *Amicus* brief, and the IMFAT granted that request.

Ms. "J" had contested a decision of the Administration Committee of the Staff Retirement Plan denying her request for disability retirement. The SAC applied to communicate views as *Amicus Curiae* in order to address what it termed "systemic issues" relating to the procedures employed by the

---

[20] *See id.*, para. 33:

> It may also be observed that the standard "may be affected" by the judgment is a broad one. Hence, the intervenor's interests need not be *determined* by the judgment but merely *affected* by it. Additionally, the Fund's position that Mr. "H" would be entitled to pursue his own application with the Tribunal should the outcome of the case be unfavorable to Ms. "G" may not be realistic. While a judgment is *res judicata* only with respect to the actual parties, in the case of a challenge to a regulatory decision, the precedent established would affect any future challenge on similar grounds to the policy at issue.

(Emphasis in original.)

The Tribunal's Judgment upheld the Fund's exercise of discretion in enacting and applying the expatriate benefits policy, denying the Applications of both Ms. "G" as Applicant and Mr. "H" as Intervenor. *See Ms. "G"*, Decision.

[21] *Id.*, para. 34.

[22] *See* "Report of the Executive Board to the Board of Governors on the Establishment of an Administrative Tribunal for the International Monetary Fund," pp. 15–16. (In respect of Article II, Section 2(c), of the Statute: "The Staff Association would not be entitled to bring actions in its own name before the tribunal.")

[23] The first sentence of Rule XV provides:

> The Tribunal may, at its discretion, permit any person or persons, including the duly authorized representatives of the Staff Association, to communicate views to the Tribunal as *amici curiae*.

SRP Administration Committee as well as the Committee's interpretation of the relevant Plan provisions.[24]

As the IMFAT's Rules of Procedure prescribed neither procedural nor substantive requirements for the exercise of the Tribunal's discretion to permit the communication of views by an *Amicus Curiae*, the SAC's request occasioned some improvisation on the part of the Tribunal.[25] The request was transmitted to both the Applicant and the Respondent, inviting their views as to whether it should be granted and, if so, whether the pleadings in the case, which ordinarily are kept confidential, should be opened to the SAC for the purpose of preparation of its brief.

The Applicant raised no objection to the SAC's participation and consented to the opening of the pleadings, including attached medical records, for the purpose of the SAC's preparing an *Amicus* brief. The Respondent, by contrast, maintained that the SAC had not identified any systemic issue, such as a "regulatory" decision of the Fund, that was properly before the Tribunal, and it "'. . . reserve[d] its position as to whether this criterion had been met.'" The Fund additionally objected to the disclosure of the pleadings to the SAC on the ground that they included confidential medical information of the Applicant.[26]

The Tribunal, finding the objections of the Fund unpersuasive, granted the SAC's request. The Tribunal in *Ms. "J"* distinguished the role of an *Amicus Curiae* from that of an Intervenor, observing that while an Intervenor is expressly entitled to "participate in the proceedings as a party," pursuant to Rule XIV, para. 3, an *Amicus Curiae* is not. Accordingly, in *Mr. "P" (No. 2)* and *Ms. "G"*, following the admission of the intervention, the Intervenor participated fully in the exchange of pleadings; by contrast, in *Ms. "J"*, the Tribunal awaited receipt of the final pleading in the case before transmitting the entire dossier to the SAC, which was then given an opportunity to file its brief. Thereafter, the Applicant and the Respondent were accorded a period, simultaneously, in which to offer their observations on the views of the *Amicus Curiae*.[27]

---

[24] *Ms. "J"*, para. 15.

[25] The President invoked his plenary authority when the Tribunal is not in session to ". . . deal with any matter not expressly provided for in the present Rules." Rule XXI, para. 3. *See Ms. "J"*, para. 16. As a result of its experience in the case of *Ms. "J"*, the Tribunal adopted as part of its 2004 amendments to the Rules of Procedure the following additional provisions of Rule XV:

> The Tribunal may permit an *amicus curiae* access to the pleadings of the parties. The Tribunal shall enable the parties to submit timely observations on an *amicus* brief.

[26] *Ms. "J"*, para. 17.

[27] *Id.*, paras. 18–19 and fn. 7.

The SAC's *Amicus Curiae* brief drew attention to a significant issue raised by the case of *Ms. "J"*, i.e. the standard of review to be applied by the IMFAT when a request for disability retirement is denied by the SRP Administration Committee. The controversy concerning the standard of review, observed the Tribunal, was "argued principally between Amicus Curiae and Respondent."[28] The Tribunal found "discerning and constructive"[29] the brief of the SAC, which took the view that decisions on disability retirement deserve a deeper level of scrutiny by the Administrative Tribunal than the "arbitrary and capricious" standard urged by the Respondent.[30] In short, while the case of Ms. "J" did not involve a challenge to a "regulatory" decision of the Fund, it did affect the staff as a whole, as well as the development of the IMFAT's jurisprudence, in setting forth a standard of review for disability retirement cases.[31]

Finally, while the Staff Association may not serve as an Applicant and the IMFAT's Rules do not make provision for class actions, the Tribunal was in 2005 seized for the first time of multiple (i.e., seven) identical Applications filed simultaneously challenging a "regulatory" decision of the Fund. The case, the first in which a "regulatory" decision was contested directly,[32] was of considerable interest, as the Applicants challenged a decision of the Fund's Executive Board affecting the staff compensation system.

To streamline procedures, the Respondent was invited to file a single Answer to the seven identical Applications. The Fund answered the Applications with a Motion for Summary Dismissal, to which the Applicants filed a joint Objection. In *Baker et al., Applicants v. International Monetary Fund, Respondent (Admissibility of the Applications)*, IMFAT Judgment No. 2005-3 (December 6, 2005), the Tribunal denied the Fund's Motion, and the pleadings resumed on the merits.[33] Following a subsequent Executive Board decision further amending the compensation system, however, the Tribunal dismissed the Applications as moot.[34] In July 2006, five new Applications were filed contesting the latter decision of the Executive Board.

---

[28] *Id.*, para. 100.

[29] *Id.*, para. 20.

[30] *Id.*, para. 100.

[31] *See id.*, para. 128. That standard of review was applied in a second case, decided the same day, *Ms. "K", Applicant v. International Monetary Fund, Respondent*, IMFAT Judgment No. 2003-2 (September 30, 2003).

[32] A "regulatory" decision may be challenged directly, i.e. in the absence of an individual decision based thereon, within three months of its announcement or effective date. Statute, Article VI, Section 2.

[33] The Tribunal concluded that the Applicants had met the threshold requirement of Article II, Section 1, of the Statute, i.e., that they were "adversely affected" by the contested decision despite the decision's not having had adverse financial consequences for the Applicants during the 2005 compensation round. *Baker et al.*, Judgment No. 2005-3, paras. 16-23.

[34] *Baker et al., Applicants v. International Monetary Fund, Respondent (Dismissal of the Applications as Moot)*, IMFAT Judgment No. 2006-4 (June 7, 2006).

Attorneys' Fees and Costs

Another important issue upon which the IMFAT has elaborated in recent years is that of assuring access to the Tribunal through the authority granted by its Statute to order the Fund to bear "totally or partially" the applicant's legal costs when an Application is "well-founded in whole or in part."[35] The IMFAT has been forthright in its approach to awards of attorneys' fees, mindful that the ". . . purpose of Article XIV, Section 4 is to provide for cost-shifting in favor of prevailing applicants, thereby increasing access to the Tribunal for aggrieved staff members."[36]

Accordingly, the Tribunal has accepted an attorney's statement of costs as a valid representation of the costs "incurred by the Applicant," refusing to inquire into the particular fee arrangement between the Applicant and his or her counsel.[37] The IMFAT also has held that costs may encompass not only the Applicant's representation before the Tribunal, but also representation in the administrative review process that, pursuant to Article V of the Statute, must be exhausted before an applicant may seek judicial review by the Administrative Tribunal.[38]

---

[35] Article XIV, Section 4, of the Statute provides:

> If the Tribunal concludes that an application is well-founded in whole or in part, it may order that the reasonable costs incurred by the applicant in the case, including the cost of applicant's counsel, be totally or partially borne by the Fund, taking into account the nature and complexity of the case, the nature and quality of the work performed, and the amount of the fees in relation to prevailing rates.

[36] *Mr. "V", Applicant v. International Monetary Fund, Respondent*, IMFAT Judgment No. 1999–2 (August 13, 1999), para. 138.

[37] *Ms. "J", Applicant v. International Monetary Fund, Respondent (Assessment of compensable legal costs pursuant to Judgment No. 2003–1)*, IMFAT Order No. 2003–1 (December 23, 2003), para. First; *Ms. "K", Applicant v. International Monetary Fund, Respondent (Assessment of compensable legal costs pursuant to Judgment No. 2003–2)*, IMFAT Order No. 2003–2 (December 23, 2003), para. First.

[38] *Ms. "C", Applicant v. International Monetary Fund, Respondent (Interpretation of Judgment No. 1997–1)*, IMFAT Order No. 1997–1 (December 22, 1997), para. Fourth. *Accord Mr. "F", Applicant v. International Monetary Fund, Respondent*, IMFAT Judgment No. 2005–1 (March 18, 2005), para. 124. The Tribunal explained the rationale for this decision as follows:

> . . . the preparation of a claim that ultimately succeeds in the Tribunal necessarily involves the presentation of that claim to, and its rejection by, the Grievance Committee. . . . unless awards under Article XIV, Section 4 of the Statute could encompass costs incurred in pressing such claims in the Grievance Committee, the statutory purpose of giving all staff members access to the Tribunal would not be well served. The Tribunal considered as well that had the claim succeeded initially in the Grievance Committee (as success in the Tribunal suggests it should have), the grievant could have had the benefit of the Grievance Committee's own fee-shifting authority [footnote omitted].

Mr. "V", para. 136. *See generally* Goldman, "The Relationship Between the International Monetary Fund Administrative Tribunal and the Channels of Administrative Review," in *Current Issues in the Law and Practice of International Administrative Tribunals: Promoting the Effectiveness of the Decision-Making Process* (35th anniversary publication of the Organization of American States Administrative Tribunal).

In awarding costs, the Tribunal has demonstrated sensitivity to the realities of the litigation process. In the case of *Ms. "J"*, in which the Applicant prevailed in full in seeking rescission of the decision denying her a disability retirement, the Tribunal awarded the full amount of legal costs submitted.[39] Notably, the Tribunal rejected the Respondent's objection that the fee award should be reduced by a sum attributed to consultation regarding a workers' compensation claim that the Applicant, during the course of the Tribunal's proceedings, conceded was not yet ripe for review. In its Order assessing the Applicant's compensable legal costs, the IMFAT observed that in its Judgment on the merits it had recognized that the workers' compensation claim was of an "intersecting nature" with the Applicant's disability retirement claim. Accordingly, the Tribunal concluded that ". . . at the applicable stage of consultation [between the Applicant and her counsel], both complaints were reasonably being considered in tandem," and that no diminution in the fee award was appropriate.[40]

In cases in which an Applicant has prevailed only in part, the Tribunal has applied a principle of proportionality to fee awards. In the early case of *Ms. "C", Applicant v. International Monetary Fund, Respondent*, IMFAT Judgment No. 1997–1 (August 22, 1997), the Tribunal denied the Applicant's challenge to the non-conversion of her fixed-term appointment but held that irregularities in the non-conversion process had given rise to a compensable claim. In assessing costs, the Tribunal concluded that "[t]he limited degree to which Applicant was successful in comparison with her total claims justifies a measure of proportionality in the determination of the costs to be borne by the Fund."[41]

In respect of a subsequent Judgment, *Mr. "F", Applicant v. International Monetary Fund, Respondent*, IMFAT Judgment No. 2005–1 (March 18, 2005), the Tribunal, in awarding costs, observed that the Applicant had not been successful on his "principal and most complex claim."[42] Nonetheless, the

[39] The Tribunal reviewed the statement of costs in light of the statutory criteria, i.e. ". . . the nature and complexity of the case, the nature and quality of the work performed, and the amount of the fees in relation to prevailing rates." Article XIV, Section 4. *Ms. "J"*, Order No. 2003–1, para. Third. *See also Ms. "K"*, Order No. 2003–2, para. Second.

[40] *Ms. "J"*, Order No. 2003–1, para. Second.

[41] *Ms. "C"*, Order No. 1997–1 (December 22, 1997), para. Fifth. *See also Ms. "C", Applicant v. International Monetary Fund, Respondent (Assessment of compensable legal costs pursuant to Judgment No. 1997–1)*, IMFAT Order No. 1998–1 (December 18, 1998), para. Third.

[42] *Mr. "F", Applicant v. International Monetary Fund, Respondent (Assessment of compensable legal costs pursuant to Judgment No. 2005–1)*, IMFAT Order No. 2005–1 (April 18, 2005), para. First. The Tribunal had sustained the decision to abolish the Applicant's position as a reasonable exercise of managerial discretion, but it awarded compensation for the Respondent's failures to: (a) take effective measures in response to religious intolerance and workplace harassment of which Mr. "F" was an object; and (b) give Mr. "F" reasonable notice of the abolition of his post. *Mr. "F"*, Judgment No. 2005–1, para. Decision.

Tribunal awarded seventy-five percent of the total costs submitted. Again demonstrating its appreciation of the litigation process and the purposes of Article XIV, Section 4, the Tribunal explained that "... the record assembled and argued by Applicant's counsel in pursuit of [the principal claim on which he did not prevail] was indispensable to the Tribunal's award to Applicant of substantial relief on other substantial counts, and ... accordingly the Fund should bear the great majority of Applicant's legal costs."[43]

Finally, in the case of *Baker et al.*, considered above, the IMFAT awarded partial costs to the Applicants on an exceptional basis. Acknowledging that Article XIV, Section 4, "... does not contemplate an award of costs in the absence of a decision on the merits of an Application," the Tribunal concluded, nonetheless, "in view of the exceptional character of the case which is of importance to the staff as a whole," that legal costs were to be awarded to the Applicants, limited to the costs incurred in the preparation of their successful Objection to the Respondent's initial Motion for Summary Dismissal.[44]

Conclusion

In sum, the IMF Administrative Tribunal, in taking decisions relating to access to the Tribunal by Intervenors, *Amici Curiae* and multiple Applicants, as well as in the exercise of its authority to award legal costs to prevailing Applicants, has demonstrated a measured, yet flexible, approach to the interpretation of its statutory mandate. Such decisions, which may be at once procedural in their presentation and substantive in their impact, highlight but a few of the developments in the Tribunal's jurisprudence over its twelve-year history.

---

[43] *Mr. "F"*, Order No. 2005–1, paras. Second and Third.

[44] *Baker et al.*, Judgment No. 2006–4, para. Costs.

INDEX

Note: Italic page numbers indicate a reference to material in French

[1] 'Abuse of discretion' has been regularly elaborated in the jurisprudence to include judgments which are arbitrary, discriminatory, improperly motivated or carried out in violation of a fair and reasonable procedure.

www.ingramcontent.com/pod-product-compliance
Lightning Source LLC
La Vergne TN
LVHW081515300926
849161LV00006B/1183
* 9 7 8 9 0 0 4 1 5 7 1 2 5 *